J. Pierpont Morgan,
Collector

Dedicated to John Pierpont Morgan, Sr., who built the Morgan
Memorial in Hartford, on the 150th anniversary of his birth in
the city, and to John Pierpont Morgan, Jr., who presented part of
his father's magnificent art collection to the Wadsworth Atheneum.

J. Pierpont Morgan, Collector

European Decorative Arts from the Wadsworth Atheneum

Edited by Linda Horvitz Roth

Wadsworth Atheneum

1987

The Wadsworth Atheneum, Hartford:
18 January–15 March 1987

The Pierpont Morgan Library, New York:
17 April–1 August 1987

The Kimbell Art Museum, Fort Worth:
15 September–1 December 1987

Publication made possible by United Technologies Corporation,
the National Endowment for the Humanities, with additional
funds from the National Endowment for the Arts.

Designed by Derek Birdsall RDI

Photographic Credits: Joseph Szaszfai, unless otherwise noted

Typeset in Monophoto Van Dijck 203
and printed on Parilux Matt Cream
by Balding + Mansell Limited, Wisbech, Cambs.

Printed in England.

Cover: Nautilus Goblet, detail.
Dresden, about 1620, nautilus about 1710.
Wadsworth Atheneum, Gift of J. Pierpont Morgan, 1917.269.

Contents

Foreword

In addition to its elucidation of the famous financier's art collection, the insight it provides into his collecting methods, and its record of some of the family history, we hope this book will also more strongly establish J. Pierpont Morgan's connection with Hartford. Most Americans associate Morgan with New York, and very few are even aware of his London connections, although in Britain his is perhaps the single best-known American name. J. Pierpont Morgan was indeed very active in both those places, but he was born and raised in Hartford in one of the oldest and most distinguished families of New England, and his benefactions initiated the modern history of the Wadsworth Atheneum in Hartford, America's oldest public art museum and in many ways because of him, one of its most distinguished. Nonetheless few people even in Hartford know the relationship of the museum's Morgan Memorial Building and the Morgan collections here with the great financier of the turn of the century.

It will correct what I believe is also a widely held and erroneous view of Morgan — that he was exclusively an indiscriminating and wholesale buyer of other people's collections, an opulent aggrandizer and not a careful practitioner of the art of connoisseurship. He did buy whole collections, but mostly for his favored museums rather than for himself, and in every case it was to take advantage of the discriminating eye of an earlier collector. The telling fact brought out in the essay by Linda Roth is that he insisted upon actually seeing everything he cared most about, and those most familiar with him seem to have held his methods in high regard.

He was, of course, operating in a very different art market. These beautiful large color transparencies which dealers routinely send around today were of course not available to collectors in Morgan's time. The whole field of art history and the museum establishment were both much smaller and less well informed as there was a comparatively minuscule body of literature and hardly any of the technical tools we have now. But if there were fewer and less reliable advisers to choose from, Morgan seems to have used the best of them. What a joy it must have been to have great resources available in a market unplagued by the scarcity which so frustrates museums and collectors alike a hundred years later. To have exhausted the supply of objects of acceptable quality, as Morgan said he had done on more than one occasion, was a far greater achievement then than now, when even if one has the money available, it is difficult to find material of museum standards to buy. This is especially true in the fields in which Morgan collected.

Of course Morgan and his contemporary fellow collectors helped create that scarcity, but for the health of America's museums it is better that they did what they did when they did it. In Morgan's case, however, it was only America's museums which profited; Britain's did not fare very well, although there might have been an important Morgan memorial museum in London as well as in New York and Hartford. (As a museum director I can only too well imagine the disappointment of the Victoria and Albert and the Glasgow Art Gallery when material long on loan to them from Morgan left for America.)

I have never believed that Europeans have a legitimate complaint about wealthy American collectors such as Morgan "looting" their patrimony. Their museums have always seemed to me quite well stocked, and America does after all share the European cultural heritage, and even outdid them at their own industrial game in Morgan's era — the real source of the complaint. The Metropolitan, though nearly thirty years younger than the Atheneum, benefited from being in New York rather than in much smaller Hartford, and also had quite a large collection even at the time of the younger Morgan's distribution of his father's collection. So they have little cause for complaint either, although I am sure they shared some of their British colleagues' anguish at losing any treasures of such great quality.

The museum professional, tied up as he is in institutional collecting policies, cannot help but envy the freedom of the private collector to pursue his own directions. One of the most fascinating aspects of Morgan's collection is its elusiveness to logical analysis. He was not an intellectual collector, driven to complete "sets," but a lover of wonderful objects, different types of which he may have pursued at different times. Nor in spite of the range of the collection was he particularly interested in creating an art historical survey. He never had to feel the pain of passing up a mouth-wateringly beautiful object because it did not fit into a rigid institutional scheme of collecting.

Morgan kept careful records of his purchases in the form of invoices, but we have few personal references to his collecting. One would very much like to know more about his collecting philosophy, and how he actually acquired some of his things. Every collector seems to have favorite anecdotes about the chase and the capture, but none at all seems to survive in his case, and it would be especially interesting to know how he felt about some of his favorite possessions. But alas all is silent except for brief hints in a few surviving letters and in the less than complete histories of his biographers.

Morgan's gifts have affected the Atheneum in many ways, one of the most lasting of which stems from his penchant for collecting decorative arts objects along with paintings. Hartford's museum is often referred to as a "little Metropolitan." The Metropolitan and the Atheneum's Morgan Building are not dissimilar in architectural style, and both collections, especially in the areas for which Morgan was primarily responsible, are extraordinarily varied. Although there is no comparison between the two museums in scale, of course, most other general art museums do incline more toward being primarily picture galleries. The somewhat personal combination of objects from the Morgan collection that came to the Atheneum helped to establish our rather eccentric and widely appreciated character as a museum.

It is unfortunate that none of Morgan's paintings or tapestries came to the Atheneum, although as Gregory Hedberg cogently speculates in his essay, this was probably his original intention. However, the Sumner Fund came to the Atheneum soon after the Morgan gift, and as it was both substantial and restricted to the acquisition of paintings, the imbalance created by Morgan's gift of decorative arts was eventually corrected and the Atheneum is now at least as well known for its European paintings as for the Morgan objects.

The Morgan gifts were soon followed by many others in the decorative arts. This was partly because Hartford was an early center for private collecting of American material, and surely partly because of the example set by Morgan and the resulting receptivity of the museum. But his benefactions were also followed by the Great Depression and then the evil days of the Second World War, and the museum began to fall behind in its ability to manage and display its collections adequately.

It is a pleasure to be able to mark the 150th anniversary of our great patron's birth not only with this splendid book, but with refurbished galleries in his building. The Morgan Memorial now has new roofs, a complete new computerized electronic security system, and for the first time in its history, adequate lighting. It has also been restored completely to the display of European art, from a former admixture of American paintings, which I am sure would also please Mr. Morgan. Work still remains on both the installations and some of the building's infrastructure, but then a museum is never really finished.

I am pleased to acknowledge the good work of all those who contributed to this book. I want especially to thank Gregory Hedberg who conceived of the idea of the exhibition and who was project director, and Linda Horvitz Roth who has been closest to it the longest.

Over the past decade United Technologies of Hartford has spearheaded the production of a significant number of extraordinary art publications. With funding already granted from the National Endowment for the Humanities, we reversed the normal procedure of a museum going to a corporation asking for funds and approached United Technologies, asking if they would undertake the production of the book for which we had the funding. With enthusiasm on the part of Raymond D'Argenio, Gordon Bowman and Carin Quinn, the somewhat modest book our budget envisioned turned into this more expansive publication, beautifully designed by Derek Birdsall of London. United Technologies also undertook full sponsorship of the accompanying exhibition in Hartford and the cost of the elaborate cases which will eventually be used for the permanent display of the objects in the museum's Morgan Memorial.

Other major financial assistance came from the National Endowment for the Humanities, which provided funds for the initial planning of the project and for research and publication of the book. The National Endowment for the Arts provided funds for the conservation of the objects, and support for sharing the collections with The Pierpont Morgan Library in New York and the Kimbell Art Museum in Fort Worth. The Kimbell also gave us advance funding that enabled us to get the project started. The J. Paul Getty Center for the Arts and Humanities supplemented funds to photograph the collection.

We are grateful to the Women's Committee of the Atheneum and the many contributors to the capital campaign which enabled the renewal of Mr. Morgan's building, some of whose names are commemorated in the galleries and some of whom are of the Morgan family.

Most of all we are grateful to John Pierpont Morgan, and to all those members of his family and his friends who, over the years and still today, have done so much for the Wadsworth Atheneum. They have continuously reaffirmed his authentic concern for the spiritual well-being of the public.

Tracy Atkinson
Director

Acknowledgments

Our intention was to evaluate the entire Morgan bequest of 1,325 European decorative arts objects and select one hundred highlights for in-depth research aimed at an eventual publication and exhibition. To do so required five years and the involvement of many talented individuals from the museum's staff and from here and abroad. Olga Raggio of the Metropolitan Museum was the first outside scholar to review the collection, followed by Sir Francis Watson, Michael Hall, David McFadden and Armin Allen, each contributing from his or her area of expertise. Once the general scope of the project was determined with help from Charles Ryskamp, Director of the Morgan Library, and Edmund Pillsbury of the Kimbell Museum, a complete analysis of the Sèvres, Meissen, silver, ivory and majolica was undertaken by Sir Geoffrey de Bellaigue, William Hutton, Helmut Seling, Christian Theuerkauff and Jörg Rasmussen, respectively. With the conception of the project, Linda Horvitz Roth moved from the museum's European paintings department to take charge of the European decorative arts collection of the Atheneum. In addition to coordinating all the curatorial aspects of the project, she directed the research on the objects and edited the publication. One of the lasting benefits of this project for the museum is the acquisition of a newly trained curator in the fields represented by the collection. Others involved directly with the project are appropriately acknowledged by Linda Roth, who coordinated the entire undertaking.

In conjunction with research on "The Morgans of Hartford," three years ago Eugene Gaddis, the museum's archivist, set out to organize all the museum's archival information on the Morgans. His findings and the documents uncovered by Mrs. Roth relating to Morgan's plans for a London museum provided important support for the essay. David Wright, archivist at the Morgan Library, Mary Kates at the Holyoke Library, and Nelson Taintor and Bill Griswold at Cedar Hill Cemetery, as well as David Parrish, Patrice Spillane, William Hosley, John Teahan, Raymond Petke, Jane Catler and Christopher Fox of the museum staff were also very helpful in providing information. Tracy Atkinson, Eugene Gaddis, and Jared Edwards kindly read early drafts, Linda Roth and Louise Lincoln expertly edited the text, and Gertrud Bourgoyne processed it. Finally, a personal acknowledgment to the late historian and author Marion Hepburn Grant whose lively conversations sparked an interest on the part of the author to delve more deeply into the Morgans of Hartford.

Gregory Hedberg
Associate Director for Collections and Exhibitions

This book reflects the combined efforts of many people whose contributions call for recognition and thanks. Some of these people helped in the exploration of J. Pierpont Morgan as a collector, while others were more concerned with investigating the individual objects in the collection. Still others provided additional intellectual, moral, financial, and technical support.

Of the first group, I would like to thank Neil Harris, Richard Guy Wilson, Alan Trachtenberg, and Barbara Balsiger for participating in a December 1983 planning meeting where we discussed the various issues to be explored in this book. Additional thanks go to Neil Harris for his direct contribution to the book. Thanks to Jeanie James, Archivist, and Marica Vilcek, Associate Curator, Catalogue Department, The Metropolitan Museum of Art, for granting access to the archives and the catalogue files of the museum and assisting with the investigation of Morgan and The Metropolitan Museum of Art. From The Pierpont Morgan Library, thanks to Barbara A. Paulson, Supervisor of the Reading Room and Diane Stiles, Assistant Registrar, for many kindnesses. Deepest thanks and gratitude go to David Wright, Archivist, whose unending support, encouragement, time, patience, and generosity made research on Morgan possible and such a rewarding experience. Thanks also go to J. V. G. Mallet, Keeper, Department of Ceramics, Victoria and Albert Museum, London, for providing access to the Morgan Registration files, and to Michelle Alten who helped compile the appendix portion of the book.

Cataloguing the individual objects of the Morgan collection was accomplished by five leading authorities in their respective fields of expertise: Sir Geoffrey de Bellaigue, William Hutton, Jörg Rasmussen, Helmut Seling, and Christian Theuerkauff. Their work began with detailed examinations of all the Sèvres, Meissen, majolica, silver, and ivory, and ended with seventy-nine informed and documented catalogue entries. A special tribute should be paid to the late Jörg Rasmussen, who nobly wrote his entries from a hospital bed in Munich. Thanks also to Dr. Tönnies Maack for helping Dr. Rasmussen with this endeavor, and to Wendy Watson for stepping in at the last moment and writing the introduction to the section on majolica. Others who helped greatly in the cataloguing process were Corinna van Meeteren and Helga Domdey-Knodler, and especially Christy Anderson, who contributed greatly to the evaluation of the French porcelain.

Thanks must go to many other scholars who graciously helped along the way: Olga Raggio for surveying the collection in 1983 and for subsequent help and encouragement; David McFadden for initial support and suggestions; Armin Allen for evaluating and appraising the massive collection of Meissen; Antoine d'Albis for helpful comments made during a visit to the Atheneum and for kind assistance during my visit to Sèvres in 1985; Tamara Préaud, Antoinette Hallé, Elisabeth Fontan, and Pierre Ennès for sharing very useful information related to the French porcelain; Clare Le Corbeiller for allowing me to examine the porcelain collection at The Metropolitan Museum of Art and many other kindnesses; Gillian Wilson, Charissa Bremer-David, and Peter Fusco for providing information on related objects at the J. Paul Getty Museum; Dwight Lanmon, David Whitehouse, and Thomas Swope for supplying information on the European glass, ancient glass, and ancient bronzes in the Morgan collection.

The conservators involved in this project allowed the objects to be shown to their best advantage: Ellen Howe provided initial advice, and Echo Evetts, John Dennis and Clifford Craine, and Rostislav Hlopoff expertly conserved the ceramics, silver, and ivories, and *Ebony Cabinet*.

There are many staff members of the Wadsworth Atheneum to whom the project owes a great deal of thanks: Stephen Kornhauser for supervising the conservation of the objects, Zenon Gansziniec for spending hours preparing the works for the conservators, and

Patricia Garland for additional guidance and assistance. Special thanks go to Gertrud Pfister Bourgoyne, who headed the secretarial team of Irene Heublein, Kathleen Keller, and Jeanette Harrison, all providing much-needed assistance with maximum good humor. Wilfred Stebbins and Raymond Petke supervised and coordinated the vast project of photographing several hundred objects. John Teahan helped track down many references, and Eugene Gaddis provided archival information and moral support. Nancy Ketchiff undertook the unenviable task of editing my essay, for which I thank her most sincerely.

For their work on the exhibition of the Morgan collection which will accompany the publication of this book, thanks go to Cecil Adams and David Parrish, who coordinated the exhibition logistics, and to Charles Froom who designed the cases. Recognition must also be given to the following Atheneum staff members: Susan Abare, Alan Barton, Claudia Bell, Michael Cappiello, James Cronin, Brenda Dranoff, Efrain Lopez, Daniel Heery, Marion LeBel, Anne Mayo, Beverly Morgan-Welch, Susan Nichols, Melissa Snow, Patrice Spillane, Muriel Thompson, Jack Trascz, Barbara Urban, Peter Waite, and Nancy Wilson. Their experience and hard work have been essential to its success.

Many people were instrumental in making the manuscript into a book. Andrea Anderson and Steven Mansbach of the National Endowment for the Humanities were most helpful and patient during the funding process. I thank Catherine Waters for initially consulting with us on the book's design. Donald Hook and Lothar Kahn translated entries and introductions from the German. Julie Perkins ably copyedited the manuscript, providing much-needed consistency and readability to a widely diverse group of essays and entries. Joseph Szaszfai, photographer, took an early interest in the project, and deserves special praise for his photographic skills, sensitivity to the objects, and tremendous patience. The Metropolitan Museum of Art, The Frick Collection, The Pierpont Morgan Library, the J. Paul Getty Museum, and the Corning Museum of Glass provided photographs for the essay and appendix portions of the book.

Of course without the administration of the Wadsworth Atheneum this project would never have been possible. Gregory Hedberg conceived of the project in 1981, shortly after he arrived at the museum and discovered much of the Morgan collection in storage. He has been the guiding force behind the project and his experience and advice over the past five years have been invaluable.

Christopher Cox, along with Gregory Hedberg, saw to it that the necessary funds were raised to carry out the project from beginning to end. Tracy Atkinson, Director, has given his support and blessings to this undertaking from the beginning. I thank him for his belief in the project and in all of us.

To Jean K. Cadogan I would personally like to express my utmost gratitude, for bringing me to the Atheneum, sharing her office, giving me advice and encouragement all along the way, and for being a true and supportive friend.

Linda Horvitz Roth
Associate Curator of European Decorative Arts
Editor

The Morgans of Hartford

Gregory Hedberg

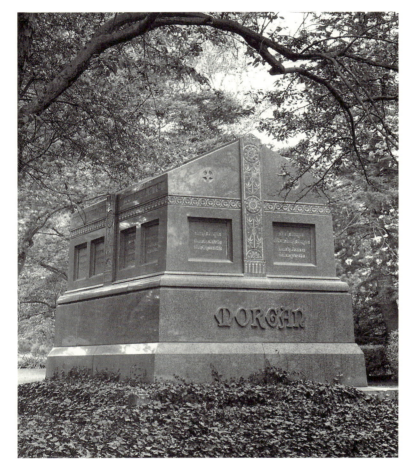

1 : George Keller, *Morgan Family Monument*, Cedar Hill Cemetery, Hartford.

2–3 : American, unknown, *Portraits of Joseph and Sarah Morgan*, about 1840, Gift of Mrs. Walter L. Goodwin, Wadsworth Atheneum, 1952.325–6.

When wealth was primarily tied to land, the great noble families and art patrons of Europe tended to remain in one place and put down deep roots. The American families that emerged to prominence in the late nineteenth century, however, were much more mobile and often relocated after one or two generations. Involved in international finance, the Morgans of Hartford were not tied to their native city in the same way the Fords were to Detroit or the Du Ponts to Wilmington; rather the nature of their business required new family centers in London and New York. Nevertheless, despite changing perspectives as the family relocated and became famous, the Morgans continued to be major patrons in their native city for four generations. The land on which Hartford's City Hall rests, the Williams Memorial Library at Trinity College, St. John's Episcopal Church and, most prominently, the Morgan Memorial wing and much of the European and American collections of the Wadsworth Atheneum testify to a century of periodic involvement of the Morgans with Hartford.

Each side of the Morgan family monument in Hartford's Cedar Hill Cemetery (Figure 1) bears the names of members of the four generations who affected Hartford in different ways, headed by the eldest son: on the north, Joseph Morgan (1780–1847) who moved the family to Hartford and laid the foundation for the family fortune; on the east, Junius Spencer Morgan (1813–1890) who first made the Morgan family name internationally famous; on the west, John Pierpont Morgan Sr. (1837–1913), the great collector and subject of this book; and on the south, John Pierpont Morgan Jr. (1867–1943) who bore the burden of distributing his father's vast art collection.

Joseph Morgan

In 1817, J. Pierpont Morgan's grandparents, Joseph and Sarah Morgan (Figures 2–3), moved down the Connecticut River by boat to Hartford from the family farm in West Springfield, Massachusetts. This farm had been held for four generations having been first settled by Miles Morgan (1616–1699) who came to the Connecticut Valley from England in 1636. Joseph Morgan immediately purchased the Exchange Coffee House in Hartford, a gathering place for river boat captains, merchants and financiers. He soon began to invest in other real estate (he eventually owned over a hundred acres inside the present city limits of Hartford) as well as other enterprises related to travel, shipping and insurance. In 1819 in the parlors of his Exchange Coffee House, the Aetna Fire Insurance Company was organized and he was one of the founders. In connection with Aetna Fire, Morgan frequently traveled throughout the United States to inspect buildings that were ruined or to evaluate others as to risk, and in doing so formed business contacts for the Morgan family nationally. After selling the coffee house in 1829, he leased a hotel on the corner of Main and Gold Streets across from the Wadsworth property on which the Atheneum would be built thirteen years later. During the 1830s he helped organize and then invested in a canal company, a steamboat line, the railroad from Hartford to Springfield, and the Connecticut River Banking Company, at the same time accumulating considerable wealth.[2]

In 1835 Joseph Morgan built a substantial three-story town house at 26 Asylum Street in Hartford. In 1841 when the town's prominent citizens raised over $30,000 for the new Wadsworth Atheneum, Morgan was among the original 134 subscribers. He pledged $200, which made him an incorporator and gave him two transmissible shares in the corporation.[3]

Joseph Morgan and Sarah Spencer (1787–1859) of Middletown, Connecticut, married in 1807 and had three children. The eldest, Mary (born 1808), married Rev. James Allwood Smith and moved to Great Falls, New Hampshire. The second daughter, Lucy (1811–1890), was a socially prominent figure in Hartford throughout her lifetime. She married James Goodwin (1803–1878), who was to become the largest taxpayer in Hartford, being connected to a variety of business ventures including Connecticut Mutual Life Insurance Company. This marriage forged an important link between the Morgans and the venerable Goodwin family, civic leaders since Hartford was founded in 1636. James and Lucy Morgan Goodwin eventually built a huge residence in Hartford that was often visited by J. Pierpont Morgan. Joseph and Sarah Morgan's third child was Junius Spencer.

Junius Spencer Morgan

Born into prosperity, Junius Spencer Morgan (Figure 4) advanced the family's position to one of international importance. He began as a merchant in Hartford, learning business acumen from his father in whose house he lived until he was twenty-seven, and from his older brother-in-law James Goodwin. In 1836 he married Juliet Pierpont (1816–1884), the daughter of a prominent Boston family, and four years later the couple moved into their own house on Farmington Avenue on Lord's Hill (a superb grandfather's clock [Figure 5] once owned by Junius and Juliet Morgan when they lived in that house was later given to the Atheneum).[4] For the initial Wadsworth Atheneum building fund J. S. Morgan was also an incorporator and pledged $100.

In 1851, four years after his father died, Junius Spencer Morgan moved the family to Boston where, with the considerable wealth he had inherited, he joined the booming mercantile firm of James M. Beebe & Company, which then became J. M. Beebe, Morgan & Company. Three years later, he accepted an invitation from fellow Yankee George Peabody to move to London and become his partner in the important international banking house of George Peabody & Company, a firm that specialized in investing European capital in American industries. A decade later Peabody retired and the well-established firm became J. S. Morgan & Company.[5] Successfully negotiating a $50,000,000 loan to the French government during the Franco-Prussian War of 1870, Morgan rivaled the Rothschilds in international finance. He lived at No. 13 Princes Gate facing Hyde Park in London and had a country estate called Dover House on ninety-two acres in Roehampton.

Having lived in Hartford for thirty-four years, Junius Spencer Morgan continued to have close ties with that city, which was becoming a major financial and insurance center due to the considerable amount of capital that had accumulated in the valley from farming and trade. He regularly visited his mother in Hartford until her death in 1859 and then continued to visit Lucy and James Goodwin, with whom he had financial dealings. These old ties undoubtedly led him to look favorably upon a request,

4: William Wetmore Story, *Bust of Junius Spencer Morgan*, 1884, Gift of Miss Caroline L. Morgan, Wadsworth Atheneum, 1914.1.

coming in 1889 from his sister's son, Rev. Francis Goodwin (1839–1923), to help the Wadsworth Atheneum, then forty-five years old and in need of major repairs and additional endowment. These needs were explained by Goodwin one night after dinner at Princes Gate and Morgan agreed to subscribe $100,000 towards a $400,000 goal. This was a significant tribute to the Atheneum for not only was it a large sum of money, but, unlike his son J. Pierpont, Junius Spencer did not make large monetary gifts. Exactly paralleling the first Morgan gifts to the museum when Junius pledged one half the amount of his father's gift, his own son, J. Pierpont, now repeated the gesture and offered $50,000.[6] The remaining $250,000 of the goal came from two thousand other contributors, including $50,000 from the Goodwins, partly in memory of Lucy Morgan Goodwin, who died in 1890.

Junius Spencer's generosity towards the Atheneum may also have resulted in part from his own interest in art. The large vaults at Princes Gate were apparently filled with silver,[7] but whether household silver or a serious collection — perhaps of English silver — is not known. Following a revival of interest in Gainsborough and Reynolds spurred by the English Rothschilds, Morgan also bought works by those artists. In 1876 he bought the celebrated Gainsborough portrait of the *Duchess of Devonshire*; however, the picture was stolen from Agnew's before it was delivered to Junius, only to reappear in 1901 (and to be bought by J. Pierpont!). Had the work not disappeared the price of over $50,000 would have made the painting the second most expensive picture in the world at the time. Junius indicated he wanted to buy it as a gift for his son — perhaps thus adding an element of casual one-upmanship to the rival Rothschilds who had recently bid on the painting.[8] In 1887 he gave the Metropolitan Museum in New York another English portrait, *The Hon. Henry Fane with His Guardians* by Sir Joshua Reynolds.[9]

In 1890 Junius Spencer Morgan died as the result of an accident near his villa in Monte Carlo. His body was brought back to Hartford and a funeral service was conducted at Christ Church. All the stores in Hartford closed along the route of the funeral procession, flags were flown at half-mast, and Junius Spencer Morgan was buried in the Morgan family plot, near the Goodwin's, at Cedar Hill Cemetery.[10]

John Pierpont Morgan, Sr.
Junius' son John Pierpont Morgan was born in Hartford on 17 April 1837, when his parents were still living with Joseph and Sarah Morgan at 26 Asylum Street. His given names come from his mother who was the daughter of the noted preacher and poet Rev. John Pierpont, then pastor of Old Hollis Street Church in Boston. Like the Morgans, the Pierponts were a long-established family of merchants and farmers, having descended from John Pierpont of London who came to New England about 1640.

Herbert Satterlee's 1939 biography provides a wealth of information on young Pierpont's early days in Hartford. He was the eldest of five children,[11] attended public and private schools in Hartford, and for a time went to the Connecticut Episcopal Academy at Cheshire. His closest friend while growing up in Hartford was his aunt Lucy's son, James Junius Goodwin (1835–1915) — whose middle name came from Morgan's father. Morgan's first business venture was "Morgan & Goodwin" founded for the purpose of making a "Diorama of the Landing of Columbus." Only twelve at the time Morgan kept a detailed account book of ticket sales to the display.

In 1851 the young J. Pierpont Morgan left Hartford with his parents, first to move to Boston and then three years later to London. He attended a private school in Vevey, Switzerland for two years, then during 1856–1857 the University of Göttingen in Germany. During these years, he corresponded each week with

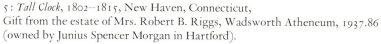

5: *Tall Clock*, 1802–1815, New Haven, Connecticut,
Gift from the estate of Mrs. Robert B. Riggs, Wadsworth Atheneum, 1937.86
(owned by Junius Spencer Morgan in Hartford).

James Goodwin in Hartford. In one letter from Germany he laments that his trunk was stolen "containing my collections of autographs worth at least $100."[12] Even in his youth Morgan was a collector and one who apparently knew what his collection was worth. Morgan and Goodwin toured Europe together in 1857, just before Morgan returned to settle in New York City. In 1862 when Morgan was twenty-four the two young men lived together in New York City and formed a partnership under the name J. Pierpont Morgan & Company, serving as the American representatives of Junius Morgan's London firm.[13]

From the time he returned from Europe in 1857 until the death of his father in 1890, J. Pierpont Morgan was establishing himself as a prominent financier in his own right and had relatively little contact with Hartford aside from his business dealings and personal friendships with the Goodwins. During this period Morgan established his own family in New York City. After a first marriage at age twenty-four to Amelia Sturges, who tragically died four months later, Morgan married Frances Tracy (1842–1924) in 1865 and they had four children: Louisa Pierpont (1866–1946) who married Herbert L. Satterlee; John Pierpont Morgan, Jr. (1867–1943) who succeeded him as head of the family firm; Juliet Pierpont (1870–1952) who married William P. Hamilton; and Anne Tracy Morgan (1873–1952) who formed the American Museum at Blérancourt, France. In 1882 the Morgans moved into a remodeled brownstone at 219 Madison Avenue, next to the present Morgan Library.

Morgan's contacts with the Wadsworth Atheneum were few during the middle twenty-five years of his life, but this began to change in the winter of 1889 when, on a visit to Hartford, he discussed with Francis Goodwin a new plan to revitalize the museum. Noting that this would interest his father, Morgan set up in May of that year the meeting in London which resulted in the generous pledges from the two Morgans. Morgan also advised Goodwin about the financial management of the institution and their discussions mark the beginning of J. Pierpont Morgan's role as a major patron of the Atheneum.

The Wadsworth Atheneum

Part library and general culture center as its name implies, the Wadsworth Atheneum (Figure 6) was central to the cultural life of Hartford when Morgan was a boy. It was founded by Daniel Wadsworth (1771–1848) who donated his superb art collection, his property on Main Street, and funds towards a new building which would contain a large central picture gallery. With additional funds from the community the Atheneum opened in 1844 with eighty paintings on view. Joseph, Junius, as well as young Pierpont Morgan all experienced at first hand the pride generated by this innovative public monument and civic art collection — the first in the country. They also saw the numerous paintings bought during the first decade of the museum as another $12,000 was raised to buy five large John Trumbulls, a magnificent Thomas Cole, the first important work by the young local painter Frederic Church, and forty-one other European and American paintings, including major works by Vanderlyn and Lawrence, bought from the recently defunct American Academy of Arts in New York. By 1851 when the Morgans moved to Boston the collection had grown to 140 works of art.

Although there is no evidence of young Morgan coming into personal contact with the art collector Daniel Wadsworth, Morgan and Wadsworth occupy parallel positions in their respective family histories; and the similarities between them may help illuminate the motivations for Morgan's extraordinary benefactions.

Daniel Wadsworth and J. Pierpont Morgan were born into families that were well established socially and economically. During their adult years, however, both men saw their families rise

6: Wadsworth Atheneum, Hartford, 1842 building.

7: J. Pierpont Morgan, Sr., 1902, Pach Brothers/Bettmann Archives.

8: Benjamin West, *The Raising of Lazarus*, 1780 (as painting appeared hung over the altar at Winchester Cathedral, Winchester, England from 1780–1900), Gift of J. Pierpont Morgan, Wadsworth Atheneum, 1900.3.

to great wealth and international prominence and they became heirs to a family dynasty. In the late eighteenth century the Wadsworth name became almost as well known nationally and internationally as the Morgan name was to become a century later, for Jeremiah Wadsworth (1743–1804), who left his huge estate to his son, was one of the foremost capitalists in the young Republic. Commissary-general for the Continental Army during the Revolution, Jeremiah Wadsworth developed an international trading business with Europe and China and was the largest shareholder in the Bank of North America in Philadelphia, the second President of the Bank of New York, and the founder of the Bank of Hartford. Upon the death of their fathers — a time when one confronts one's own mortality, as well as perhaps experiences a release from a very dominating personality — both Morgan and Wadsworth started to collect art avidly and for both it became an obsession.[14]

While their parents had concentrated on building up the family wealth and creating a dynasty, in their later years Daniel Wadsworth and J. Pierpont Morgan concerned themselves with giving away their possessions and perhaps with securing the newly-won status and reputation of the family. Just weeks before their seventieth birthdays, they each declared their intention to provide funds to erect a large building for the purpose of displaying art, that would also be an eternal monument to the family name. In their wills they each made provisions to utilize the new building to house their own art collections.

The parallels that can be drawn between Wadsworth and Morgan are not simply coincidences; both men followed a pattern frequently observed in succeeding generations of a famous family. As explored in Thomas Mann's 1901 novel *Buddenbrooks*, after the establishment of great wealth and social standing, the next generation — frequently the third in traditional societies but more commonly the second in this century — often turns to art. There are numerous historic parallels to Morgan and Wadsworth. As J. Pierpont has so frequently been compared to Lorenzo de'Medici, so Junius Spencer Morgan can be compared to Lorenzo's grandfather Cosimo de'Medici who made the family famous, and Joseph Morgan can be seen to parallel Lorenzo's great-grandfather, Giovanni di Bicci de'Medici, the little-known founder of the family fortunes in Florence. The rival Rothschild banking family or Morgan's cousins, the Goodwins, also provide parallels to the Morgans as later generations of these families turned to art. England in the eighteenth century produced a plethora of third-generation art collectors, and there the common practice was to retain the collections in the family and pass them down from generation to generation — like titles. In the United States, on the other hand, when the art collector boom hit with later generations of Havermeyers, Clarks and Rockefellers, it had become a public spirited custom, of which Daniel Wadsworth was among the progenitors, to give collections to civic institutions.

Of course many magnificent art collections do not follow the Medici, Wadsworth and Morgan pattern and were assembled by self-made men, such as Henry Ford (1863–1947), Samuel H. Kress (1863–1955) or Benjamin Altman (1840–1913), often after they had rapidly achieved fortune and position. Interestingly, Henry Clay Frick (1848–1919) does not fit the general progression from wealth to fame to collection, for he started collecting art as a young man, before he made his fortune. Perhaps this early interest explains why Frick is among the most distinguished collectors America produced. While Morgan's collecting and museum building was also influenced by contemporary historic trends and ideas, his personal position as perpetuator of the newly created Morgan family dynasty also needs to be considered.

After the death of his father in 1890, Morgan (Figure 7) took control of J. S. Morgan & Company, London, as well as his father's property including Princes Gate and Dover House. His position as

America's premier banker was then solidified as he played central roles during the financial panic of 1893, the United States Treasury crisis of 1895 and the billion-dollar steel merger of 1901. Collecting art now became his recreation as well as his great passion.

The chronology and details of Morgan's collecting activities are discussed here by Linda Roth. Among his contemporary collectors in America Morgan was quite unusual for his primary interest in objects and decorative arts rather than paintings (probably only five per cent of his collection consisted of paintings). He was, however, less unique in this respect among other Hartford-born collectors, for the city was a focal point for collecting objects, particularly American, during the latter part of the nineteenth century. Local collectors of Morgan's generation such as Horace Fuller (1835–1905), Gurdon Trumbull (1841–1903), Stephen Terry (1842–1889) and Albert Hastings Pitkin (1852–1917), all of whom eventually gave their collections to the Wadsworth Atheneum, are often cited as among the first in the nation to collect decorative arts.[15]

While slowly evolving a master plan for his collections as he assembled them, Morgan gave away only a small part of his collection during his lifetime. He donated only one significant work of art directly to Hartford. That work, a large and important painting of *The Raising of Lazarus* by Benjamin West had hung since 1780 on the high altar of Winchester Cathedral in England (Figure 8).[16] It was removed to make some repairs and then sold to Morgan in 1900. One of the most famous treasures owned by the Atheneum since it first opened was a *Portrait of Benjamin West* by Sir Thomas Lawrence, yet the museum did not own a painting by West himself. Morgan apparently sought to rectify this situation by acquiring the work and immediately giving it to the Atheneum. In 1900 he also bought the famous Sebastiano del Piombo portrait of *Christopher Columbus* and, feeling it should remain permanently on view in what was then the country's only national museum, he gave it to the Metropolitan Museum the same year. It is interesting to note the clear logic behind these gifts, and how Morgan appears to have carefully balanced what he gave to the Metropolitan with what he gave to the Atheneum.[17]

The Morgan Memorial (1893–1915)
The construction of the Morgan Memorial building of the Wadsworth Atheneum (Figure 9) at once more than doubled the size of the seventy-year-old institution and launched a new era for the museum. The inscription on the floor of the grand staircase of the Memorial reads "THIS BUILDING HAS BEEN ERECTED IN LOVING MEMORY OF JUNIUS SPENCER MORGAN / A NATIVE OF MASSACHUSETTS / A MERCHANT OF HARTFORD 1836 . . . 1851 / AFTERWARD A MERCHANT OF LONDON / BORN APRIL 14, 1813 DIED APRIL 8, 1890." What the inscription does not say is that the patron behind the project was J. Pierpont Morgan, that it took twelve years to assemble the plot of land on which the Memorial rests and seven more years to construct the building, and that the total cost of over $1,400,000 represents the largest of Pierpont Morgan's gifts.[18]

Morgan apparently wanted to create a significant memorial to Junius Spencer Morgan in each of the four cities in which his father had lived, namely Holyoke, Massachusetts, near the Morgan farm where Junius was born, Hartford, Boston, and London. In Holyoke, Morgan gave funds in 1899 to build a new library as a memorial to "Joseph Morgan and Junius Spencer Morgan, natives of Holyoke." For Hartford, in light of their mutual patronage of the Atheneum and interest in art, a memorial connected to the Atheneum was a logical choice. For Boston a sensible project presented itself and Morgan decided very quickly: in 1901, he gave $1,000,000 to Harvard University to erect three buildings at the medical school, "as a memorial to Junius Spencer Morgan, a native of Massachusetts

9: Benjamin Wistar Morris, Morgan Memorial, from southwest, 1908–1915, Wadsworth Atheneum, Hartford.

and for many years a merchant of Boston." What he intended to do in London, where his father lived for thirty-six years, is not clear. Yet in letters at the Victoria and Albert uncovered by Linda Roth and discussed in her essay, Morgan clearly indicates that in June of 1904 he was planning to create a museum at Princes Gate (previously his father's house) to house his own art collection. One might speculate that this edifice would have become the London memorial to his father, or at least that it would have perpetuated the London family house as the Morgan Library building preserved the family locus in New York. Late in 1905, however, Morgan concluded that even after enlarging the house at Princes Gate (he had bought the property next door) it would not be large enough for "his entire collection" — presumably meaning his entire London collection. The idea for a London museum may also have been dropped because Morgan finally succeeded in obtaining a site large enough for his growing collection in Hartford, where it appears he started to think in similar albeit grander terms to what he had planned for London. His London plan of a building associated with the father containing art collected by the son is exactly what Morgan eventually erected in Hartford, but now on a public as opposed to a domestic scale.

A series of letters recently uncovered by Eugene Gaddis indicates the sequence of events for the Morgan Memorial. As early as 1893 Morgan had begun buying the land immediately south of the Wadsworth Atheneum and had noted the possibility of erecting an addition in the future. He may have been prompted to such action when Rev. Francis Goodwin told him that the adjacent buildings were a fire hazard (Goodwin undoubtedly knew what to say to the grandson of an Aetna Fire inspector).[19] He bought parcels in 1893 and 1900, but a crucial piece of property on Main Street owned by St. John's Church presented a major obstacle. Finally, after Morgan agreed to contribute $100,000 towards a new church in West Hartford, the congregation voted in late October, 1905, to sell the land. Two months later Morgan indicated to Sir Purdon Clarke that he was abandoning plans for a museum in London.[20]

Another event that occurred in 1905 and may have served as a catalyst for Morgan to act decisively was the death in late August of Elizabeth Hart Jarvis Colt (1826–1905), one of the wealthiest women in America and widow of Hartford's famous gun inventor and manufacturer Samuel Colt. Having started collecting in the 1850s and being particularly active after her husband died in 1862, she was perhaps the first woman in America to buy major paintings and sculpture on her own. In her will she left a bequest of 730 works of art and funds to erect a building or wing in conjunction with the Atheneum to bear her name and to house her collection. As the Wadsworth trustees planned to build the Elizabeth Hart Jarvis Colt wing, Morgan formally clarified his intentions in a letter of 8 January 1907, to Rev. Francis Goodwin:

"*Dear Sir:*

Referring to the conversations which I have had from time to time with you, during the past few years, you are aware of the fact of my long cherished idea of erecting, in connection with the Wadsworth Atheneum, some building which would be a memorial to my father, whose early years of business life were passed in Hartford and whose remains now rest in Cedar Hill cemetery. To this end, I have, from time to time, secured two or three tracts of land adjacent to the old property, which have been turned over to the Atheneum, or are now held by you for its benefit.

It is upon a part of this that I desire to erect a building on which I am prepared to expend an amount not exceeding five hundred thousand dollars.

The conversations that I have had with you and with your architect, Mr. Morris, have led practically to an agreement between us as to the ultimate character of the building, and whatever further is needed in that line I am prepared to decide whenever we have another conversation, which has been delayed by my illness . . .[21]

10: Benjamin Wistar Morris, drawing showing plan for Morgan Memorial and Colt Gallery, Hartford, 1907.

Benjamin Wistar Morris (1870–1944), a noted New York architect who was also Rev. Francis Goodwin's son-in-law, was selected to design both the Morgan Memorial and Colt Gallery. His 1907 drawing (Figure 10) shows how the two buildings were planned to complement one another. The new Colt Gallery connected the original Wadsworth building to the new Morgan Memorial. To provide a transitional link between the two main structures, the Colt Gallery was set back and built in an English Tudor style to match more closely the 1842 Wadsworth building, while the Morgan Memorial was to contain the new main entrance to the museum and would be in a grander English Renaissance style. The Colt Gallery, which would contain a mixture of European and American art collected by the Colts, may also have been conceived as a transition between the American art contained in the Wadsworth building and the European art intended for the Morgan Memorial.

After the site was cleared, the cornerstone was laid on 23 April, 1908 and construction began. In the fall of 1908 Morgan visited Hartford with his granddaughter to see the Goodwins and discuss how the construction was progressing. He had just weathered the great economic panic of 1907 and his collecting activities greatly accelerated — perhaps with an eye towards filling the new building. As president of the board of trustees of the Metropolitan, he was also directing the construction of a new wing for the Hoentschel collection (now the Morgan Collection) of French art which Morgan had given to the museum in 1906.

In Hartford after eighteen months of construction, the front and most lavish part of what eventually was to be a much larger building had been completed, and on 19 January 1910 Morgan took several members of his family on a special train from New York to attend the dedication and opening of the new Morgan Memorial. At this time the building contained tapestries on loan from Morgan and some paintings from the museum's own collection (Figure 11).[22] During the next three months 95,000 people visited the new Memorial. After the 1910 section of the building was completed with no expense spared in its construction (there were nine different types of marble used in the grand entrance way and staircase — Figure 12), twenty-one additional galleries to the east were begun. These galleries, more modest in appointment, tripled the exhibition space of the Atheneum and changed the scale of the project: from a distinguished memorial wing it became in itself a large new art museum. The addition clearly would only be useful, though, if Morgan intended to increase the holdings of the museum. Early in 1912 as these new galleries were being readied, the vast quantities of decorative arts and paintings that had been held by Morgan in London started to leave England *en masse*. In October of that year Morgan went to Hartford to make a complete inspection of the additional galleries being constructed and to discuss the details with the architect.[23] Then in November he surprised Edward Robinson, Director of the Metropolitan, by telling him that he had "no intention of giving or bequeathing his collection to the Metropolitan Museum."[24] Nevertheless, the completion of the Memorial was far enough away to provide time for a New York showing of London material, some of it en route to Hartford, and plans were made for a temporary exhibition at the Metropolitan in 1914 to show the combined London and New York portions of the Morgan Collection.

The Morgan Collection and Hartford

What was to happen to Morgan's art collection after the New York exhibition? Morgan obviously intended to send part of the collection to Hartford when the new galleries were finished, just as he had sent tapestries for display in the already completed part of the Memorial. Before the Metropolitan exhibition even took place, however, Morgan died in Europe. According to the terms of his

11: Morgan Memorial galleries, completed 1910.

12: Morgan Memorial, base of grand staircase, completed 1910.

will, the permanent distribution of his vast collection was left to his son. Presumably following Morgan's own plan, almost all the material that had been on loan to the Metropolitan for years went to that museum, while Hartford received most of the decorative arts that had been kept in London. Several distinct groupings of ancient bronzes and glass also went to Hartford. Despite Morgan's thoughts of creating a museum in London, he gave little to that city.[25] Although Morgan's will refers to the disposition of his "paintings, miniatures, porcelains and other works of art . . . which would render them permanently available for the instruction and pleasure of the American people," the demands of the estate were such that the majority of the tapestries and paintings were retained or sold.

Did Morgan actually intend to place a significant part of his painting and tapestry collection in the Morgan Memorial? The floor plan of the Morgan Memorial as approved by Morgan in 1906 clearly calls for large painting galleries as well as a Tapestry Hall (Figure 13). The decorative arts and ancient material that did come to Hartford were perfectly suited for display in the sixteen small side galleries built on the first and second floors of the Memorial. The six main galleries at the front and rear of the building, however, with skylights and large fixed seating units in the center, were clearly intended to be painting galleries, and the central core of the building was a hall with huge walls for tapestries. If Morgan did not plan to give some tapestries and part of his seventeenth- and eighteenth-century European painting collection to complement the seventeenth- and eighteenth-century European decorative arts that did come to the museum, one must conclude that he was willing to have the most prominent galleries in the Morgan Memorial (for which he bought the land, financed the lavish construction, and personally endowed) display works of art collected or donated by others. The paintings then owned by the museum were primarily American — not an area of interest for him — and well suited for display in the recently refurbished Wadsworth building with the Wadsworth bequest. Actually the museum did not own enough paintings to fill the large galleries in the Memorial and there were no tapestries in the collection.

If Morgan had meant the Morgan Memorial to be filled with art that he personally had collected, he would have been following a pattern found frequently in Europe and America from the mid-nineteenth century to the present, as well as his own idea for London. It is common for collectors to want to keep together at least part of what they have assembled as a legacy of their accomplishment. This was true of Mrs. Gardner in Boston, Frick in New York, Walters in Baltimore, Phillips in Washington, Du Pont in Wilmington and many others.[26] The closest parallel to Morgan's plans for Hartford, may be found in his fellow New York City residents and collectors, Robert Sterling Clark and his wife Francine who selected Williamstown as the out-of-town site for their museum because of early family associations with Williams College — a city location being next to impossible for the museum they wanted to found. Helen Clay Frick was another New Yorker who selected an out-of-town site associated with her father, in this case her hometown of Pittsburgh, on which to build a museum for the art she collected.

While Morgan was able to create his own library in New York, it was much more difficult to find an appropriate site with adequate space and light either in London or New York for a significant part of his fine art collection — paintings require top floor galleries with skylights and tapestries need huge walls. Then too, a separate fine arts museum in New York would have been quite an affront to the Metropolitan to which Morgan was very loyal. By conceiving of a logical division of his collection among the Metropolitan Museum, the Pierpont Morgan Library and the Morgan Memorial, however, Morgan established a legacy in diverse ways. He was a

13: Morgan Memorial, tapestry gallery, completed 1915 (shows Greek lions given by Morgan and tapestries on loan).

model for his fellow multimillionaire collectors through his gifts to the Metropolitan Museum to expand America's comprehensive national museum.[27] Simultaneously he created his own library in New York filled with objects that are better stored away than displayed. And, in his hometown, on a large and central tract of land, he erected a building that could accommodate a significant part of his collection for a unified and permanent display as a personal legacy. The mixture of objects, paintings and tapestries that would fill the Morgan Memorial in Hartford would not be encyclopedic — the goal for the Metropolitan — but would have a more personal, eclectic character resembling that of a great English country house. While most of the material that went to the Metropolitan is from collections Morgan bought *en masse* from Gréau, Ward, Quakenberg, Hoentschel, Le Breton, Marfels and others to represent entire areas of Western art, his paintings, tapestries, Sèvres, and ancient bronzes were bought singly and hence were a more appropriate memorial to his abilities and taste as a collector.[28]

If Morgan had indeed intended to fill the Morgan Memorial completely with items from his own collection, then the motivation behind the vast project can be seen to reflect more broadly his natural instincts, as one of the most avid collectors America ever produced, to preserve intact part of what he had assembled. This was in addition to the noble but less passionate motives of a son erecting a memorial to his father or a native being very generous to his hometown. In 1912 Pierpont Morgan arranged to donate to the Atheneum a very large portrait of himself painted that year by Carlos Baca-Flor, a reminder that the Morgan Memorial was not to commemorate Junius Spencer Morgan alone.[29]

Morgan's reputation as a fine art collector would be much greater today if the demands on the Morgan estate had not been larger than anticipated,[30] and perhaps if his son had been concerned as he was with keeping part of the fine art collection together under the Morgan name. Through sales from the estate numerous paintings and other works of art were ultimately made available to the American people, as Morgan had wished, however the credit line does not name Morgan but rather the Metropolitan's Joseph Pulitzer Bequest Fund, or Gift of Mellon, or Widener or Frick. Works such as Fragonard's series *The Progress of Love*, Reynolds' *General Burgoyne*, Greuze's *Wool Winder*, Rembrandt's *Nicolas Ruts*, Goya's *Don Pedro, Duque de Osuna*, and Constable's *The White Horse*, plus Limoges enamels and Renaissance bronzes — all now at the Frick Collection but brought to America by Morgan, are today seen as reflecting Frick's and not Morgan's distinguished taste as a collector.

J. Pierpont Morgan died in Rome at the age of 75. During his final hours his mind wandered and he talked of boyhood days in Hartford.[31] After his death — no other event in 1913 received as much world press — his body was brought to Hartford for burial in Cedar Hill Cemetery, and when the funeral procession passed the Morgan Memorial, it crossed to the opposite lane in deference to Morgan's generosity to the city. Compared to his peers, his estate was surprisingly small, reduced by his lavish spending, collecting and philanthropy.[32] After Morgan's death, construction continued in Hartford. In 1915 the newly expanded Junius Spencer Morgan Memorial galleries were opened (see Figure 9), and in 1917 some 1,325 works of art from the J. Pierpont Morgan collection were given to the Atheneum. Due to Morgan's efforts the museum was now the fifth largest in America.

John Pierpont Morgan, Jr.
John P. Morgan, Jr. was admitted into his father's firm in New York City in 1892 at the age of twenty-five. From 1893 until his father's death, however, he lived principally in London, handling affairs previously directed by his grandfather, and became head of the

14: William Wetmore Story, *Alcestis*, 1881, Gift of J. Pierpont Morgan, Wadsworth Atheneum, 1914.4.

family firm, after 1913. He helped oversee the separation of the deposit banking business of J. P. Morgan & Company from the investment banking field, the part of the business assumed by some partners forming a new investment bank, Morgan-Stanley & Company. Morgan remained head of the commercial bank.

In 1890 he married Jane Grew (1868–1925) of Boston. "Jack & Jessie" as the Morgans were called, lived more informally than the older Morgans and had four children, Junius Spencer, Jane Norton, Frances Tracy and Henry Sturgis. They had a house at Glen Cove, New York, and when in New York City, the Morgans lived near J. Pierpont's house and library at Thirty-seventh and Madison. Although he continued to have contacts with Hartford, the family center had decidedly moved to New York City and London. Morgan was more focused as a collector and philanthropist than his wide-ranging father. Encouraged by Belle da Costa Green at the Morgan Library, he specialized in collecting rare books and manuscripts (occasionally at prices that would have shocked even his father) which he then donated. The library was expanded under Morgan's direction and incorporated as a public institution in 1924.

John P. Morgan, Jr. was entrusted with the task of distributing the vast art collection, presumably following some expression of Morgan Sr's intentions although the only written guideline, in Morgan's will of 1913, is a general statement of his desire and intention to make his collection permanently available to the American people; the Wadsworth Atheneum, the only museum mentioned, was agreeable to him to effect part of this purpose, but he left the disposition entirely up to his son.[33] The first crates arrived in Hartford in 1914 and contained American sculpture — two busts by Hiram Powers, the bust of Junius Spencer and a large marble of *Alcestis* by William Wetmore Story (Figure 14), works of art probably originally bought by Junius Spencer Morgan. Some works were then sold, others retained by the family. The remainder of the fine art collection was divided and in the summer of 1916, 1,325 objects arrived in Hartford and were installed in the Memorial.[34]

While the highlights of the European decorative arts collection generously given to the Wadsworth Atheneum by Pierpont Morgan Jr. are represented here, the superb collection of eighty-two ancient bronzes (Figure 15) which Morgan also gave to the museum should not be overlooked. Reflecting Morgan's general collecting patterns and the domestic scale of Princes Gate, some objects given to the Atheneum can be grouped as focused collections in their own right: English salt-glaze ware from Staffordshire (Figure 16), Venetian glass, ancient glass, or Roman pottery. Also included in the bequest were smaller lots of ancient gold jewelry, paste gems and enamels, as well as French porcelain from factories other than Sèvres. While perhaps ninety-five per cent of the items fall into groups (see Appendix I), others were probably purchased singly and stand on their own, such as the *Ebony and Silver Cabinet* (cat. no. 15); a pair of magnificent Greek marble lions; a Roman bathtub; and an elaborate Chinese export enamel centerpiece. The nature of the objects that came to the museum from the Morgan bequest helped to establish the distinct character of the Atheneum as a combination of diverse special collections.

During this period the Atheneum also received gifts from other members of the Morgan family. Caroline Morgan, daughter of the senior Morgan's sister Sarah, gave the superb bust of her father Junius Spencer Morgan by William Wetmore Story (Figure 4) and a large painting by the British artist Sir Benjamin Williams Leader. The most spectacular gift to come to the museum from other members of the family was the magnificent donation in 1923 of Albert Bierstadt's painting *In the Mountains* (Figure 17) given by John Junius Morgan in memory of his mother Juliet Pierpont Morgan, sister of Morgan Sr. Appropriately, one Morgan family heirloom came later as a gift from the Goodwins. When Walter L. Goodwin died in 1952, Mrs. Goodwin gave the museum a pair of portraits of Joseph and Sarah Morgan (see Figures 2–3), the first generation in Hartford who were great-grandparents to both Walter Goodwin and J. Pierpont Morgan Jr.

The Nutting Collection

The story of the Morgan family's generosity to Hartford has a dramatic finale, and it involves American, not European, decorative arts. Most American collectors during the period after the Civil War were, like Pierpont Morgan himself, chiefly interested in European art. There slowly developed a group of collectors in New England (and particularly in Hartford), however, who turned their attention to Americana. They cited the thin veneer of European furniture as the product of a decadent civilization, while the solid oak furniture of the early American craftsmen reflected nobler virtues. The most vocal and prominent spokesman for this revival of interest in American pilgrim-century furniture was Wallace Nutting (1861–1941). He wrote numerous books on the subject and launched several commercial ventures, one of which was the manufacture of reproductions of early American furniture and another which featured hand-colored photographs of restored rooms, usually complete with Pilgrims. In the early 1920s Nutting assembled a large collection of seventeenth- and eighteenth-century furniture, kitchen utensils, looms and spinning wheels, pewter, looking glasses and ironwork with the aim of selling it *en bloc* to one of the new collectors of Americana. Henry Ford was the first prospect, but apparently Nutting's desire to have the collection bear his name was unacceptable to a newly famous man such as Ford.

William B. Goodwin (1866–1950), the Atheneum's curator of colonial American furniture and decorative arts at the time, was eager to have the collection in Hartford. In the fall of 1924 Goodwin with his younger brother Charles A. Goodwin (1876–1954), both children of Francis Goodwin, asked their cousin J. P. Morgan, Jr. to buy the entire collection for the museum, to be displayed in the basement galleries of the Morgan Memorial. Although the material reflects a complete change in taste from what interested his father, the collection appealed to Morgan's interest in early American history. In a letter to William Goodwin, Morgan observed: "My interest in the collection . . . is entirely from the standpoint of history, although some of the pieces are really beautiful in themselves." The purchase of the Nutting Collection enabled Morgan to make a contribution to the Morgan Memorial independent of his father. Perhaps he also thought the Nutting collection was a more appropriate gift to Hartford, known for its widespread and avid interest in Americana, than some of the European paintings or tapestries that Morgan Sr. may have once envisioned in the Memorial. In any case Morgan very generously bought the collection for $200,000 and gave it to the museum in 1926, a year after it had been installed and opened to the public with great fanfare.[35]

Acquiring an entire collection of almost one thousand objects was just the sort of thing that J. Pierpont Morgan Sr. would have done. But his son's attitude towards the name of the collection represents a marked change. Whenever Morgan bought a formed collection it was renamed the Morgan Collection. In a 1926 letter to Charles A. Goodwin, now president of the board of trustees, however, his son offered the Nutting collection as a gift to the Museum and added:

> It is Dr. Nutting's expressed desire that the Collection should be called the "Wallace Nutting Collection," and with this wish I think it would be wise to accede, if the Atheneum has no objection . . ."

That Morgan Jr. would not insist that the collection bear his name perhaps reflects the more securely established position of the fourth generation of a family dynasty. Unlike his father, Morgan Jr. was born with a famous name.

15: Egyptian, *Seated Bronze Cat*, Gift of J. Pierpont Morgan, Wadsworth Atheneum, 1917.521.

16: Salt-glaze Teapot, Staffordshire, England, about 1750, Gift of J. Pierpont Morgan, Wadsworth Atheneum, 1917.377.

17: Bierstadt, *In the Mountains*, Gift of John Junius Morgan in memory of Juliet Pierpont Morgan, Wadsworth Atheneum, 1923.253.

18: Nutting Collection, Gift of J. Pierpont Morgan, 1926 (as originally installed in basement of Morgan Memorial, 1925).

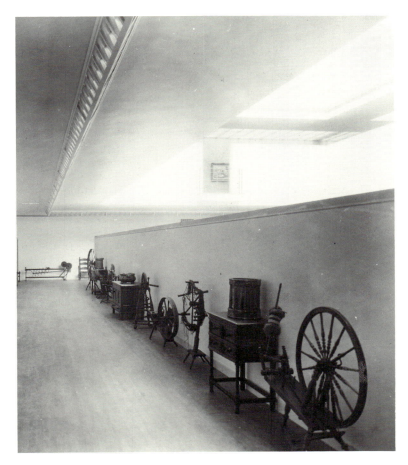

19: Nutting Collection (as installed by A. Everett Austin, Avery Memorial, 1934).

20: Nutting Collection (as installed by William Hosley, Avery Memorial, 1984).

The treatment of the Nutting Collection changed dramatically during Pierpont Morgan Jr.'s lifetime, only a few years after it was initially installed in the basement of the Morgan Memorial (Figure 18) according to specific themes outlined by Nutting. In 1934 it was moved to the museum's new Avery Building (Figure 19) in what may prove to have been the first modernist installation of American decorative arts. A. Everett Austin, Jr., director of the museum from 1927 to 1944 (and husband of Helen Goodwin, the granddaughter of Francis Goodwin) was the genius behind this installation, which treated the objects not as historical artifacts but as works of art, emphasizing their formal qualities. Fifty years later the collection was again reinstalled reflecting a warmer post-modernist aesthetic (Figure 20).[36]

J. Pierpont Morgan Jr. remained on the board of the Atheneum after the purchase of the Nutting Collection, but contact between the Morgan family and the Atheneum decreased. In 1928 five large tapestries that had been on loan to the Atheneum were removed to the new Morgan Library annex; another group of tapestries left in 1932. When the Avery Memorial building of the Wadsworth Atheneum opened in 1934, the Morgan Memorial went out of use for the next decade; the size of the painting collection did not warrant so many galleries open during the Great Depression and World War II, and the tapestry hall was now empty. The Memorial was reopened in the mid-1940s. By now the painting collection had increased enough to justify three buildings, and a set of large tapestries were given by Elisha Hilliard in 1945. Pierpont Morgan Jr. died in 1943 and his ashes were interred in the family plot at Cedar Hill where his wife had been buried in 1925.

A century after his grandfather and great-grandfather first donated funds to the museum, Morgan left a portrait of *Robert Rich, Earl of Warwick*, attributed to Van Dyck, to the Atheneum. Other extraordinary paintings he owned at the time of his death — including works by Rembrandt, Gainsborough, Constable, Reynolds, Lawrence, Turner, Rubens, Greuze and others, all formerly in his father's collection — were then sold, several to the Frick Collection.

Postscript

The Morgans launched a new era for the Wadsworth Atheneum. Their generosity perhaps helped to stimulate many other benefactions. Magnificent donations from Samuel P. Avery, Jr. (another New York City decorative arts collector who found Hartford and the Atheneum a suitable site for a memorial) added 1,400 objects and another building equal in size to the Morgan Memorial. Other collections were offered to the museum and although the professional staff was very small, the superb quality of the objects made saying no unthinkable. The Pell collection of ceramics, the Mead basket collection, the extraordinary Gould collection of American paintings, the Schnakenberg ancient collection, Van Gerbig glass, Miles and Hammerslough silver collections, and many others added tens of thousands of works to the collection, by gift or bequest. At the same time the Sumner Fund permitted the purchase of some 800 European old master, contemporary and American paintings. From the Goodwin family, which produced many later collectors as well as artists, architects and art patrons, came an 1873 parlor with superb Herter Brothers furniture from the huge house built by James and Lucy Morgan Goodwin following the latest English ideas of James's brother Francis Goodwin. Early American furniture was given by William B. and Mary Arabella Goodwin; a large and distinguished collection of marine objects came from Charles A. Goodwin; magnificent modern art was donated by the family from the estate of Philip L. Goodwin (the architect for the Museum of Modern Art in New York). A fifth building was added — opposite a court and parallel to the Morgan Memorial — named in tribute to James

Lippincott Goodwin (1881–1967), the son of Pierpont Morgan Sr.'s closest childhood friend and first partner, James Junius Goodwin.

Within the last ten years the trustees and staff have undertaken an ambitious program to revitalize the Wadsworth Atheneum and the Morgan Memorial. Structural problems had developed in the older buildings, including the Morgan Memorial, and large parts of the collection were no longer accessible to the public. Recognizing that operating costs would increase after the buildings were renovated and exhibition space increased, the trustees first doubled the operating endowment. Roofing was replaced, the buildings rewired, and new security and fire detection systems installed. Such extensive alterations presented to the professional staff the opportunity to rethink the entire installation of the museum. For years American paintings had been hung in the Morgan Memorial galleries, despite the grand European flavor of the architecture. In planning the reinstallation, the idea naturally evolved of making the Morgan Memorial a European wing. After fifty years of Sumner fund purchases the Atheneum has hundreds of superb European old-master paintings of its own. With an eye to filling some of the large galleries in the Memorial the Atheneum was the first museum in the country to buy major Italian and Spanish Baroque paintings.[37] The highlights of the museum's holdings in European paintings, some of the type once owned by Pierpont Morgan Sr., are now hung in the newly renovated painting galleries in the Morgan Memorial. Meanwhile, newly restored tapestries have been hung in the central hall and the Morgan decorative arts and ancient objects installed in the side galleries on the first and second floor. Now installed in a manner that was probably first envisaged decades ago by its founder, seventy-five years after Morgan's death the Morgan building is indeed a proper memorial to Hartford's most famous son and the most ambitious collector America ever produced.

Notes:

[1] The generations are as follows: Miles Morgan (1616–1699) married as second wife Elizabeth Bliss, daughter of Thomas and Margaret Bliss of Hartford; their son Nathaniel (1671–1752) married Hannah Bird of Farmington; their fifth son Joseph Morgan (1702–1773) married Mary Stebbins of Springfield; their son Joseph Morgan II (1755–1813), a captain in the Revolutionary War, married Experience Smith; their son was Joseph Morgan (1780–1847).

[2] See Herbert L. Satterlee, *J. Pierpont Morgan: An Intimate Portrait* (New York, 1939), pp. 1–5.

[3] On the other original incorporators of the Atheneum, see Eugene R. Gaddis, "Foremost upon this Continent: The Founding of the Wadsworth Atheneum," *Connecticut History* 26 (November, 1985), pp. 99–114.

[4] This tall clock, 1802–1815, inscribed Merriman & Co., New Haven, Connecticut, may have been a gift to Junius from Joseph Morgan who also gave him the house. Museum records document the clock (a gift from the estate of Mrs. Robert B. Riggs, 1937.86) to Junius Spencer Morgan's house, further noting it was owned by Joseph Morgan.

[5] Born in Massachusetts, Mr. Peabody moved to London in 1827 and soon prospered in investment banking, setting up the network taken over by Junius Morgan. During his lifetime Peabody founded Peabody Institute in Baltimore, and gave substantial funds to Harvard and Yale.

[6] The sequence of events is described in a November 1913 memorandum by Rev. Francis Goodwin in the Atheneum's archives (see note 19). Earlier donations by J. S. Morgan include a generous contribution in 1886 to the Hartford Orphan Asylum to establish the Sarah Morgan Fund in memory of his mother. He also donated to Trinity College, the newly-established Yale Law School, Guy's Hospital in London and the National Nurses Pension Fund, England (see D. Appleton, *Cyclopedia of American Biography*, vol. 4 [New York, 1888], p. 402).

[7] Satterlee, 1939, p. 536.

[8] Obviously in international banking the Rothschilds provided a model for the Morgans and perhaps also initially in their collecting activities. In 1874, the Vienna-born Baron Ferdinand de Rothschild started Waddesdon Manor — later a model for the Frick Collection — with French furniture and English portraits, particularly Gainsborough; yet the Baron was outbid in his attempt to buy the *Duchess of Devonshire*. Lionel Nathan de Rothschild (1808–1879) who bought Tring Park estate, also bought English portraits including a superb Reynolds in 1872. (J. S. Morgan may have sent his son to Göttingen as it was earlier the school of this head of the English Rothschilds.) Gerald Reitlinger, *The Economics of Taste* (New York, 1961), pp. 186–189, 193, 197.

[9] J. S. Morgan also had his portrait painted by the English artist Frank Holl (1845–1888), and his bust (Fig. 4) executed by William Wetmore Story (1819–1895), both works now in the Atheneum. J. S. Morgan also bought a rare Walter Scott manuscript, his son then bought nineteen, and J. P. Morgan, Jr. bought one (Douglas and Elizabeth Rigby, *Lock, Stock and Barrel: The Story of Collecting* [New York, 1944], p. 289). J. S. Morgan had also recently expressed an interest in his own family roots in New England by commissioning a statue at Court Square in Springfield, Massachusetts, of Miles Morgan, who had been very prominent in colonial politics. The inscription on the statue by J. S. Hartley reads "Miles Morgan / an early settler of Springfield / died 1699 aged 84 / erected in 1882 by one of his descendents of the fifth generation."

[10] Cedar Hill Cemetery opened in 1864 and the Morgan lot was purchased on December 11, 1872. Probably at that time the bodies of Joseph Morgan and Sarah Spencer Morgan were moved from Old North Cemetery, Hartford. After the burial of Junius Spencer Morgan on 6 May 1890, the remains of J. Pierpont Morgan's mother Juliet Pierpont Morgan, died 1884, and his younger brother, Junius S. Morgan, died 1858, were moved to Cedar Hill from an earlier plot in London. The Morgan family monument was designed by George Keller (1842–1935), a noted Hartford architect, to represent Morgan's interpretation of the Ark of the Covenant. A smaller version of the design was erected for the Pierpont family monument in Mount Auburn Cemetery, Cambridge, Massachusetts.

[11] The siblings were Sarah Spencer (1839–1896) who later married George H. Morgan from another branch of the Morgan family; May Lyman (1844–1919) who married Walter Hayes Burns in 1867 and settled in London; Junius Spencer Morgan (1846–1858) who died in London at age twelve; and Juliet Pierpont (1847–1923) who married John B. Morgan.

[12] Satterlee, 1939, pp. 17, 22, 36, 88. Morgan also collected pieces of stained glass as a young man.

[13] After a decade of working with Morgan, James Goodwin returned to Hartford in the mid-1870s to pursue his own family business (his father, James Goodwin, was one of Hartford's wealthiest citizens), but the two continued to be very close — like brothers — according to Satterlee. Satterlee, 1939, pp. 22, 71, 92, 116, 147, 149, 153.

[14] Jeremiah Wadsworth was also undoubtedly admired by all three generations of Morgans for his financial acumen. In 1907 J. Pierpont Morgan, Sr. donated to the Atheneum a large collection of letters written by Jeremiah Wadsworth. For Daniel Wadsworth, see Richard Saunders, *Daniel Wadsworth, Patron of the Arts* (Hartford, 1981).

[15] Elizabeth Stillinger, *The Antiquers* (New York, 1980). Other object collectors with close Hartford connections include Henry Wood Erving (1851–1941), George Dudley Seymour (1859–1945), and Francis Patrick Garvin (1875–1937). While Morgan's preference for objects as opposed to paintings is rightly viewed as a personal one, there might also be a Hartford, and perhaps an Atheneum, connection here. While it is unlikely Morgan personally knew any of the numerous Hartford area collectors of Americana, they all experienced one common influence, namely they were all raised in a town that, unlike any other at the time in America, had a public museum already filled with paintings and monumental sculpture (the Metropolitan and Boston Museum of Fine Arts were founded only in 1870). Moreover, even before the opening of the Atheneum in 1844, the earlier Hartford Art Gallery before it closed in 1840 had a collection of sixty-eight paintings with regular shows

from 1797. Just as creative artists take for granted the type of art they were born into and explore new areas, so too collectors repeatedly move to collect in areas not staked out by the preceding generations. The most important American parallel to Morgan in terms of collecting primarily ancient and European objects was Henry Walters (1848–1931) of Baltimore — the son of a painting and sculpture collector. Another parallel was Samuel P. Avery, Jr. (1847–1920), the son of a famous painting dealer and print collector, who in turn assembled a large collection of objects and decorative arts. (Avery also parallels Morgan in being a New Yorker who gave his collection and established a wing at the Wadsworth Atheneum). Morgan, born into paintings and sculpture, turned to objects, and given the opportunities presented by school and his family's business abroad, to European objects. Perhaps reacting to all the local Hartford interest in decorative arts and the Morgan gifts of some 2,300 objects and only three paintings, when Frank Sumner left the Atheneum a bequest of over one million dollars in 1927 to buy art for the collection, he saw the need to specify in his will that the income be used to acquire "paintings only."

[16]In addition to the new lavish catalogues of parts of his collection, Morgan Sr. also gave to the Atheneum several major books, including the forty-nine volume set of works on the birds of the world by John Gould given in 1899 in memory of Junius Spencer Morgan. He also gave the museum *The North American Indian* by photographer Edward Curtis (1868–1952), eventually a set of twenty volumes with 700 copperplate photogravures. Beginning in the 1890s Morgan financed Curtis' project to record the vanishing native cultures. Later volumes were given by Morgan Jr., starting the museum's small photograph collection.

[17]In 1906 as Morgan planned a new wing for the Atheneum, he bought the Hoentschel collection for the Metropolitan for over $1,000,000, approximately the same amount he was spending in Hartford. See Calvin Tomkins, *Merchants and Masterpieces: The Story of the Metropolitan Museum of Art* (New York, 1970), p. 166. If some paintings and tapestries were to go to the Memorial, the values of the collections going to the Atheneum and to the Metropolitan would have been closer.

[18]J. Pierpont Morgan gave the Atheneum $1,328,375 in cash during his lifetime — about half of which was spent on constructing the Morgan Memorial, a third for endowment, a sixth on land acquisition — plus $100,000 to St. John's Church to clear a site for the Memorial. To put this into perspective in terms of other cash gifts, the best estimates gathered by Linda Roth from clippings in the museum's archives and elsewhere indicate that J. Pierpont Morgan gave away close to $10,000,000. The major gifts include $1,350,000 to the Lying-in Hospital in New York; $1,000,000 to Harvard University; $560,000 to St. George's Church in New York where he was a warden for many years; $500,000 to the building fund of the Cathedral of St. John the Divine in New York and an equal amount to the New York Technical School; $175,000 for a botanical park in New York City; $150,000 to the New York Yacht Club; $125,000 to Palisades Park; $100,000 each to the Y.M.C.A., House of Rest for Consumptives, St. John's Church, Hartford and Holyoke Library in Massachusetts; and gifts of $50,000 or less to the Metropolitan Club in New York, the New York Public Library, Hartford Hospital, St. Paul's Cathedral, London for lighting (perhaps as a London memorial to his father) and Cooper-Union. As he spent considerable time over the years in Rome, Venice and Aix-les-Bains, other funds went to the American Academy in Rome, towards a new campanile in Venice and a hospital in Aix-les-Bains. Funds also went to various departments at the Metropolitan Museum, Trinity College, Hartford, Yale University, and George Peabody College in Nashville (founded with funds left by J. S. Morgan's London partner).

[19]In a November 1913 memo in the Museum's archives Francis Goodwin, President of the Board of Trustees from 1890 to 1919, outlined the sequence of events:

In 1889 the Wadsworth Atheneum having no sufficient endowment and some of its more interested friends having died, it became necessary to make an effort to secure contributions to repair and extend the buildings and to provide an adequate fund for its maintenance.

It happened at that time that J. P. Morgan was making me a visit and in the course of conversation inquired particularly about what was being done for the Atheneum and I told him of the plan which had been made for its resuscitation. He said to me, "This is a matter that would interest Father and if you should go out to London while I am there in the spring I will see that you have the opportunity to bring it to his attention." In May of the same year I was in London and dined with Mr. Junius Spencer Morgan at Princes' Gate with J. P. M. After dinner we went into the library and he said to me, "Now is your opportunity to talk to Father about the Atheneum." I went very fully into the whole history of the matter and explained in detail what we desired to do. As a result, Mr. J. S. Morgan stated that he would subscribe the sum of $100,000. Whereupon J. P. M. came behind where I was sitting and whispered to me, "and I'll give you $50,000." These were the two first subscriptions of the fund which was afterwards, by other contributions, increased to over $400,000. In January 1893,

J. P. M. came up to the opening of the re-constructed buildings and while here he asked me incidentally if I had everything to my mind. I said that there was only one thing that troubled me and that was that the Watkinson Library building stood almost upon the southern boundary of the Atheneum property and, in case the adjoining land was sold, our light would be in part cut off and the fire risk greatly increased. Shortly after, I was told by a lawyer that he was preparing the deed of that adjoining property and upon expressing my regret and alarm, he said I had no cause to fear although he was not at liberty to disclose the name of the purchaser. A few days later I received a letter from J. P. M. enclosing the deed of the property.

The Letter from Morgan to Goodwin in the museum's archives dated 19 January 1893 reads:

My dear Sir,
When I was in Hartford at the reopening of the Athenaeum, I was impressed by the fact that the building was cramped on the South side by the too near approach of the buildings adjacent. With the view of remedying this, I have ventured to purchase 63 feet on Main Street . . .
I desire to present this to the Wadsworth Athenaeum, and consequently enclosed herewith the necessary deeds for that purpose . . .
In making this gift I make no conditions, I would only suggest that the buildings upon the property now, be torn down, the land graded to correspond to the rest, and left until such time as the Trustees may hereafter decide to build an addition to the present structure.
Yours very truly,
J. Pierpont Morgan

The additional structure to which Morgan refers may indicate his own idea to erect an addition, or perhaps even more likely he was aware, through Goodwin, of Mrs. Colt's plan to eventually provide funds for a Colt wing and hence helped out by buying the land well in advance. As to his later plans for the Morgan wing, a competitive sense to outshine Mrs. Colt in his hometown (or nationally to rival what Walters was building in Baltimore and Frick in New York; or internationally to follow the Wallace Collection which opened in 1900), may also have been a factor; as a collector Morgan was extremely competitive.

[20]See Linda Roth, note 27. Morgan bought the following properties for the Atheneum and the city: a lot belonging to the Charles H. Brainard estate just south of the Wadsworth building was purchased in 1893 for $25,000; the Merrill house on Main Street just south of the Brainard property was bought in 1900 for $42,000 (the Colt Memorial sits on this and the Brainard properties); the Austin Dunham place on Prospect Street was bought for $30,000 in 1900 (the rear of the Morgan Memorial is on this property); after a $100,000 donation, St. John's Church sold their property on Main Street in 1905 for $70,000 (this is where the entrance to the Memorial now rests); after the first section of the Memorial opened, in 1910 the Fanny Bartholemew property on Prospect and the Brace property on Main Street were purchased for $30,000 and $60,000 respectively to remove some nearby unsightly buildings. This is the land upon which the Hartford municipal building now rests and as recorded in trustee minutes of June 1911, Morgan intended that title of this land to be transferred to the city "for some worthy municipal building or for a public square, at their discretion." A new municipal building, dedicated in 1914, in a late Georgian style was designed by Davis & Brooks to complement the Morgan Memorial across a street laid out on the remainder of the Morgan parcel.

[21]Morgan letter, Atheneum archives. Although here Morgan indicates he wanted to spend no more than $500,000, two months later it was estimated that the cost would be $620,000 due to the fact that the cost of the finest pink Tennessee marble had gone up. The decision to erect both buildings in the English style may reflect the influence of Francis Goodwin who in the 1870s began to effect numerous Hartford projects with his strong personal preference for contemporary English architecture. Goodwin may also have suggested William Burgess as architect for Trinity College in Hartford. His interest in contemporary English aesthetics is reflected in a recent gift to the Wadsworth Atheneum of a rare collection of photographs, mostly by Harry Bedford Lemere, of English interiors and houses collected by Francis Goodwin and later used extensively by Henry Russell Hitchcock. Behind the scenes, Goodwin was a master architectural planner for Hartford and the city's park system. Although not documented, he may have discussed with Mrs. Colt a building or wing of the museum for her collection, perhaps during the 1890 fundraising effort.

[22]At this time Morgan gave the Atheneum 2,200 shares of United States Steel Preferred worth over $250,000 as an endowment. Satterlee, 1939, p. 520 describes the opening ceremonies which were followed by a large lunch party at James Goodwin's. On the Memorial, see also *The New York Architect* 4 (February 1910).

[23]At the same time Morgan promised to give Trinity College in Hartford a new library, in memory of Morgan's friend Bishop Williams. This event occurred during a ride after lunch with James and Francis Goodwin. Satterlee, 1939, p. 554.

[24]See discussion in Roth's essay. Note: this was after Robert de Forest called for new construction by noting in the Metropolitan Museum Bulletin of 1912 that the museum had no space to show the Morgan Collection permanently.

[25]Some stained glass was given to South Kensington, however, the great Raphael, the *Colonna Madonna*, which had been on view at the National Gallery in London went to New York. Why did Hartford increase and London decrease in importance for Morgan's plans for his collections as indicated by his actions starting in 1905 and in his will? The main reasons appear to have been Morgan's desire to have a large part of his collection together, coupled with financial and site considerations, more than anything negative occurring in London. Francis Goodwin was obviously very effective in orchestrating events in Hartford, while there was apparently no one assisting or urging something major be done in London. Actually, Mr. Morgan's preferred man in that city, Sir Purdon Clarke, the director of the South Kensington Museum, was hired by the Metropolitan Museum as director early in 1905 at Morgan's suggestion.

[26]While more modest collectors like Mrs. Colt added galleries to existing museums or simply donated collections, in Morgan's era those who were more ambitious often thought in terms of creating their own art museums in the context of their own family residences (like the Pitti Palace), perhaps utilizing an addition (like the Uffizi). Wadsworth's Atheneum was built next to his own house on the site of his father's house, while in 1873 E. B. Crocker erected a gallery next to his house in Sacramento, California. Others early to utilize a family residence were Wallace in London, Gardner in Boston, Frick and Morgan in New York, the Tafts in Cincinnati, Du Pont in Wilmington, and T. B. Walker in Minneapolis. These house museums serve to focus attention on the founders to a degree generally not found in the mixed collections of a large civic museum. In general, later collectors who wanted to form their own museums thought in terms of public accessibility and appropriate site and hence independently of the private family locus — Kimbell in Fort Worth, Getty in Malibu, Norton Simon in Los Angeles, and De Menil in Houston. (Philip Johnson may be returning to the earlier pattern with his "house" museum in New Canaan, Connecticut.) Morgan first thought along the lines of the more traditional house museum in New York and London; for Hartford the newer idea of a public family Memorial, separate from any residence, only slowly evolved.

[27]When Morgan was president of the Metropolitan Museum he had gotten Henry Walters of Baltimore, John G. Johnson (1841–1917), a native of Philadelphia, and Henry Clay Frick to join the Board, realizing each one of these men had his own agenda and ties elsewhere, as Morgan had to London and Hartford. Yet Morgan also probably hoped that they would follow his example and support what was then the country's only national museum in New York as well.

[28]The portrait measures $81\frac{1}{4} \times 78\frac{1}{2}$in. In a letter in the Atheneum archives of 9 August 1912, to Alfred Clifford in Hartford, Benjamin Morris described a meeting with Morgan at his library in New York where he learned of his plan "to give to the Wadsworth Atheneum one of three portraits of himself which have been painted in triplicate for him by the Peruvian painter Carlos Baca-Flor:

> . . . One copy is for the Metropolitan museum, one for the Wadsworth Atheneum, but I have not been advised of the destiny of the third . . . Mr. Morgan desires that this portrait, together with that of his father which is already in the Morgan Memorial, be placed . . . at the head of the stairs . . .
>
> I discussed with Mr. Morgan other locations for these pictures, but, in view of his very positive statement that he desired his own picture and that of his father's to be in the same room . . . though he did not say this in so many words, in positions of equal importance . . .

[29]It is of course possible that Morgan again paralleled Daniel Wadsworth and was quite willing to have his named building filled with art collected by others. However, Wadsworth's Atheneum was not a memorial, his own collection was quite small and eighty per cent of the funds raised to build the original Wadsworth building came from others, hence it was public. (Similarly the Metropolitan's buildings were erected with public funds and that museum had a policy, often broken, against keeping collections separate.) Morgan, on the other hand, had a vast collection and in Hartford paid for the entire building, land, and endowment himself. Moreover, he was one of the most passionate of collectors, and spent almost half of his available funds on art. Morgan obviously had a desire to keep his books, manuscripts, prints and drawings together under one roof, and abandoned the idea of a London Museum at Princes Gate because he could not display his entire collection there — hence it seems clear he was thinking in terms of keeping part of his collection together. While it is generally thought that Morgan kept some of his collection in London to avoid American import duties on works of art (repealed in 1909), this did not prevent him from bringing the million dollar Hoentschel collection from Paris and countless other works of art to New York before 1909. More likely some of the fine art collection remained in London to keep it separate.

[30]See also Calvin Tomkins, 1970, pp. 179–181.

[31]Satterlee, 1939, p. 583.

[32]Not including the art collection (worth according to Morgan about $50,000,000), the amount of Morgan's estate was a little over $68,000,000. This was a smaller amount than left by Frick, Harriman, Andrew W. Mellon or fellow Metropolitan Museum trustee George F. Baker, and far smaller than the estates of Thomas Fortune Ryan and Payne Whitney. Although as famous, Morgan was not as wealthy as John D. Rockefeller, Sr. or Andrew Carnegie, who each gave away 350 to 500 million dollars. Morgan not only made less money in finance than the captains of industry, but he also spent a good deal of what he earned. See Frederick Lewis Allen, *The Great Pierpont Morgan* (New York, 1949), pp. 148–149.

[33]Morgan Jr. also determined what part of the collection needed to be sold or retained by the family. Widener bought two of Morgan's great tapestries for $500,000, and Frick paid $5,000,000 for ceramics and bronzes, most of which stayed in New York while some are now at The Frick Art Museum, Pittsburgh. A number of spectacular paintings as well as Limoges enamels were also bought by Frick. Perhaps Morgan was aware of Frick's own plans to open his house eventually as a public museum. If so, then the items sold to Frick through Duveen would eventually go on public view and thereby be in keeping with the senior Morgan's wish to make them permanently available to the American people, although under another name. Several paintings were also sold in the mid-1930s to the Metropolitan Museum, the Frick Collection, and to Mellon for the National Gallery — again sales that would result in Morgan items being available to the American people. Other paintings were sold after the death of Morgan Jr. — see the listing of sales in Appendix II.

The vast number of items given to the Metropolitan and the Morgan Library by Morgan Jr. are outlined in Appendix I: briefly, manuscripts, documents, books, prints and drawings — roughly 20,000 items collected by Morgan Sr., stayed at the Morgan Library. Approximately 7,000 objects that had for the most part been on loan to the Metropolitan Museum for years, ranging from ancient Egyptian to the Renaissance, were given to that museum by Morgan Jr. in 1917. (Morgan decided not to give the museum the Garland Collection of Chinese ceramics as the museum had just received the magnificent Altman Collection, and through Duveen it was sold to Frick, Rockefeller, and Widener.) Only a few paintings were given to the Metropolitan, the one of greatest consequence being the Raphael *Colonna Madonna* — when Morgan bought it for £100,000 ($484,000) it was the most expensive painting ever sold — which filled a major gap long noted in the museum's collection. Some French eighteenth-century paintings were also given to the Metropolitan in 1917 to complement the paintings and decorative arts given in 1906 with the Hoentschel collection. Some Dutch paintings were also given at this time, perhaps because they had previously been on loan (see Satterlee, 1939, p. 436).

[34]Morgan Jr. initially considered putting the works on loan, but then decided otherwise. The trustees received a letter from 23 Wall Street dated 17 February 1917, and now in the Atheneum's archives. After quoting his father's will, Morgan Jr. wrote:

> It has been a great satisfaction to me to send to the Wadsworth Athenaeum at Hartford various articles now shown in cases in the rooms of the Morgan Memorial. These articles consist largely of ceramics and porcelains, classical and early Venetian glass and Italian pottery of the seventeenth century, and include also the French and Meissen porcelains of the eighteenth century of which my Father left so large and complete a collection. There are also certain classical and Roman bronzes, and a collection of ivories of the seventeenth century.
>
> In pursuance of my Father's intention, I now make final disposition of these articles by giving them into your hands to be kept as a permanent exhibition for the benefit of the people of Hartford, the collection to be known as the "J. Pierpont Morgan Collection."

Most of these objects had been on loan to the South Kensington Museum or displayed at Princes Gate until 1912. Morgan Jr. also gave $50,000 to be added to the endowment for general purposes and $20,000 for cases to display the collection.

[35]See William N. Hosley, Jr., "The Wallace Nutting Collection at the Wadsworth Atheneum, Hartford, Connecticut," *Antiques* (October, 1984), pp. 860–874.

[36]After being installed in the 1960s in the Wadsworth Building the Nutting Collection was reinstalled in 1984 in the Avery Building, this time after a professional survey of the collection by William Hosley and using a professional designer, Charles Froom.

[37]In 1930, under the directorship of A. Everett Austin, the Atheneum bought two large Luca Giordanos and the next year a major Strozzi. During the 1930s and 1940s other works by Zurbarán, Valdés Leal, Murillo, Rosa, Caravaggio, Orazio Gentileschi; as well as Poussin, Claude Lorrain and others were purchased with the museum's Sumner Fund. As later acquisitions built on this strength, including the 1985 purchase of a major Scarsellino, today the museum is a pilgrimage site for those interested in Baroque painting.

J. Pierpont Morgan, Collector

Linda Horvitz Roth

John Pierpont Morgan is known to the world as one of the great financiers of the late nineteenth and early twentieth centuries. His contributions to American business in these years were impressive: he helped to bring order out of chaos in the transportation industry by substantially reorganizing the American railroad system; he secured much needed gold for the American Treasury in 1896; he was instrumental in the growth of the steel industry; and he successfully averted national financial disaster during the Wall Street Panic of 1907.

As with most public figures, Morgan's image was and remains open to criticism. Contradictory motives often were assigned to his actions and he was both applauded and reviled for his bold business achievements. Many viewed him as a man with a gargantuan appetite for money and power, which he would do anything to satisfy. The distance of years, however, has shown that Morgan was something between a saint and a devil.[1] Certainly he strove to attain money and position. Yet it appears that he also was inspired by public-spirited motives. Morgan had an idealistic vision of what America could become. Although he spent a portion of every year in Europe, he was fiercely patriotic, and this spirit would guide him in nearly all his affairs. He believed that his actions (like the reorganization of the railroads) would contribute to the greater good of "his" young nation.

In addition to his business activities, Morgan had a "hidden" career: that of art collector, a pursuit familiar to some historians but not well known today to the wider public. The same principles and drive which had guided him in business also formed his collecting methods. His success in business guaranteed him enough wealth and power to live as comfortably as he desired. It also enabled him to surround himself and his family with beautiful things, including works of art. Yet it would seem he collected for something larger than his immediate gratification, in the same way that he acted in business for more than personal gain. His collecting appears to have been rooted in that same idealistic and patriotic vision of America that had guided his business life. Undoubtedly he believed that American culture should rise to a level worthy of its political and economic stature, and that, as in business, he had the ability to contribute toward this end.

Other wealthy Americans were collecting art by the late nineteenth century, but again, as in business, Morgan surpassed everyone else. His was not a highly idiosyncratic collection, as were those of William Randolph Hearst or William H. Vanderbilt. Instead, Morgan's collection reflected a focused desire to bring to America the best of historic European culture; he always knew that some day this collection would be a gift to the people and to the nation.

Morgan's collecting can rightly be called a career; during the last twenty-three years of his life he devoted an increasing amount of energy to it. After the turn of the century, when his daily business affairs were in the hands of his capable partners, his major activity was that of the art collector — no longer the financier. By 1907 he spent most of his time buying works of art. Although the focus had changed, the methods had not. Morgan surrounded himself with experts and trusted advisors, relying on them to search out and screen works of available art. But the final decision to purchase always rested with him. Art collecting was far more than a hobby to Morgan, far more than something to occupy his leisure time: it was an activity with a purpose and a plan.

Once Morgan's stature as a collector becomes apparent, questions arise concerning his collecting activities: What did he collect and what motivated these selections? Why, for example, did Morgan limit himself to European art? Isn't this paradoxical in a man with such faith in America? Questions also surface about Morgan's methods: How did he manage to gather such a collection together? What parallels existed between his business and aesthetic organizations? Ultimately, one wonders where he kept it all? Was this enormous collection in one place — did Morgan keep his objects around him, to see and enjoy with regularity, or were they spread about in warehouses and loaned to museums?

Perhaps the most important question is the hardest to answer: why did Morgan form such a collection? Morgan never wrote about his motivations, goals, hopes, and dreams, either in business or in art. Perhaps collecting was part of an insatiable desire to acquire things, like stocks and railroads. Perhaps it was merely a way to boost his personal status and display his wealth and power. Or was the catalyst behind this second, hidden career truly that public-spirited and idealistic desire to contribute toward the building of America's culture?

John Pierpont Morgan began collecting art rather late in his life, only after his father, Junius Spencer Morgan, died in 1890. Some authors have ascribed this fact to a son's filial desire not to outdo his father, but it was probably owing to more pragmatic, financial considerations.[2] During the first three decades of his adult life, Morgan was busy building his career, developing into an extremely successful financier. By 1880 he was the father of four children and the owner of a large brownstone house at 219 Madison Avenue, on the corner of Thirty-Sixth Street. Yet not until his father died did he become a truly wealthy man backed by a powerful financial organization.

Before 1890 Morgan had purchased only odd pieces of art, but in 1891, when he was 54 years old, he began more systematic purchasing, focusing on rare books, historic autographs, manuscripts, and first editions. He was especially interested in author's manuscripts and in autographs and letters of the kings and queens of England.[3] During these first years he kept his collection in a small basement room at the Madison Avenue brownstone or in the vault of his Wall Street office, but it was not long before his collections spilled out of these spaces.[4]

It is difficult to document Morgan's collecting in the early years, from 1890 to 1896. Invoices for his purchases survive only from 1896, and are not numerous until 1900. Any information that might have been culled from letters is lost because Morgan had burned, two years before his death, all of the correspondence that he had sent to Junius and others over three decades. The best source of information about this period of Morgan's life is the thorough, although often biased, biography written in 1939 by Herbert Satterlee, Morgan's son-in-law.

Morgan's purchases are most clearly identified in the summary of his collection found in the Metropolitan Museum of Art's *Bulletin* of 1913, the year of his death. This describes the objects that were then being prepared for the only comprehensive exhibition of his collection ever to take place. There were approximately 4100 works in the 1914 exhibition, most of which Morgan had shipped from England in 1912, after America's import tax on works of art was repealed (about one-third of these later came to the Wadsworth Atheneum). The exhibition did not include the many pieces, especially Oriental, Egyptian, and Merovingian works that Morgan had sent directly to the Metropolitan over the years. Still, there was an encyclopedic range of objects representing to a large degree the entire history of Western art before 1800: about 550 enamels, from ninth-century Byzantine cloisonné works to eighteenth-century snuff boxes; 260 Renaissance bronzes, mostly statuettes; ancient material, including glass, jewelry, and the over eighty bronzes now in the Wadsworth Atheneum's collection (Figure 1); about 150 examples of Renaissance and Baroque silver and silver-gilt, many from Germany (see cat. nos. 15–26) and Italy; approximately 260 watches and clocks; about 140 pieces of jewelry and objects in crystal and amber, mostly from the Renaissance; Renaissance majolica numbering about 120 (see cat. nos. 1–14); 350 examples of French eighteenth-century porcelain (see cat. nos. 59–79); 330 pieces of German eighteenth-century porcelain, mostly figures (see cat. nos. 38–58); forty-three works in sixteenth- and seventeenth-century Venetian glass; thirty-nine Gothic to eighteenth-century tapestries, as well as tapestry covered furniture; over thirty pieces of French eighteenth-century furniture, many decorated with porcelain plaques; approximately 225 medieval through Baroque ivories, from various schools (cat. nos. 27–37); about forty-five small carvings in wood or stone; twenty-seven pieces of Italian sculpture, and fifty pieces of French eighteenth-century sculpture; almost 900 miniatures; and over fifty European paintings dating from the fifteenth to the eighteenth centuries.[5]

This impressive listing suggests that Morgan had put together his own "museum." It also reveals that he was in many respects an "old master" collector, a type that became prominent in America during the 1880s and 1890s.[6] Most of these collectors sought accepted masterpieces by well-known, respected Renaissance and Baroque artists. They also collected decorative objects, but usually as adjuncts to their paintings.[7] These collectors generally did not buy works by contemporary artists, either European or American.

Morgan conforms in many ways to this pattern of collecting. He bought old masters in such established areas as Italian Renaissance painting, seventeenth-century Dutch and Flemish painting, and works from the English school. While Morgan's purchase of a group of early Sienese paintings, considered too primitive by most Americans in this period, deviated from the established pattern, he was not alone among old master collectors in his decision not to buy

1: *Draped Warrior*, Greek, sixth century B.C. Wadsworth Atheneum, Hartford, Gift of J. Pierpont Morgan, 1917.815.

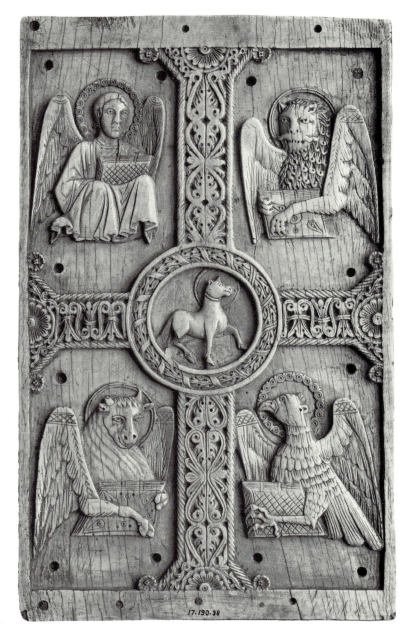

2: *Ivory Plaque from a Book Cover*, German or (?) North Italian, tenth century. The Metropolitan Museum of Art, Gift of J. Pierpont Morgan, 1917.

popular nineteenth-century French Salon and Barbizon landscape paintings. Similarly, he refrained from purchases of American or contemporary art. A distance of time and space seemed to be a prerequisite for the art that Morgan and many of these collectors coveted.

The vast majority of Morgan's collection consisted of decorative arts, dating from antiquity through the eighteenth century. Unlike other old master collectors, Morgan did not assign a secondary status to these objects. His interest in three-dimensional objects, often made of precious materials, led to a collection of decorative arts such as porcelain, enamels, and glass, which was extraordinary in volume as well as in the geographic area and time span it covered. Morgan not only sought these objects from the Renaissance and Baroque periods, but collected ancient glass and sculpture, and even the more unusual Merovingian antiquities, Byzantine and later medieval enamels, and Gothic ivories and metalwork (Figure 2).

An interest in decorative arts, however, was not new. Many of Europe's greatest princely and mercantile collectors, including such families as the Medici and the Rothschilds, bought "the minor arts." It was only in the nineteenth century that a serious schism between the major and minor arts even appeared: both areas historically had been viewed with respect and reverence. In buying from these two areas on a vast scale Morgan was, in fact, following in the traditions of earlier collectors.[8]

During the years 1890–1913, when Morgan was assembling paintings and decorative arts, he was also building a collection of thousands of mostly European books, manuscripts, autographs, prints, and drawings (not included in the Metropolitan's 1914 exhibition) rarely equaled by any other collector (Figure 3). This material is now all in The Pierpont Morgan Library (1900–06) in New York, a building specifically constructed for it.[9]

It is remarkable that Morgan should be able to collect this much in so short a period. He did not accomplish this in solitude, but depended on the help of an army of dealers and experts. As early as 1900 Morgan's custom was to see dealers every morning, especially when he was in Europe; they would come to his house in London or to his suite of hotel rooms in Paris or Rome, offering him "unique" and "priceless" works of art.[10] Dealers combed Europe for objects — even entire collections — that he might buy, endeavoring to keep his name out of the transactions in order to keep the price down. George Williamson, who advised Morgan on miniatures and sometimes acted as his agent, reported that he always kept Morgan's name quiet "because your name has a somewhat staggering effect upon persons who sell things."[11]

Morgan also bought at auction; a dealer would bid for him in return for a commission, usually of five per cent. Generally, Morgan would discuss these purchases in advance with the dealer, who would report back to Morgan with the results.[12] Thomas Kirby, a New York dealer, reminded Morgan in a letter of 1909 that when bidding for him he always used a code name.[13] Unfortunately it often was not possible to keep Morgan's identity out of a sale, which on at least one occasion was purported to have had less than happy results. Edward Robinson, the Director of The Metropolitan Museum of Art, in a letter to Morgan's librarian Belle da Costa Greene in 1913, discussed an ancient cameo glass cup which Morgan had purchased and which the Museum believed was a modern forgery (Figure 4). Apparently this object had been on the market earlier and Metropolitan Museum officials had advised Morgan not to buy it. Robinson wrote, "probably Mr. Morgan forgot all this [prior advice] in the glamour which attended the auction sale in Paris last year, the sale being a special one at which I believe only this cup was put up, and which, curiously enough, coincided with the time of Mr. Morgan's visit to Paris."[14] Morgan's commanding presence in the art market made him a target for dealers and impoverished nobility who all sought to profit from his pocketbook. In this case, the cameo glass cup had been on the market for some time; it appears someone had faith it could be sold to Morgan if the right kind of publicity and ambience were created for its sale. This was an accurate assumption.

Mr. Robinson, in his note, laments the fact that Morgan "forgot" the Metropolitan's earlier advice about the cup, but in the end Morgan proved to be correct in his decision. Now known as the *Morgan Cup*, this ancient work of art is in the collection of the Corning Museum of Glass in Corning, New York, having been sold after Morgan's death by the Pierpont Morgan Library. Current scholars acknowledge it to be genuine and an extremely important example of the ancient glassmaker's art.[15] It would be fascinating to know if Morgan really had forgotten the Metropolitan Museum's advice or whether he did not agree with their appraisal. Even if he had forgotten, he must have recognized the quality of the piece when he bought it at the Paris auction. Regardless of the outcome of this particular incident, it appears that Morgan, like other collectors, was in continual danger of being deceived by unscrupulous sellers.

Morgan was careful to take many steps which helped him find his way through the maze of the world art market. In most cases, remarkable though it may seem considering the volume of his purchases, he would not buy something without seeing it first. In a letter to Belle Greene, the dealer Charles Wertheimer wrote he had sold a reliquary that he had hoped to sell to Morgan because she had told him Morgan would not buy the work without first seeing it. Wertheimer decided he could not risk holding on to the object in the hope that when Morgan came to London the next year he would buy it.[16] While Morgan might have lost a few opportunities this way, he obviously believed it still was preferable to examine works of art firsthand.

Morgan learned from his business career to take advantage of the expertise of others before making final decisions. In his collecting career he also used a variety of experts, dealers, museum curators and directors, and gifted amateurs to counsel him and screen many of the objects he was asked to buy. Among his more prominent advisors were Sir Hercules Read, keeper of the department of British and Medieval Antiquities in the British Museum; Wilhelm von Bode, the distinguished director of Berlin's Kaiser Friedrich Museum; William M. Laffan, editor of the *New York Sun* and an expert on Chinese porcelains; and, later, the entire staff of the Metropolitan Museum of Art where Morgan was President of the Board from 1904. Bishop William Lawrence, a long time friend and the author of unpublished memoirs about Morgan, stated: "If through a personal visit of Mr. Lithgoe [sic] or Mr. Winlock [Egyptian experts for the Metropolitan Museum] an inspection was worth while [sic], Mr. Morgan halted at no difficulties to study the object for himself."[17] While Morgan did rely a great deal on experts, he never relinquished control of his purchases to anyone, preferring to be intimately involved and believing in his own abilities to recognize quality. This paralleled his business method.

Satterlee describes one manner in which Morgan used his advisors and other experts to his advantage. Often, when he was offered individual objects, he would ask the dealer to leave it at his house "on approval." Once there, he would show it to dealers and experts, listening to all their comments and opinions, good and bad. Only then would he make a decision to purchase or return it. Satterlee remarks that "none of the dealers liked this method but none of them dared to object to it."[18]

Of course it was not possible to use this method for objects bought at auction or with large groups of objects. In these cases he would have to rely more heavily on individual advisors or dealers.

It would have been very difficult for Morgan to accumulate such

3 : Master of Marguerite d'Orleans, "Betrayal of Christ," from a *Book of Hours*, fragment, France, probably Tours, about 1445, M190, f. 42. Courtesy of The Pierpont Morgan Library, New York.

4 : *The Morgan Cup*, Roman Empire, late first century B.C. — first century A.D. The Corning Museum of Glass, Corning, New York.

a vast collection in so short a time by buying every object individually. It is not surprising, therefore, to find that he was also fond of buying groups of objects, especially entire private collections. There was a great advantage to buying collections *en bloc*: he could take advantage of another collector's time-consuming, painstaking gathering of first-rate objects. Even if Morgan had to accept a few bad pieces with the good it was worth it, for the law of averages would be on his side. Time has borne this out.

Unfortunately this *en bloc* approach also left Morgan open to criticism. Roger Fry, the English art critic and one-time curator of paintings at the Metropolitan, said that Morgan was a "cheque-book collector . . . . he bought in batches."[19] The *Burlington Magazine*, in an obituary of Morgan, characterized him as a great collector but not a connoisseur:

> *It was the conquest of the most precious objects of all ages and countries that tempted his active spirit. And this continual conquest, carried on in the hurly-burly of his financial campaigns, left him but little leisure for that prolonged contemplation of the intimate beauties of his spoils which is the delight of the connoisseur.*[20]

Certainly with such an immense collection, scattered among various homes and institutions, Morgan would not have been able to appreciate on a daily basis everything he bought. Yet he was a far cry from a "department-store collector" like William Randolph Hearst, whose personal ambitions and desire to display his wealth and power led him to buy trainloads of objects, almost indiscriminately. Hearst bought so much that during his lifetime much of it was warehoused and, after his death, part had to be sold through Gimbel's department store in New York City. Morgan, on the other hand, bought voraciously, but never without regard for the quality of the objects and a relatively firm idea of how they fit into his collections.

According to some of Morgan's contemporaries, he sometimes was carried away by his passion for acquiring beautiful objects. Sir Hercules Read wrote to Belle Greene in 1911 that Morgan "sadly wants a restraining hand at times, and will cumber himself with things he would be better off without, quite apart from the fact that they cost him a good deal of money."[21] Morgan's enthusiasm and ambition periodically caused him to get caught up in the excitement of buying; he would occasionally purchase objects not in the best condition or of the finest quality. Although he had a genuine appreciation for beautiful materials and craftsmanship, he was not the careful connoisseur who slowly gathered his collection together one exquisite piece at a time.

Morgan was a man with an ambitious plan: to amass a collection comparable to those assembled by the great patricians of earlier centuries. He wished to surround himself with beautiful works of art, works that also had a place in history. Morgan himself would become part of that history when he bequeathed the collection to the American public. According to his wishes, Morgan's art was divided principally among The Pierpont Morgan Library, The Metropolitan Museum of Art, and the Wadsworth Atheneum. As Bishop Lawrence recognized, Morgan was more than a crass acquisitor:

> [I]*n the gathering of works of art, he doubtless took pleasure in acquisition. He liked to find the best and to know the best . . . . That the chief motive in the gathering of his collections was the love of acquisition, anyone who knew him would immediately deny. He had a love, almost a passion, for beautiful and interesting things for their own sake.*[22]

Morgan's specific purchases lead to this same conclusion.

Everything about Morgan's collecting was a natural outgrowth

5: McKim, Mead and White, *The Pierpont Morgan Library, Exterior*, New York, 1900–1906. Courtesy of The Pierpont Morgan Library, New York.

of his background. He was raised in an old New England family with a healthy respect for the value of money, a trait he retained even when paying enormous sums for works of art.[23] Morgan's invoices and correspondence indicate he did refuse some objects because they were too expensive. Morgan's solid religious faith had been introduced to him early by his maternal grandfather John Pierpont, a fire and brimstone preacher in Boston, and was maintained throughout his life through his activities in the Episcopal Church. A sense of restraint and moderation characterized Morgan's way of life, exemplifying these conservative New England religious and commercial roots. Extensive traveling in Europe, beginning during Morgan's school days in Switzerland and Germany, brought a cosmopolitan influence to his life which tempered these New England traits. Still, when he turned to collecting art, Morgan did so without ostentation; he never built himself a showy domestic palace filled with an unintelligible aggregate of art and decoration.

Collecting on a vast scale presented certain logistical problems, however. As early as 1899 there was less and less room in his home on Madison Avenue to keep his works of art. He already stored some items in a warehouse on Forty-second Street, but this was not a satisfactory solution to the problem, for he always wanted his objects to be on view. In 1900, therefore, he began planning a library for his ever-growing collection of books, manuscripts, autographs, prints, and drawings. He commissioned the architectural firm of McKim, Mead & White to design the structure, insisting that it contain a study which he could use as an office and where he could meet dealers and business associates. The result, The Pierpont Morgan Library, was a Renaissance style palazzo made out of perfectly hewn blocks of pinkish-white marble (Figure 5). It was monumental in every detail, and provided a more appropriate setting for his collections than did his more domestic brownstone at 219 Madison Avenue.

The Library came to house all of Morgan's literary collections and a small part of his art collections. However, he kept most of the latter in Europe, where they were bought. There were many reasons for this, foremost among them a pragmatic concern: as noted earlier, until 1909 works of art brought into America were taxed. Morgan was instrumental in eventually persuading Congress to pass a bill which allowed works of art over 100 years old to enter the United States duty free. Meanwhile, however, it was far too costly to send everything he bought in Europe to New York.

Much of Morgan's collection was in the house he inherited from his father at Princes Gate, London, which he expanded in 1904 by incorporating the townhouse next door. Bishop Lawrence provides a good description of its interior. A brief excerpt of that description gives an idea of how the collections were displayed in the house:

Glancing at two glorious Turners, one at each side of the large door, we passed into the next room, a perfect example of Louis XVI, walls, rugs, furniture and ornaments of the richest of that day. Across the hall . . . we entered the Fragonard Room, whose walls were drawn in by the builder to meet the exact dimensions and designs of the panels. In the centre stood a table covered with a glass cabinet filled with beautiful jewelled boxes. A glimpse of the portrait of the most attractive boy that one has ever seen, probably by Velasquez, drew one into the Louis XV Room, where were beautiful cabinets and examples of Sevres.[24]
(Figure 6)

Princes Gate was filled with priceless paintings, porcelains, silver, gold, and hundreds of miniatures, which he kept in tables with shallow drawers in the drawing room. As much as space permitted, his collections were an integral part of his domestic environment,

6: Jean-Honoré Fragonard, *The Meeting*. Copyright The Frick Collection, New York.

7: Study, Princes Gate, London, August 1902, from a previously unpublished photo album, newly discovered. Courtesy of The Pierpont Morgan Library, New York. Faintly visible on the bookshelf are the pair of *Tub Carriers* now in the Wadsworth Atheneum (cat. no. 24). On the far right of the bookshelf is a coconut shell *Owl*, also in the Atheneum's collection (1917.278 — now thought to be nineteenth century). In other still unpublished photographs of Princes Gate in this album one can see several pieces of Sèvres displayed on the furniture.

kept in rooms where Morgan could enjoy them all the time.

It appears that Morgan at one time had different ideas about his art collection's place in Princes Gate. Bishop Lawrence wrote in 1914 that "for whatever use Mr. Morgan had for museums as such, he had no interest in making his house a museum."[25] Yet in 1904, when Morgan requested that the South Kensington Museum, London (now the Victoria and Albert), continue to house many of his objects which were on loan, he told them: "I have recently acquired the premises adjoining my house in Princes Gate, and after considerable structural alterations have been made I hope to remove my collections there and thus form a museum."[26] A year later, however, he returned to the South Kensington Museum to extend the loan. Morgan told Purdon Clarke, Director of the Museum, that even after having Princes Gate enlarged and remodeled, there still was not enough room to house his entire collection, which was still growing. Therefore, he wished to keep exhibiting much of it at the museum.[27]

Did Morgan's desire to create his own museum reflect his long-term intentions for the collection, or was it an interim plan, meant to be implemented only until American duty laws were changed? Would that he had said more about this, for it would have clarified his purpose in forming his collection and his views on the public role of art and collectors. In any case, it appears that as early as 1904 Morgan viewed his collection specifically in a museum context. However developed his plan may have been, though, it proved to be impractical and was abandoned.

Other groups of objects were kept at Dover House, his country house outside of London, and in the Library in New York. However, overflow remained, much of which was taken up by the South Kensington Museum. From 1901 Morgan sent object after object to be exhibited there on temporary loan; by 1912 these numbered 1,618 objects.[28] Many things were sent directly from the dealers to the museum, which had mixed feelings about accepting this huge and expanding loan; they had no commitment from Morgan that he would ever give any of it to the London museum. One staff person was concerned about the commercial advantage that Morgan could gain by having the museum exhibit his private collection.[29] Yet in spite of these concerns the South Kensington Museum agreed to be the second London home for Morgan's objects, where they were available for public inspection. Morgan was a frequent visitor to his collection.

It is possible to track Morgan's purchases over seventeen years, from 1896 until his death, by reviewing the extant invoices and letters in the archives of the Morgan Library. In 1896, for example, he was buying Renaissance and Baroque goldsmiths' work and ivories, Limoges enamels, and European porcelain. Information for 1897 and 1898 is scant, but in 1899 Morgan's activities include purchases of miniatures, rock crystal, jewels, Louis XVI furniture, a great deal of eighteenth-century porcelain, and very important paintings (such as Fragonard's series *The Progress of Love*, now in The Frick Collection). He continued to buy these same groups of objects in the following years. The first extant invoice for Renaissance bronzes (a group of fifty-four) dates from 1901. This was also the year that Morgan bought the *Duchess of Devonshire* by Thomas Gainsborough, for which he is said to have paid a very high price. Medieval objects appear in 1902, and ancient works of art in 1903.

The years 1904 through 1906 show increasing expenditures by Morgan, some owing to the redecoration of Princes Gate after the purchase of the house next door. Like many other collectors of this period, Morgan often employed dealers as decorators, especially the firms of Duveen and Daniell in London — distinctions between dealers and decorators not being as clearly drawn at the beginning of this century as they are now. He actually had two accounts at Daniell, one for household items and one for fine arts. Reflecting the level of spending during these years, the total of one bill from Duveen dated 4 January 1906 was $131,627.75.[30]

Morgan kept buying porcelain, silver and ivories, miniatures, enamels, tapestries, paintings, jewels, rock crystal, ancient and Renaissance bronzes, jewelled boxes, and of course books and manuscripts throughout the first decade of the century. It is difficult to detect any pattern to these purchases or any indication that his tastes changed measurably during these years. There is some reason to believe, however, that Morgan would "finish" collecting certain types of things and move on to other areas. For example, Bishop Lawrence recounts that Morgan's sister once asked him whether he would be visiting a certain dealer in Greek antiquities on one of their trips to Naples. He is said to have answered, "'I am not going there any more; I have done with Greek antiques, I am at the Egyptian.'"[31] Lawrence also recalls a remark made to him by Morgan that "when he had collected every piece of French porcelaine of the finest that could be found outside of the museums, he stopped."[32] Further written support for this is found in a letter from the dealer Durlacher to Belle Greene in 1909, in which he says that "Mr. Morgan is now through with his bronze collection, so he says."[33] Morgan continued to buy many categories of works, however, throughout his collecting career, which suggests he was not operating by any rigid system. The frenzied pace of acquisitions seems to have kept up until 1911 and 1912, when the files reveal fewer invoices.

*   *   *

Morgan's invoices also help to illuminate how and when the part of the collection now housed at the Wadsworth Atheneum was acquired.[34] In the case of the Sèvres porcelain, for example, Morgan bought from several dealers, including Cartier and Seligmann in Paris, and Daniell and Duveen in London. That the Sèvres was kept at Princes Gate is clear from Bishop Lawrence and from previously unpublished photographs in the archives of the Morgan Library; it was mostly in the Louis XV Room, some in vitrines and some just on top of furniture (Figure 7). Functional services were kept in a basement china room.[35] A few things seem never to have been delivered, such as two late *jardinières* which remained with Seligmann in Paris until 1918.[36]

Morgan bought a fairly well-rounded selection of Sèvres, although one is not aware that he made any attempt to document systematically shapes, colors, and patterns. He seems to have been fond of yellow ground pieces (which were very rare), which explains the many single yellow cups and saucers in the collection. He also bought quite a few unglazed biscuit figures (cat. no. 70), many modeled after designs by the French sculptor Falconet. This is not surprising for he also collected many full-size French eighteenth-century sculptures.

Invoices for his French porcelain, as for most other kinds of objects, often show important provenances for the items purchased. Germain Seligman, the son of one of Morgan's favorite dealers, remembered that "to him, pedigree is also of importance, if for no other reason than the historical continuity which is so much a part of the aura surrounding works of art."[37] Morgan consistently was intrigued by objects with interesting histories, which perhaps helps to explain his extraordinary fondness for portrait miniatures. Even the ever-critical Roger Fry conceded that "a crude historical imagination was the only flaw in his otherwise perfect insensibility."[38] Sometimes the provenances and historical associations were unusually optimistic, as in the case of the Atheneum's pair of Vincennes *Potpourris* Morgan purchased in 1896 (cat. no. 59), reputed to have been given by Marie Antoinette and Louis XVI to the Abbes de Ronceray.[39] These pieces date from 1751, making such a provenance impossible. However, the

8: *Potpourri Vase (Vaisseau à Mat)*, French, Sèvres, about 1761. The J. Paul Getty Museum, Malibu.

9: *Louis XV*, French, Mennecy-Villeroy, about 1750. Wadsworth Atheneum, Hartford, Gift of J. Pierpont Morgan, 1917.1509.

Mounted Green Vase (cat. no. 64) appears to have belonged to Louis XV's mistress Madame de Pompadour.[40]

Invoices also reveal that Morgan purchased his French porcelain piece by piece and not *en bloc*, in some cases spending as little as forty-five pounds and sometimes, as with the Atheneum's pair of large green ground *Vases* (cat. no. 67), as much as £10,000.[41] His chief advisors in this area undoubtedly were J. H. Fitzhenry, himself a porcelain collector, and the Count de Chavagnac, who wrote Morgan's catalogue of the French porcelain. According to Bishop Lawrence, Morgan claimed to have picked up examples of French porcelain bit by bit, "'in shops in Paris and out-of-the-way places . . . until some years ago I made up my mind that I had gotten everything that there was of the finest quality that could be purchased now and that was not already in museums.'" When he wanted them catalogued, he engaged the Count de Chavagnac, "the best expert." He asked the Count to evaluate the collection and to "'send into the market every piece that is not genuine or not of the rarest quality.'" Lawrence relates that as a result, Morgan sold about forty pieces.[42]

Although some of Morgan's French porcelain was kept by the family until 1944, when it was sold (Figure 8), almost 300 pieces came to the Atheneum. They are of very high quality, many exceptionally beautiful and rare. Morgan also bought many pieces of Sèvres-mounted furniture and, from the same group of dealers, an important group of eighteenth-century French porcelain from the factories at Mennecy, Chantilly, and St. Cloud, many of them figural groups (Figure 9).

The story of Morgan's acquisition of Meissen porcelain is very different. Though the same dealers sold him a few pieces, most of his collection was purchased from Henry Duveen. In 1899 he bought four cabinets of Meissen from Duveen's London shop—161 pieces at a cost of £17,000.[43] Over the next few years he made other purchases from Duveen, usually in groups of five to ten pieces. Unlike other collections Morgan purchased *en bloc*, in this case it was not a collection gathered over a lifetime by a connoisseur but a group of works gathered together by a dealer. This forced him to rely solely on the dealer's knowledge and integrity, rather than on a previous collector's skill and connoisseurship. Recent scholarship has determined that many of the Meissen pieces are not of the same quality and condition as other works in his collection. While he bought numerous first-rate examples of the Meissen factory's art, others are less interesting both in design and decoration.

A peculiar aspect of Morgan's collection of Meissen is that it consists almost entirely of figural groups. Among the best of these are the crinoline groups, designed by one of the major artists at the factory, Johann Joachim Kaendler (cat. nos. 38–57). Morgan did buy a few large sets of vases known as *garnitures de cheminées*, one of them visible in a photograph of Morgan's study at Princes Gate (Figure 10). However, there is very little representation of Meissen tableware in the collection, which in fact was a major part of that factory's production. Again, as with the Sèvres, we find that Morgan was not systematic in his purchases, even within a confined area such as Meissen. He kept his over 350 figural groups at Dover House, curiously apart from the rest of his collections. We know that in 1907 he bought an expensive pair of satinwood cabinets to house them in the drawing room.[44]

The invoices for Italian Renaissance majolica show that, again, Morgan purchased objects individually or in small groups. He bought from the familiar group of dealers which included Jacques Seligmann, Durlacher Brothers, J. & S. Goldschmidt, as well as Lowengard in Paris and Imbert in Rome. He bought a wide variety of schools from the fourteenth through the sixteenth centuries, including a group of early Orvieto pieces later given to the Atheneum that now appear to have been made in the nineteenth century. These he bought from Imbert, but there is nothing to indicate that the dealer knew they were not period. Morgan also bought a very interesting Gubbio plate in 1907 from Seligmann for $18,000 (Figure 11). It is decorated with three different coats of arms, a fact duly noted in the invoice. Also noted is the plate's pedigree of three ex-collections.[45] Unfortunately, the rim of the plate does not belong with the center, the two parts having been put together sometime before Morgan bought it; the three coats of arms do not belong together, nor does the decoration of the rim match the decoration of the center. In this case Morgan made a fairly expensive but understandable mistake, for in these years art historical scholarship, particularly in the decorative arts, was in its infancy, and even the best experts were liable to be fooled. As late as 1959 this plate was thought to be correct when it appeared in an exhibition in Detroit on *Decorative Arts of the Italian Renaissance*.[46]

We know from Roger Fry that at least once, in 1907, but probably with more frequency, Morgan went out into the Italian countryside to buy objects. In this particular case, he went to see a majolica service which belonged to a pair of sisters who lived near Perugia. Fry says that "Morgan was always pleased by the idea of buying family heirlooms from the family itself, the object seemed to convey with it some of the distinction of impoverished nobility."[47] One must take with a grain of salt this last comment, for Fry did not like Morgan and insisted on seeing him in the worst light. The story does confirm, however, that at least occasionally Morgan did hunt down objects himself, not always relying on his dealers.

Morgan sent some of the majolica to New York to be put in his Library, which was decorated in the Renaissance style and hung with many of his Renaissance paintings (Figure 12). Most of it, however, went to the South Kensington Museum to be placed with his other loans. In the 1905 *Inventory* there were forty-eight pieces listed.[48]

Invoices also indicate that Morgan began buying goldsmiths' works and ivories fairly early, for entries appear in one of the earliest surviving invoices, dated 1896. At this time he was acquiring both sixteenth- and seventeenth-century pieces, somewhat unusual in a period that tended to ignore many aspects of Baroque art. Included in this part of the collection are many rare objects, such as nautilus shell cups, cups made of ostrich eggs mounted in silver-gilt, and beautifully mounted, carved ivory tankards and covered cups. These are mostly German, but also include some Austrian and Dutch works, among them an extraordinary carved ivory relief of *The Fall of Man* from Vienna (cat. no. 27). He also collected English silver and silver-gilt, but these were not included in the Wadsworth Atheneum gift (some pieces were given to the Metropolitan Museum while others were kept by the family and later sold).

Many of the silver pieces were part of a collection assembled by German banker Consul Gutmann, and purchased by Morgan through the dealer J. & S. Goldschmidt for £75,000 in 1902. There was some discussion about payment for this collection, for although Morgan usually paid for works of art a year after he bought them, Gutmann would not accept this arrangement and Morgan paid the full price immediately. Gutmann wrote to Goldschmidt that he would "never have consented to sell his collection to [sic] such a low price except to Mr. Morgan, on account of the ready money, because dealers or museums are not able to pay at once as Mr. Pierpont Morgan!"[49] It is likely that many items were sold to Morgan with this idea in mind.

Aside from a few pieces that were kept at Princes Gate, most of the silver and ivories went to the South Kensington Museum. The museum, in turn, sent those from the Gutmann collection to the Glasgow Art Gallery for long-term exhibition, for the curators felt the collection repeated many things the museum already owned and would take up too much valuable space in the gallery.[50]

10: Study, Princes Gate, London, August 1902, from a previously unpublished photo album, newly discovered. Courtesy of The Pierpont Morgan Library, New York. Visible on the mantlepiece is a garniture of five Meissen vases now in the Atheneum's collection (1917.1194-1198) and two ivory tankards (the one on the left probably 1917.311, the other impossible to identify from the photograph).

11: *Majolica Plate*, Italian Deruta, sixteenth century. The rim and center of this piece are from two separate dishes — they must have been put together in the nineteenth century. Wadsworth Atheneum, Hartford, Gift of J. Pierpont Morgan, 1917.454.

12: Interior, West Room, The Pierpont Morgan Library. Courtesy of The Pierpont Morgan Library, New York. One can identify the majolica plate on the far left of the bookshelf as belonging to the Atheneum (cat. no. 9).

It is clear from documentary evidence that the South Kensington Museum had hopes that at least part of this vast group of objects would be placed there permanently. However, it appears that Morgan had always envisioned his collection in America: not only was he closely allied with the Metropolitan Museum, as its president, but in 1905 he began to plan the Morgan Memorial of the Wadsworth Atheneum, probably to house part of his collection. In 1912, therefore, three years after the duty laws were changed, he began transferring the thousands of objects from Europe to New York.

Just where the collection was to go in the United States had not been determined in 1912. Most people assumed that Morgan would give it to the Metropolitan Museum of Art, where he had been president since 1904. In fact, he had been active in the museum since its beginnings in the 1870s, and by 1897 had begun giving it "lavish" gifts and loans.[51] Among them was the Garland Collection of Oriental porcelain in 1902, bought when Garland died and the objects which had been on loan to the museum were in danger of being sold. Morgan also purchased the Hoentschel collection of eighteenth-century French decorative arts and woodwork for the museum in 1906, and the Gaston LeBreton collection of French faience in 1910 (the latter was not accessioned into the museum until 1917) (Figure 13). In 1911 and 1912 he purchased the Hoentschel collection of medieval art and placed it on loan with the Metropolitan. Furthermore, for many years he was an active and generous supporter of the Egyptian department and its archaeological excavations. His energetic role in the young museum was inextricably bound to his activities as a collector.

Morgan's greatest collecting years coincided with his years of involvement with the Metropolitan Museum. Calvin Tomkins, in his history of the museum, notes that when Morgan assumed the presidency in 1904 there was a fundamental change in conception about how the museum was going to function. There was to be a new emphasis on acquiring a great collection of masterpieces; in the Annual Report of 1905, probably reflecting Morgan's influence, the trustees stated that their aim was

not merely to assemble beautiful objects and display them harmoniously, still less to amass a collection of unrelated curios, but to group together the masterpieces of different countries and times in such relation and sequence as to illustrate the history of art in the broadest sense, to make plain its teaching and to inspire and direct its national development.[52]

Attempting to form a great collection of masterpieces, related in time and place, was in many ways what Morgan was doing with his own collection. While the range of his collections was broad within the scope of Western European art, it never reflected a completely scholarly representation of Western European artistic production, not even within specific areas of concentration such as French porcelain. Yet it is likely that Morgan and the Metropolitan Museum were at least familiar with ideas of "scientific" or systematic collecting, an approach gaining currency in late nineteenth-century America during the period known as "The American Renaissance."[53]

These ideas were fundamental not only to the Metropolitan, but to the growth of the American museum movement in general, in which Morgan took an active part. As president of the museum, he was in a very strong position to carry out a plan for bringing together an historically related group of great masterpieces. From the account offered by Tomkins and other evidence from The Pierpont Morgan Library Archives, it is clear that Morgan wielded great power in the museum: he was instrumental in hiring Purdon Clarke from the South Kensington Museum to be the director in 1905, and had a great deal to say about hiring Dr. William Valentiner as curator of Decorative Arts in 1908.[54] He frequently purchased works of art for the museum without consulting the staff or trustees (and for which they would have to raise the money afterward.)[55]

His involvement with the Metropolitan often made it difficult to distinguish Morgan the private collector from Morgan the public collector and benefactor. In part this is owing to the questions still surrounding his intentions for his personal collection. Clearly it was an issue during his tenure at the Metropolitan, for in some respects he was in competition with the museum. According to Satterlee, in buying works of art Morgan "exercised his own taste and frequently did not know until the cases were unpacked in New York and he saw the things again, whether he would keep them where he could see them daily, or add them to the collections of the Museum."[56] One of his last major conflicts with Roger Fry was in 1909 over a painting by Fra Angelico that they both wanted to buy. Unknowingly, the dealer who owned the painting sold it to both Fry and Morgan, believing that they were both acting on behalf of the Metropolitan. However in this instance Morgan had been acting on his own behalf.[57]

The same question arises repeatedly —did Morgan have a grand plan? Aline Saarinen believes Morgan meant to "gather for America an undreamed-of collection of art so great and so complete that a trip to Europe would be superfluous. And he would give this vast and splendid compendium to the Metropolitan Museum."[58] There is much to suggest that she is correct, although the plan was never carried out in this manner. For example, in most cases Morgan's personal collection did not overlap areas in which the museum was actively buying, such as Egyptian art, monumental ancient art, and arms and armor. When he did buy objects to give or loan directly to the museum, he would thereafter continue to acquire for them in these areas. This certainly is true in the case of Chinese porcelains and French faience. It appears that Morgan avoided duplication, indicating that he expected at least some of his collection would go to the Metropolitan.

Central to American thinking of this period was the idea that it was the duty of leading Americans to contribute toward the creation of a great republic which could compete culturally with Europe. The noted American architect Stanford White claimed that it was perfectly acceptable to import great quantities of art for private consumption, adding that it was the right of all dominant nations, as exercised throughout history, to plunder works of art from earlier generations.[59] Morgan, in effect, was the master plunderer, snatching up objects and whole collections from all over Europe, for himself and for the Metropolitan. Satterlee, like Saarinen, wrote that Morgan's plan was "that the public should get the benefit of all the art and beauty that it was possible to gather and bring over to the United States."[60] To this end Morgan looked toward Europe and the art of the past as the providers of culture, a conservative viewpoint shared by many during this period. He believed it was the duty of the privileged few to "ensure the moral superiority of America," and elevate aesthetic standards in the "belief that culture and art were indexes of civilization."[61] America would achieve cultural and moral superiority through Europe, not independently at home.

These ideas may partially explain why Morgan did not buy American art, either contemporary or earlier works, and why, outside of the design and decoration of his Library, he never patronized American artists. Appropriately enough, the two artists whom he employed for the Library, Charles McKim as architect and H. Siddons Mowbray for the interior murals, both looked to Europe and the art of the Renaissance for inspiration. McKim built Morgan a Renaissance palazzo and Mowbray decorated it with murals in the Italian Renaissance style.

It is not surprising that Morgan has often been compared with the great Medicis of the Florentine Renaissance. The appellation

13: *Broth Basin with Cover (Ecuelle)*, French, Moustiers, eighteenth century. The Metropolitan Museum of Art, Gift of J. Pierpont Morgan, 1917.

"An American Medici" was used as early as 1909, as the title of an article on Morgan and his collections in *Putnam's Magazine*.[62] Francis Taylor warned against comparing Morgan and Lorenzo de'Medici too closely, explaining that they differed greatly in personality and temperament. Yet Taylor did credit them both with endowing their contemporaries with a new appreciation for the significance of art.[63] Strictly speaking, Morgan can only be compared to nineteenth-century perceptions of the Medici, which in many ways differed from sixteenth-century reality.

Morgan's collection did resemble those of the Renaissance merchant princes in its combination of great paintings and decorative arts. It differed from these Renaissance collections, however, in its absence of contemporary works of art — Morgan, unlike the Medici, did not patronize artists of his day. Still, Morgan and many other late nineteenth-century American collectors believed their goals to be similar to those of Renaissance princely collectors: a desire to display their prestige and wealth, but also a sense of moral duty to elevate public taste, to teach the public what was "good."[64] If Morgan's plan was to gather together the greatest collection of art in modern times, bringing it to America for the benefit and education of the people, then he might indeed have thought of himself as "An American Medici." Roger Fry, taking a dim view of this comparison, was quick to note that Morgan viewed himself "as a modern counterpart of a gorgeous Renaissance Prince."[65]

This attitude may help explain why Morgan privately published lavish catalogues of his collections, often written by the best experts in the field (Figure 14). Printed in very limited editions, these catalogues were painstakingly produced, a few extravagantly bound in tooled leather. These Morgan would send to a small group of individuals or institutions, among them many of the crowned heads of Europe. That the production and distribution of the catalogues was important to Morgan is proven by the wealth of correspondence on this subject in the archives of the Morgan Library. Morgan carefully restricted the recipients of his catalogues, and it was deemed a great privilege to be one of the chosen few. The tradition of collectors having private catalogues printed of their collections goes back to the days of the Renaissance *Kunstkammern*,[66] and it was only appropriate that this modern prince, reflecting pride in what he accomplished, should continue the tradition.

If Morgan was endowed with the ideals of the "American Renaissance," then the decision to bring his collections to America was the only possible one he could have made. Importation duties were no longer an issue by 1912, and the threat of death duties imposed by the British government on any part of Morgan's collection still in England at his death was an added incentive to remove everything to New York.[67] It still had to be determined where these collections would be housed. This issue caused great controversy.

It had been assumed by most people (certainly by the press) that Morgan's collections were to end up at the Metropolitan Museum. Even Satterlee believed this, writing that in 1911:

> [Morgan] *was planning to bring together at New York as a gift to the public (through the Metropolitan Museum) all the splendid collections that he had been gathering at home and abroad, so that craftsmen, students, and art lovers of all the coming generations should get technical and cultural benefit from them all without having to go to the East or the West overseas.*[68]

Discussions took place beginning in 1911 between Morgan and officials at the Metropolitan about where the collections would be exhibited when they arrived. The problem was whether to put them in galleries that were already being built, or to attempt to get

COLLECTION OF J. PIERPONT MORGAN

BRONZES
ANTIQUE GREEK, ROMAN, ETC.

INCLUDING SOME

ANTIQUE OBJECTS IN GOLD AND SILVER

INTRODUCTION AND DESCRIPTIONS

BY

SIR CECIL H. SMITH

PARIS

LIBRAIRIE CENTRALE DES BEAUX-ARTS

MCMXIII

14: Title Page, Catalogue of Ancient Bronzes commissioned by Morgan, privately printed, 1913. Wadsworth Atheneum, Hartford.

the city of New York to appropriate more money for a new wing specifically devoted to the Morgan collection. Morgan did not make any decision on this matter in 1911, and not until November 1912 did the museum discover that it might not receive the expected gift. In a memorandum now in the Metropolitan Museum Archives, Edward Robinson, Director, recounted for the record an interview with Morgan on November 29:

> [Morgan] *wished it distinctly understood by the City authorities and whoever else ought to know of it, that he had no intention of giving or bequeathing his collections to the Metropolitan Museum. He said that the value of these collections at the present time was about fifty million dollars, and he regarded this as too large an asset to take out of his estate . . . [He] did not wish the City to grant the money asked for this year upon the understanding that it was to be devoted to the permanent housing of his collections, and then learn afterward that the collections were not to become the property of the Museum . . . This was the first intimation Mr. Morgan has ever made to me of his ultimate intentions with regard to his collections.*[69]

It is difficult to document what went on during the year between the discussions in 1911 and this memorandum in November 1912. There was extensive opposition in the New York papers and among city officials about the taxpayers' money being used to Morgan's advantage, although Satterlee claims that Morgan was not so discouraged by this as to send his collections straight to Hartford.[70] Yet it must have had some effect on Morgan's thinking, for when he died in the spring of 1913 he had left his collections to his son, J. P. Morgan, Jr.

Article XXXII of the *Last Will and Testament of John Pierpont Morgan* deals specifically with the disposition of his vast collection of art:

> *I have been greatly interested for many years in gathering my collections of paintings, miniatures, porcelains and other works of art, and it has been my desire and intention to make some suitable disposition of them or of such portions of them as I might determine, which would render them permanently available for the instruction and pleasure of the American people.*

Morgan left his collections to his son, claiming that he had not had the time to carry out this purpose himself:

> *I hope he will be able, in such manner as he shall think best, to make a permanent disposition, or from time to time permanent dispositions, of them or of such portions of them as he may determine, which will be a substantial carrying out of the intentions which I have thus cherished. It would be agreeable to me to have "The Morgan Memorial" which forms a portion of the property of the Wadsworth Athenaeum at Hartford, Connecticut, utilized to effectuate a part of this purpose.*[71]

The will is dated 4 January 1913, with a codicil of 6 January. If he had been considering giving his collections to the Metropolitan Museum at one time, he had changed his mind by early 1913. It is difficult to draw further conclusions.

The actual disposition of Morgan's collections, then, was left up to his son. He took some time to make his decision, but decided to allow the Metropolitan's planned exhibition of them to take place in 1914. He made it clear to the museum officials that the loan was to be considered temporary, and in discussions with Edward Robinson in September, 1913 it was apparent that he had not yet decided the fate of the collections.[72] Without warning, however, one year later, he informed Robinson that he would begin taking certain parts of the collection out of the exhibition and out of the museum — the first things to go being the Fragonard panel

paintings and the Garland Collection of Chinese porcelains. He stated that the museum did not now need this latter collection because they had received another collection of Chinese porcelain from Benjamin Altman.[73]

There is little question, then, that the decision concerning Morgan's collection rested with J. P. Morgan, Jr. Some of the objects were to be given to the Metropolitan, some to the Morgan Memorial of the Wadsworth Atheneum, and some were to remain with the family or be sold. The material in the Library was to stay there and eventually the building and the collections were given to the public.

The decision to sell some of the collection apparently was owing to financial considerations: to help pay heavy estate taxes that were levied. The Garland collection, the Fragonards, forty-five Renaissance bronzes, Limoges enamels, and much of the French furniture from Princes Gate were sold to Henry Clay Frick (through Duveen) (Figure 15). French and Company purchased the tapestries. Many pieces of the Italian majolica were also sold, while some of the Sèvres, many paintings, and the English silver remained in the family for several years until J. P. Morgan, Jr.'s death in 1943, when they too were sold.[74] The miniatures were sold by the family in 1935.

In 1917 the Wadsworth Atheneum was given 1,325 objects from the Morgan collection, including ancient glass and bronzes, Italian Renaissance majolica, seventeenth- and eighteenth-century silver-gilt and ivories, seventeenth-century Venetian glass, eighteenth-century English ceramics, and eighteenth-century German and French porcelains. The Metropolitan received many of the remaining works of art, exclusive of what was in the Library, sold, or kept by the family. The choice of objects to remain at the Metropolitan was made by J. P. Morgan, Jr., the curator Joseph Breck, and the trustees of the museum.[75] There was probably considerable advice from Belle Greene.[76] It appears that when the division was made, the existing strengths of the Metropolitan's collection were considered — as in the case of the Chinese porcelains. Also considered was which objects the museum and Morgan thought were too rare to be replaced — these stayed in New York. Finally, the division seems to have been roughly chronological: much of the early material, especially from the Medieval and Renaissance periods, was given to the Metropolitan, while the later Baroque and Rococo objects were sent to Hartford. The Gutmann collection, for example, was split in two, with most of the post-1600 works going to the Wadsworth Atheneum. The rest of the collection was available for distribution to the family, or for sale.[77] We also learn that at one time Jack Morgan contemplated putting the objects in the Atheneum on long-term loan but that because of tax liabilities within the State of Connecticut he was persuaded to present them as a gift.[78] Thus on February 9, 1917, J. P. Morgan, Jr., fulfilled his father's wishes:

In pursuance of my Father's intention, I now make final disposition of these articles by giving them into your hands to be kept as a permanent exhibition for the benefit of the people of Hartford, the collection to be known as the "J. Pierpont Morgan Collection."[79]

One of the greatest gifts in the history of the Wadsworth Atheneum, this collection has served Morgan's ultimate purpose of bringing the best of European culture to America.

15 : Massimiliano Soldani, *Virtue Triumphant over Vice.*
Copyright The Frick Collection, New York.

Notes

[1] The best general biography of Morgan is Frederick Lewis Allen, *The Great Pierpont Morgan* (New York, 1949). It is the most balanced account of Morgan to date.

[2] Francis Henry Taylor, in his book *Pierpont Morgan as Collector and Patron: 1837–1913* (New York, 1970), p. 17, believes that Morgan did refrain from collecting while his father was alive. Calvin Tomkins, however, in *Merchants and Masterpieces: The Story of the Metropolitan Museum of Art* [1970] (New York, 1973), p. 97, felt that it had to be a matter of money, for until 1890 Pierpont Morgan was still just the son of a rich man.

[3] Herbert L. Satterlee, *J. Pierpont Morgan: An Intimate Portrait* (New York, 1939), p. 258. Satterlee was Morgan's son-in-law, and had firsthand contact with him for many years. This biography is full of very useful information, but is somewhat biased in its presentation.

[4] *Ibid.*, pp. 270–71, 339.

[5] Edward Robinson, *Bulletin of the Metropolitan Museum of Art* 8, no. 6 (1913), pp. 116–17. There is also a list of objects in Morgan's collection made out by a confidential agent of the United States Treasury, probably in 1912 when the collection was being sent from Europe to New York, which lists 4,307 objects, broken down into twenty categories. *The Archives of The Pierpont Morgan Library*, New York (*APML*), Metropolitan Museum File II (1912–1916). The value of the objects is listed at £6,408,498.

[6] William George Constable, *Art Collecting in the United States of America* (London, 1964), pp. 91–140.

[7] *Ibid.*, p. 97.

[8] The last quarter of the nineteenth century witnessed a lessening of the gap between the major and minor arts. This was owing, in part, to British artists and theorists like William Morris and John Ruskin, who believed that artists should be craftsmen and craftsmen should be artists. They looked to the decorative art of the past for inspiration and guidance. These concepts were embraced by American artists of this period as well. Morgan's collector's interest in the decorative arts may owe something to such ideas. See Dianne H. Pilgrim, "Decorative Art: The Domestic Environment," in *The American Renaissance: 1876–1917* (Brooklyn, New York, 1979), p. 111; also Constable, p. 98.

[9] See George K. Boyce, "The Pierpont Morgan Library," *The Library Quarterly* 22, no. 1 (January, 1952). See also Frederick B. Adams, Jr., *An Introduction to the Pierpont Morgan Library* (New York, 1964), revised by Charles Ryskamp in 1974. A detailed discussion of this portion of Morgan's collection is beyond the scope of this essay.

[10] Satterlee, p. 342.

[11] *APML*, Williamson file I, letter George C. Williamson to J. Pierpont Morgan (JPM), 24 July 1908.

[12] *APML*, Durlacher file, invoice dated 30 April 1902, Durlacher Brothers. It is not known whether all dealers received a five per cent commission on works bought at auction. In transactions not involving the auction houses, Morgan usually paid dealers a ten per cent commission.

[13] *APML*, A Miscellaneous file, letter Thomas E. Kirby to JPM, attached to an invoice from American Art Association, New York City, dated 26 February 1909, explaining that in bidding for Mr. Morgan he always used a code name.

[14] *APML*, Metropolitan Museum file II, letter Edward Robinson to Belle de Costa Greene, dated 29 January 1913.

[15] See Robert Charleston, *Masterpieces of Glass* (New York, 1980), p. 35; *Glass from the Corning Museum of Glass: A Guide to the Collections* (Corning, N.Y., 1965), pl. 8; Sidney Goldstein, Leonard S. Rakow, and Juliette K. Rakow, *Cameo Glass* (Corning, N.Y., 1982), pp. 98–99; illus. p. 21, detail p. 12.

[16] *APML*, Wertheimer file, letter Charles Wertheimer to Belle Greene, dated 18 November 1910.

[17] Bishop William Lawrence, *Memoir of John Pierpont Morgan (1837–1913)*; written in the form of a letter to Herbert L. Satterlee, 6 January 1914 (Boston, 1914), p. 80, mostly unpublished typescript in the archives of the Morgan Library, printed with the kind permission of his son, the Right Reverend Frederic C. Lawrence.

[18] Satterlee, p. 433.

[19] Virginia Woolf, *Roger Fry* (New York, 1940), p. 137.

[20] "Editorial," *Burlington Magazine* 23, no. 122 (May, 1913), p. 65.

[21] *APML*, Sir Hercules Read file, letter Sir Hercules Read to Belle Greene, 10 June 1911; Aline Saarinen, *The Proud Possessors* (New York, 1968), p. 61.

[22] Lawrence, pp. 57–58.

[23] Satterlee, *passim.*

[24] Lawrence, p. 52. This description of Princes Gate runs from pages 49–59. Taylor quotes much of it on pages 21–28.

[25] Lawrence, p. 50.

[26] Letter from JPM to the Director, Board of Education, South Kensington, 18 June 1904 (J. Pierpont Morgan Files, parts 3 & 4, The Victoria and Albert Museum, London).

[27] Note from Sir Purdon Clarke, Director of South Kensington Museum, 21 December 1905 (Morgan Files, parts 3 & 4, V&A).

[28] Complete loan list (Morgan Files, parts 7 & 8, 1912–1936); In 1905 there were 934 objects in the "Loans and Gifts, Inventory of Objects" (dated 11 November 1905, Morgan Files, V&A).

[29] Minutes from the Board of Education, South Kensington, Storekeeper's Office, 21 May 1902: "Indeed considering the increased commercial value which objects acquire through being exhibited on loan at the museum, which is assumed to place a sort of stamp of authenticity upon them, too great care can hardly be exercised in accepting objects on loan" (Morgan Files).

[30] *APML*, Duveen file, invoice dated 4 January 1904, Duveen Brothers. In today's currency this would be equal to somewhere between ten and thirty times this amount.

[31] Lawrence, p. 58.

[32] *Idem.*

[33] *APML*, Durlacher file, letter Durlacher to Belle Greene, dated 14 July 1909.

[34] Morgan is usually identified with the city of New York, where he spent most of his adult life. Yet he was born in Hartford and always retained strong feelings for his native city. When his estate was settled in 1917, many of the several thousand works of art in his collection came to the Morgan Memorial of the Wadsworth Atheneum.

[35] *APML*, "An Inventory of the Furniture, Books, Linen, China and Glass, Silver and Silver Plate Ware, Wine and Cigars and other Effects on the Premises. No. 13, Princes Gate S.W., late the property of J. Pierpont Morgan, Esq., Deceased" (London, 1913), pp. 127–37.

[36] *APML*, Seligmann file 4, 1914–1918, invoice, expenses for forwarding two *jardinières* to New York City, dated 19 April 1918.

[37] Germain Seligman, *Merchant of Art: 1880–1960* (New York, 1961), p. 73.

[38] Woolf, p. 141.

[39] *APML*, Daniell file, invoice dated 17 July 1901, A. B. Daniell & Sons, London.

[40] See catalogue entry to follow, no. 67.

[41] *APML*, Wertheimer file, invoice dated 19 April 1909, Charles Wertheimer.

[42] Lawrence, p. 26.

[43] *APML*, Duveen file, invoice dated 3 June 1899, Duveen.

[44] *APML*, Daniell file, invoice dated 4 July 1907, Daniell.

[45] *APML*, Seligmann file I, invoice dated 10 January 1904, Seligmann.

[46] *Decorative Arts of the Italian Renaissance, 1400–1600*, The Detroit Institute of Arts (18 November 1958–4 January 1959), n. 117.

[47] Woolf, p. 143.

[48] 1905 Inventory, V&A.

[49] *APML*, J. & S. Goldschmidt file, letter Goldschmidt to JPM dated 16 May 1902.

[50] Minutes from staff meeting dated 12 June 1902, Morgan Files, V&A. Some staff members felt that the quality of the Gutmann collection objects was not as good as that of similar pieces already in the South Kensington collection.

[51] Satterlee, p. 321.

[52] Tomkins, p. 99; "Annual Report," *Bulletin of the Metropolitan Museum of Art* 1 (November, 1905), p. 2.

[53] Richard Guy Wilson, "The Great Civilization," in *The American Renaissance*, pp. 11–74. Constable does not believe Morgan attempted to achieve an historical sequence in his collection, but rather aimed at amassing a collection of masterpieces; see Constable, p. 109.

[54] *APML*, Metropolitan Museum file, 1906–1911, letter dated 6 February 1906. JPM outlined in detail to Sir Purdon Clarke what he thought his duties should be and which areas of the collection would fall into the new decorative arts department. He wished to discuss at a later date the installation of the Hoentschel collection which he had just given to the Museum.

[55] Tomkins, p. 107.

[56] Satterlee, p. 440.

[57] Tomkins, p. 109.

[58] Saarinen, p. 72.

[59] Wilson, p. 15, quoting Lawrence G. White, *Sketches and Designs by Stanford White* (New York, 1920), pp. 24–25.

[60] Satterlee, p. 535.

[61] Wilson, p. 29.

[62] Gardner Teall, "An American Medici: J. Pierpont Morgan and his Various Collections," *Putnam's Magazine* 7, no. 2 (November, 1909), pp. 131–43.

[63] Taylor, p. 3.

[64] Pilgrim, p. 111.

[65] Woolf, p. 137.

[66] Barbara J. Balsiger, *The Kunst- und Wunderkammern: A Catalogue Raisonné of*

Collecting in Germany, France and England, 1565–1750 (Dissertation written for University of Pittsburgh, Department of Fine Arts, 1970, reproduced by University Microfilms, Ann Arbor), pp. 508–40.

[67]There was a possibility that if Morgan's art collections were still in England at the time of his death, they would be subject to heavy estate taxes which his heirs would have to pay.

[68]Satterlee, p. 537.

[69]Memo from Edward Robinson, recounting conversation of 29 November 1912, *The Metropolitan Museum of Art, Archives.*

[70]Satterlee, pp. 537–38.

[71]*APML, Last Will and Testament of John Pierpont Morgan,* died 31 March 1913, will dated 4 January 1913, codicil dated 6 January 1913.

[72]Edward Robinson, memorandum dated 3 October 1914, relating a conversation which took place the previous year, *The Metropolitan Museum of Art, Archives.*

[73]*Idem.*

[73]*Idem.*

[74]Sales catalogues of these later sales are recorded in the Appendix of this book.

[75]"Information about the Morgan Collection," typescript dated 17 May 1945, *The Metropolitan Museum of Art, Catalogue Department.*

[76]*APML,* Wadsworth Atheneum file, *passim.*

[77]"Information about the Morgan Collection," p. 4.

[78]*APML,* Wadsworth Atheneum file, letter, Francis Goodwin to JPM, Jr. dated 17 April 1916.

[79]*APML,* Wadsworth Atheneum file, letter to the Trustees of the Wadsworth Atheneum, from JPM, Jr., dated 9 February 1917.

Collective Possession: J. Pierpont Morgan and the American Imagination

Neil Harris

"It is preposterous to suppose that because a man is lucky in the stock market he is incapable of appreciating the very best things in art. He is not incapable; only he keeps his interests separate."
Simeon Strunsky, "Morgan" from *Post-Impressions*

The career of John Pierpont Morgan continues to fascinate the curious. In just two decades, during the 1870s and 1880s, his feats of financial management and consolidation brought him mythic status throughout the Western world. The Morgan touch — single-minded, far-seeing, concentrated — seemed never to fail. The Morgan style — terse, fierce, and audacious — made for lively journalistic copy. And the Morgan face and physique, crowned in later years by that diseased and disfigured nose, captivated photographers and caricaturists.[1]

The image of the all-powerful financial wizard whose decisions swayed empires and whose authority rivaled princes grew during the next twenty years. But it was supplemented in the two decades preceding World War I by another, newer reputation: the equally ruthless art acquisitor, the predatory treasure-hunter, the compulsive buyer whose wealth and ambition were transforming the world's art markets. Morgan's expenditure of tens of millions on a bewildering range of objects — books, paintings, miniatures, manuscripts, tapestries, porcelains, bronzes, textiles, furniture — shared the romance of the secret banking cabals and international agreements he was continually accused of masterminding. The annual trips to Europe, the forays to Egypt and the Middle East, the sudden raids on priceless hoards, all reaped their share of newspaper headlines.

The Morgan legend was aided, curiously enough, by the career of his banker son who bore the same name. In the minds of many Americans only the vaguest distinction separates John Pierpont, the railroad organizer of the 1870s, from J. P., the financier who appeared before the Pecora Committee in the 1930s, a midget seated on his knee. The name confusion has only added to the mystique.

But Pierpont Morgan himself was part of a larger story. His life and career suggest that the easy psychologizing of some Gilded Age analysts is insufficient to explain the collecting mania that overtook America in the late nineteenth and early twentieth centuries.[2] The well-educated, socially secure, personally fastidious son of a millionaire banker cannot be described by the phrases used to evoke self-made industrialists who found art either a road to respectability or a happy release from over-stimulation. And these dismissals are equally inadequate when applied to many of the industrialists as well. Morgan did not invent the collecting type as a subject for inquiry; he was merely its most energetic and puzzling representative. Morgan was, wrote one museum director, "the greatest figure in the art world that America has yet produced.... Never in the course of the history of collecting either in the United States or abroad has any private man . . . made so important or so generous a gift of art to the public."[3] He stood above the fray, but his collecting years, just a little more than twenty, witnessed a transformation of more general practices and attitudes. How this transformation occurred must be addressed before Morgan's own part is understood. He led the dance, but he did not dance alone.

*   *   *

When Pierpont Morgan began to collect seriously after the death of his father in 1890, several generations of American collectors had come and gone. And the institutional devices for receiving these accumulations had been revolutionized.

During much of the first half of the nineteenth century, American art collectors tended also to be art patrons; their interest assumed a patriotic air.[4] They not only imported art works from Europe (benefiting from local auctions and foreign tours), they grew friendly with contemporary painters and sculptors and helped support the American art enterprise during its most fragile era. Portraitists, landscapists, genre and history painters benefited from the interest of figures like the Baltimorean Robert Gilmor, the New York grocer Luman Reed, and from merchants like Charles M. Leupp, Robert M. Olyphant, and Jonathan Sturges. Dutch, Spanish, French, and Italian canvases, some of them spurious old masters, mingled in their collections with works by Thomas Cole, Asher B. Durand, William Sidney Mount, and Samuel F. B. Morse. Interest in art as such was suffused by a concern for national advancement. And this suggested support of the living. Only a few collectors took a systematic interest in representing the evolution of art, or attempted to assemble a body of chosen masterpieces. Exceptions like Thomas Jefferson Bryan and James Jackson Jarves, however celebrated and mourned by later generations of critics and historians, remain exemplary only from the standpoint of an interrupted tradition.[5] Their collecting ambitions, like their finances, suffered heavy blows.

Between the Civil War and the early 1890s many things changed. Trends were set which would mature during Morgan's collecting years. For one thing the links between collecting and interest in contemporary American work attenuated. Patron and collector split off. Americans attracted to nineteenth-century painting found French, German, and English art more agreeable than their own. A Gallic tone pervaded private galleries.

Continentals like Corot, Meissonier, Troyon, Cabanel, and Ziem represented the acme of sophistication. Some American purchasers took personal interest in foreign artists, visiting them during their travels and writing letters of appreciation.[6] But although they occasionally picked up some American art and came to know a few native artists, there was little true enthusiasm unless the Americans were working abroad or had achieved European reputations.

Collecting ranks, moreover, were now invaded by the very rich. Antebellum collectors tended to be wealthy, but they were not dominated by vast fortunes. In the 1870s and 1880s, however, names like Vanderbilt, Belmont, Widener, and A. T. Stewart swelled the lists of art buyers. Expensive houses being built on Fifth Avenue, in North Philadelphia, on Chicago's Prairie Avenue, and in Boston's Back Bay often sported their own galleries. Dealers and auction houses, sometimes American-owned but often agents of European firms, appeared to serve these needs. By the 1860s Samuel T. Avery was buying and selling art at his rooms on Broadway and Fourth Street, aided by two Baltimoreans resident in Europe, George A. Lucas and William T. Walters.[7] In the 1870s Thomas E. Kirby came north to New York from Philadelphia, and began his lengthy auctioneering career with the American Art Association. The French dealer Durand-Ruel invaded New York in 1886 with several hundred paintings, exhibiting them at the American Art Association. Sales of the John Taylor Johnston, George I. Seney, A. T. Stewart, and Mary Morgan collections brought in hundreds of thousands of dollars, although the most popular items tended to be by contemporary Europeans.[8]

The switch to European art and *objets*, the entry of the new millionaires, the dispersion of collecting focus, the higher prices, and the multiplication of dealers were seconded by a significant institutional development: the growth of the American art museum. By the 1880s the Museum of Fine Arts in Boston, the Metropolitan in New York, and the Art Institute of Chicago had begun to receive the collections (and bequests) of interested friends. Still housed in what would prove to be temporary homes, crowded with objects, experimenting with modes of self-government and staff appointments, happily welcoming casts, photographs, and personal gatherings of doubtful quality, the American museum had become a source for municipal pride and held out the promise of a better day.[9] Merchants, bankers, realtors, industrialists, and socialites mingled on its boards.

While Morgan was acquiring his financial fame, then —securing the basis of his fortune and strengthening the role of his House— the components of the art acquisition system were falling into place. But however the system was prepared for and anticipated before 1890, it was the next twenty-five years that would bring the basic changes.

The real impact of the art invasion rested on several things: first of all, fuller acknowledgment of the cultural power of the art object; second, greater understanding of the collector's role and the operations governing the art market; and third, an improved science of validation. As all this happened, America became not simply the refuge of human liberty, an asylum for millions of European immigrants, but also a storehouse of European art, the magnet for the privileged as well as the dispossessed. This was accomplished in the full light of publicity, as newspapers, magazines, and fiction of the day revealed. Journalists, novelists, and critics found the international competition for art, like the race for empire, a spectacle of considerable significance. They singled out for attention its various ingredients: the collectors, the expensive objects, the dealers, and the great museums. The paradoxes as well as the triumphs of this great transfer of ritual images and cult objects from one hemisphere to another formed a subject of consuming interest.

As a literary issue art was not new to Americans of this era. For decades American writers had depicted the desperate and sometimes farcical efforts of painters, craftsmen, sculptors, and architects to create objects of beauty for an indifferent and sometimes hostile audience. American artists confronted various constraints: the small range of older examples available in their own country, the inadequacies of specialized training, an apparent poverty of local subject matter, and the corruptions of emigration and transplantation. These themes had gradually entered the mainstream of national fiction.

But as the century closed and a new one dawned, it became increasingly fashionable to examine art collectors themselves, to consider the people who enjoyed the chase for objects, and to raise problems posed by such absorption. Theodore Dreiser, Edith Wharton, Robert Herrick, Henry B. Fuller, and above all, Henry James examined the nature of collecting. Europeans had explored the subject earlier, but more recent American experiences gave the theme a new intensity here.[10]

The collecting motif surfaced, appropriately enough, in an early Henry James novel, *Roderick Hudson*, published in New York in 1876. Though James here concentrated on a subject he would explore again and again, the plight of the working artist, he also considered the collector's needs. He did this by describing Rowland Mallet, the wealthy New Englander who supported young Hudson's tragic journey to Italy. Mallet reflected an older, antebellum tradition; he was both patron and collector. While he conceived his duty to involve supporting living artists, he also believed in the civic obligation to "go abroad and with all expedition and secrecy purchase certain valuable specimens of the Dutch and Italian schools." This done he could then "present his treasures" to an American city willing to create an art museum.[11]

Collecting exerted some romantic appeals. Mallet imagined himself standing "in some mouldy old saloon of a Florentine palace, turning toward the deep embrasure of the window some scarcely-faded Ghirlandaio or Botticelli, while a host in reduced circumstances pointed out the lovely drawing of a hand." Here he would rescue for his countrymen some priceless legacy locked away from public view. But this fantasy hardly undercut the more utilitarian ideal which animated Mallet. As an art collector he tended to be rational rather than impassioned. Eager to be useful, he lacked "the simple, sensuous, confident relish of pleasure." Aware of this handicap Mallet longed for a painter's or sculptor's sensibility in place of his own "awkward mixture of moral and aesthetic curiosity." As it was "he could only buy pictures and not paint them; and in the way of acquisition he had to content himself with making a rule to render scrupulous justice to fine strokes of behaviour in others."[12] James centered his drama upon the artist's struggle rather than the patron's obsession. The task of acquisition had not yet acquired its aura.

Other American writers concentrated less on the ineffectuality or frustrated aestheticism of the collector, and more on the ignorant vulgarity of self-made businessmen, using art to shore up shaky reputations. They had great fun. Finley Peter Dunne's Mr. Dooley found the new rich announcing their virtue by buying art. Until the top blew off the stock market the American millionaire had "bought his art out iv th' front window iv a news an' station-ry shop or had it put in be th' paperhanger." But having made their money here, the rich turned abroad to spend it. "Ye don't catch Higbie changin' iv anhy iv his dividends on domestic finished art. He jumps on a boat an' goes sthraight acrost to th' central depo." That depot was, of course, a Europe filled with clever dealers and enterprising fakers lying in wait for ambitious Americans. But the final victim was the community. The rich man might fill his home with the spoils of his travels, but when he died "he laves his pitchers to some definceless art museum."[13]

Another Chicago writer, Henry B. Fuller, also accepted as given the vulgarity of American collectors, but he added to his portrait the suggestion of civic duty that James had raised. In one Chicago collector's home room after room was "heaped up with the pillage of a sacked and ravaged globe," but its owner continued to study and learn. "I want to keep right up with the times and the people," Susan Bates told a young visitor. "We haven't got any Millet yet, but that morning thing over there is a Corot . . . people of our position would naturally be expected to have a Corot."[14]

The journalist and story writer Richard Harding Davis, writing in the early 1890s, also had sport with New Yorkers who "buy all those nasty French pictures because they're expensive and showy."[15] But he acknowledged the presence of another type, the sentimental art patron, taking more pleasure in nostalgic landscapes by a native painter than in the expensive pictures already imported from Europe. American landscapes could still evoke youth and innocence. But the European art brought higher prices.

Pompous, self-righteous, ignorant, and overbearing collectors made easy targets. The changes that could be rung on this theme were obvious by the 1890s, and were quickly joined to attacks on commercialism, materialism, and personal egotism. Americans abroad searched for canvases like carpeting. "Monet is making a great stir now," declared a visiting Chicagoan in Robert Herrick's *Gospel of Freedom*. "Mrs. Stevans has three of his. We must have at least one, and some Pizarros, and a lovely red Regnoir.[16] Yet pretension, greed, social climbing, and the shopping habit did not sum collectors up, particularly by the early twentieth century. The passions raised were too powerful, the human-object relationships too complex to be limited to lampoons and broad caricatures. Collecting represented dreams and fantasies of deep meaning, and suggested sensitivities and yearnings barely hinted at in conventional analysis.

Theodore Dreiser's epic portrait of Frank Cowperwood attempted one glimpse into the collector's passion. Cowperwood, modeled on the international traction tycoon Charles W. Yerkes, remains one of the compelling figures of the period's fiction. Dreiser developed his character within three different novels, published during the course of more than thirty years. But the first two portions of this *Trilogy of Desire* appeared during the Morgan era, and close upon Yerkes's death.

As Dreiser presented it, Cowperwood's early delight in pictures mingled powerful, undefined, semiconscious desires with a very self-conscious assault on respectability. Art could help the young Philadelphia businessman just getting established. But art also "fascinated him." Admiring nature "without knowing why, he fancied one must see it best through some personality or interpreter."[17] Cowperwood's passion for pictures grew; he paid more and more for them. And he developed a taste for fine furniture, for tapestries, porcelains, and oriental art as well.

The pull to art seemed primal. But intelligent planning and social goals also entered his calculations. "What could be greater, more distinguished than to make a splendid authentic collection of something?" Cowperwood wondered as he thought of representing the evolution of art within his own collection, on a scale possible only in great museums. This ambition came twenty years earlier to Cowperwood than to other collectors; Dreiser gave him special prescience. The logic seemed unassailable. Judgment and discrimination must "result in value as well as distinction? What was a rich man without a great distinction of presence and artistic background? The really great men had it."[18] So Cowperwood's passion could contain both a traditional quest for recognition and a compulsive urge for beauty, accompanied, to be sure, by a stunted if not primitive sense of moral issues.

The forced dispersion of his art at a public auction symbolized

Cowperwood's Philadelphia downfall as poignantly as it revealed his superior judgment. The low prices suggested a taste that ran ahead of its time. In art as in business, Cowperwood possessed genius. A move to Chicago, the site of *The Titan*, the second volume, brought a resurgence of his collecting interests. Again he used art to push the road ahead, but his objects formed a courting arena as well as an outlet for personal sensuality. Cowperwood's sexual appetite was stimulated by women who appreciated his taste, who could discuss his art with him. His search for monumentality soon expressed itself by slavish devotion to the assembled objects. Cowperwood saw himself wandering in rapt communion with his pictures, his missals, his jade, and his sculpture. "The beauty of these strange things, the patient laborings of inspired souls of various times and places, moved him, on occasion, to a gentle awe." Wearied after strenuous days battling in the marketplace, he entered his gallery at night. Turning on the lights, he seated himself before "some treasure, reflecting on the nature, the mood, the time, and the man that had produced it," meanwhile exclaiming "A Marvel! A Marvel!" The businessman as artist, a theme midwestern novelists were exploring at just this time, was perhaps more easily expressed in the collecting than in the creating mode.[19] The patient and loving assembly of objects could draw on the imaginative urges and aesthetic leanings that also fed the artist's dream.

The relationships linking commercial sagacity, personal passion, cultivated taste, and high ambition were even more thoroughly explored in the fiction of Henry James. James designed a gallery of collecting types to populate the novels and short stories he wrote during a thirty-five-year period.[20] They assumed distinct shapes. There was the pilgrim abroad, Christopher Newman, who twenty minutes after buying the first picture of his life became conscious of "the germ of the mania of the 'collector,'" and began to think art patronage "a fascinating pursuit."[21] There were the Europeans themselves, penniless patricians like Valentine de Bellgarde, insatiable accumulators whose "walls were covered with rusty arms and ancient panels."[22] There were revolutionaries like Hyacinth Robinson, too poor to collect themselves but converted to the cause of civilization by "the splendid accumulations of the happier few," the "monuments and treasures of art," in which Europe so abounded.[23] There were the elect like Mrs. Gereth for whom "things" were the sum of existence. "She could at a stretch imagine people's not having, but she couldn't imagine their not wanting and not missing."[24] There were finely honed American tycoons like Adam Verver, engaged in a pursuit for perfection which applied "the same measure of value to such different pieces of property as old Persian carpets, say, and new human acquisitions." Here, at bottom, was the aesthetic principle "planted where it could burn with a cold, still flame; where it fed almost wholly on the . . . idea (followed by appropriation) of plastic beauty."[25] And there was, even more typically, the Yankee millionaire of *The Outcry*, Breckinridge Bender, in pursuit less of beauty than of some "*ideally* expensive thing," member of a conquering horde armed "with huge cheque-books instead of with spears and battle-axes."[26]

This spectrum of gifted, haunted, obsessive, and reckless types raised endless questions about the ties between taste and moral values, questions which later generations of critics are still trying to answer. Given James's knowledge of the Anglo-American scene it was possible that some impressions of Morgan may have entered several of his characters, notably the aspiring spirits of Adam Verver and Breckinridge Bender. James's subtle inquisition into the new connections between people and things, his portrayal of a world so encouraging to acquisition and cataloguing, probably did not penetrate the consciousness of most Americans. But the real counterparts to his fictional creations did march through magazine

THE FLIGHT OF THE OLD MASTERS.

1 : Hy Mayer, "The Flight of The Old Masters," The New York Times, 27 February 1912, p. 16, section V. Copyright © 1910 by The New York Times Company. Reprinted by permission.

and newspaper pages, dazzling readers by their wealth and their grasp.

Among those so accessible in the first decade of the twentieth century was Mrs. Isabella Stewart Gardner in Boston, importing carefully chosen masterpieces while quarreling incessantly with the customs service and occasionally resorting to elaborate smuggling methods, which also made good newspaper copy.[27] By marriage and descent Mrs. Gardner was a millionaire. Benjamin Altman of department store fame collected on his own money, as did the Pittsburgh industrialist now resident in New York, Henry Clay Frick. The Philadelphia contingent included a Morgan associate, Edward T. Stotesbury, P. A. B. Widener, butcher, traction magnate, and corporate investor; and the eminent lawyer John G. Johnson, whose painting collection was larger, more distinguished, and less expensive than that of most of his fellow collectors. Charles L. Hutchinson and Martin Ryerson in Chicago, George Eastman in Rochester, Charles L. Freer in Detroit, Mrs. Collis Huntington in California, Charles Taft in Cincinnati, Otto Kahn, Jules Bache, Charles Yerkes, Clarence Mackay, and Mrs. Louisine Havemeyer, all enjoyed considerable public attention by reason of their avid pursuit of great art at large prices.[28] Without delving as deeply as did the novelists into psychological motives, newsmen were attracted by the new sport. The fortunes available outdistanced the combined national art budgets of several nation-states, and of depressed European curators entrusted with the growth of their collections.

Some comparisons make understandable the outrage and adulation greeting the new money. Before 1910 no picture had ever sold in America for more than $65,000, and this price was reached only occasionally. True, a Meissonier reached $66,000 at the A. T. Stewart sale of 1888, but it was accompanied by a self-portrait. Another nineteenth-century French painting, this time by Troyon, brought $65,000 at the Henry auction in the spring of 1910. But when Charles Yerkes's art collection was auctioned off in the spring of 1910, a spate of new records were set. A Corot brought $80,000, Turner's *Rockets and Blue Lights* managed $120,000, and a Frans Hals staggered the crowd at $137,000. All in all the Yerkes treasures garnered more than $2,000,000, some three-quarters coming from the painting sale, and $350,000 from rugs and tapestries. Headlines trumpeted the astonishing prices art could command.

But these figures paled alongside the sums Americans paid in Europe, not only for paintings but for decorative objects and groups of antiquities. In 1911 Henry Clay Frick parted with more than $1,000,000 in exchange for just three pictures, including a $500,000 Gainsborough. Otto Kahn purchased a Frans Hals family group for something more than $400,000, and Mrs. Huntington paid, that same year, about as much for a single Velasquez. A stunned *New York Times* observed that twenty years earlier $25,000 had been a handsome tribute for a single art work.[29]

Morgan helped set the new levels. To keep the Garland Collection of Oriental ceramics at the Metropolitan, he paid $1,000,000. In 1902 he spent $500,000 on a set of fifteenth-century tapestries once belonging to Cardinal Mazarin, having already purchased some Gobelins for more than $300,000. The Hoentschel collection of decorative art which he gave to the Metropolitan and various pieces from the Rodolphe Kahn collection in Paris commanded similarly staggering sums. This great price inflation occurred in a relatively short period, between the turn of the century and 1912 or so. Along with awe for the magnitude of the rise were questions about its meaning.[30]

The *New York Times* stood among the questioners. Even in 1904 it was wondering why the picture of a cow could fetch so much more cash than the cow herself, to say nothing of the pasture she grazed in. The price for such a canvas may well have constituted a simple tribute to technical skill, like the sums paid by spectators to see a man "keep ten brass balls in the air at once."[31] But the pricing logic reflected other things also. "Unique and nearly unique works of art which are desired by many tend to rise in value proportionately with the great modern fortunes," the *Times* observed. "The buyer foresees . . . that great fortunes can be made hereafter," but the finest works of art can be "bought at all, only now and then. It is the law of supply and demand in a highly accentuated form."[32] Any businessman could understand this formula; it made the swollen prices less surprising. The rich, the *Times* would argue several years later, could afford to ignore previous price levels, because art values were practically incomputable. The price for Rembrandt's *Night Watch* could one day surpass Holland's national debt.[33]

It was more than economic analogy that encouraged a tolerant view of collecting extravagance. Civic aims allowed it. At an earlier moment of national life these expenditures might well have generated greater hostility. And some reformers continued to criticize the huge prices, juxtaposing them with mass poverty. "Shall Fortunes Be Limited By Law?" remained a debate subject.[34]

Art, however, seemed a relatively wholesome outlet for the wealthy, one of the approved vents for great fortunes. As Morgan assumed the presidency of the Metropolitan Museum, the *New York Times* predicted that when the world had forgotten "the master mind which has directed the great railway combinations" it would still cherish his memory as an art collector. Art was the "monument which will carry his name 'down the corridors of time.'"[35] It was good to see rich men spending their money on "objects other than" yachts and automobiles, the *Times* observed several years later.[36]

Invested with public significance by the national press, American collections appealed as a civilizing force, an instrument for local pride, and a permanent tourist attraction. The Metropolitan's Hudson-Fulton Loan Exhibition of 1909, arranged in connection with a New York City pageant, revealed impressive American holdings of Dutch art. Visiting Germans were astonished by the Rembrandts, Vermeers, and Hobbemas they encountered. Max Friedlander of the Prussian Royal Art Museums plaintively noted that America had outstripped Germany in the number of Frans Hals canvases, and already contained seventy of the world's 650 known Rembrandts.[37] "We are gradually reaching the condition where New York is a true market for art," rejoiced the *Nation*, where the well-to-do fearlessly bought "objects of almost any description."[38] Privately owned art revealed national supremacy as clearly as steel production and coal tonnage did. And with almost the same ease of quantification.

International competition provided a justification for collecting energy beyond recreation for the rich or investment opportunity. The masterpieces purchased by millionaires were being taken away from France, Germany, Italy, and Britain. As European art lovers wrote angry letters to their newspapers, as legislatures debated (and occasionally passed) prohibitions against the export of art treasures, American readers devoured stories of humiliation and envy. "Fear for Europe Art Gems," ran one story in the *Times*. Morgan's election to the Metropolitan presidency induced alarm waves all over Europe. George Cain, director of the Musée Carnevalet in Paris, Adolpho Venturi of Rome's National Gallery, Siegfried Lillienthal, Berlin art critic, along with professors, journalists, and gallery keepers, pressed for action.[39] "American collectors are the terror of foreign curators," the *Times* reported happily.[40] "How We Strip Europe of Her Treasures of Art," became a popular theme for weekend writers[41] (Figure 1).

Occasionally Europeans rallied to their art. In Britain public subscriptions saved a few treasures. The Duke of Norfolk's Holbein, offered for sale in 1909, seemed safe only when a volunteer came up with £40,000 at the last moment.[42] British peers posed particularly mercenary demands that the nation ransom their great possessions from American millionaires. By 1911 the English were discussing imposition of an export tax on old masters. If (as was argued) as much as $10,000,000 worth of art left the country annually, a ten per cent duty might raise the funds for protection.[43] Even Wilhelm von Bode of Berlin, a museum director who with the Kaiser's help had bought heavily in France, Italy, and England, complained about American raids. However, he observed reassuringly, Americans bought paintings with a yardstick. In selecting only those making for a big show, they left behind more elegant if unpretentious pieces for discriminating European buyers.[44]

Others, like Lord Clanricard, an Irish landlord, charged Americans with gullibility as well as vulgarity. Two-thirds of the old masters imported here were fakes, he insisted.[45] Not all Americans lacked judgment, however. When Morgan acquired the Amherst Caxtons for his library, and a gorgeous catalogue of his holdings appeared, British connoisseurs bewailed the exhaustion of their "bibliographic and artistic treasures for the benefit of America," and hinted about "joint action of patriotic amateurs."[46]

The hundreds of stories like these brought immense satisfaction to American nationalists who reminded Europeans that their own art represented centuries of financial domination and military looting. "We ourselves largely took it away from somewhere, didn't we?" asked an English lady in a James novel. "We didn't *grow* it all."[47] American collectors were merely returning the favor. Movement was actually good for much of the art, boasted *The New York Times*. "The plaintive wail of the British writer on art, the arrogant ignorance of the German Kunstkritiker, and the groans of the French expert" filled the air of Europe, suggesting that the "objects thus changing hands were lost to the world." In fact they often stepped from dark, inaccessible nooks into commodious galleries generously organized for "the many. Sooner or later they reach the art museums of this big bustling country, where they are more needed than in Europe."[48] The American art collector, harmless, even benevolent, had been transformed into a "bogyman" by the Berlin art establishment, rattling bones to chill the blood of connoisseurs. The terrible picture emerged of Europe's treasures "taking ship for Yankeeland, never to return!"[49] In fact Europe's museums were already so crammed their art could barely be seen. Instead of complaints, American collectors deserved congratulations.

By purchasing undervalued schools and carrying off architectural fragments, the *Times* insisted, Americans increased European appreciation for their own art. When Burgos citizens rose angrily to protest removal of a staircase from the Casa de Miranda, the *Times* advised them to be grateful to Americans who had so stirred their pride and prodded them into protecting their heritage.[50] Swipes at Yankee meatpackers and grocers only encouraged American journalists the more to flail away at the snobbism of European connoisseurs, unwilling to spend the money to protect their treasures in an open market and unable to acknowledge that they were being bested by intelligent and discriminating (as well as wealthy) art buyers.[51]

To be sure, the millionaires were now laying siege to highlights of some celebrated collections. Americans, declared Jacques Seligmann, one of Morgan's favorite dealers, cared for "great age, for historical associations, for aquisitions that command the admiration and respect of museum experts, above all for pieces that reveal their beauty and character increasingly with disinterested familiarity."[52] This flattery may have been calculated, but a more neutral observer, recently appointed Director of the Berlin National Gallery, denied that selling Americans art was like casting "pearls before swine. I make bold to say," he announced in 1911, "that the present-day artistic taste of Americans . . . will rank in all respects with European communities."[53] The recent concentration upon pedigreed masterpieces was one piece of evidence. Another was the prices. Some enthusiasts suggested that museums add purchase prices to the labels. This sight would reinforce "the value of the lesson taught."[54] Even the Director of the Metropolitan, Sir Caspar Purdon Clarke, liked the idea, arguing that it would aid curatorial reputations.[55]

Fraud, of course, continued on its way. In Paris *La Patrie* reported (in 1910) that more than 15,000 fake old masters had been shipped to America during the previous twelve months. These included, it added slyly, 2,849 Corots, 1,812 Rembrandts, and 6,204 Teniers, along with hundreds of harpsichords once belonging to Marie Antoinette.[56] Reputable dealers denied that anything so horrendous could take place, but there were some extraordinary episodes. Spurious noblemen arrived in American cities with equally spurious pictures they presented to gullible buyers.[57] Mrs. Charles Hamilton Paine, the widow of a Boston broker and a resident of Paris, spent hundreds of thousands of dollars on sham art objects manufactured by a doubtful Comte d'Aulby. The English-born Comte printed for Mrs. Paine a handsome catalogue in English and French, listing the royal provenance of the pictures he had sold her, adding after each, "Now belonging to the illustrious amateur of art, Mrs. Charles Hamilton Paine."[58] With his self-designed uniforms and his own order of nobility, the Comte was a figure of notoriety in Paris, but this did not impair his ability to dominate Mrs. Paine. Eventually he was arrested for fraud. He had many colleagues.

American canvases were also subject to dispute. The most notorious incident provoked the trial of a New York art dealer, William Clausen, accused by a local collector of having manufactured a series of paintings by Homer Martin, an American landscapist. The lengthy and complex trial featured contradictory testimony from artists, critics, and connoisseurs. "Is there no quarter from which an authoritative announcement may come," plaintively asked *The New York Times*, "or must every man make up his mind for himself?"[59]

The sensational charges and countercharges, the revelation of dishonest dealers and active forgers, and the searching out of international networks did more than provide easy newspaper copy and still more publicity for the collecting passion. They also encouraged popular discussions which continue today. What was a real masterpiece? In 1910 the modern science of attribution was barely a few decades old. Giovanni Morelli's reexamination of Italian art works in German galleries helped revolutionize connoisseurship, but it was published as late as 1880. Disciples like Gustave Frizzoni, Jean Paul Richter, and Bernard Berenson were soon establishing the principles and techniques for more careful judgments about authorship.[60] Scientific tests appeared to validate the age and origin of some decorative art objects. The expert, self-important and self-confident, was making novel claims. Scholarship, research, and systematic analysis replaced exquisite and undefinable sensations as the basis for conclusions. Of course scientific connoisseurs did make mistakes. They revised their opinions. And some dealers and collectors continued to insist that taste offered a better guide than extended scholarship. Nonetheless, by the early twentieth century art works had to earn their labels, and this added to both the risks and the excitement of collecting.

The highly publicized changes of attribution, however, posed problems. Why should the simple change of an artist's name so affect the value and importance of a work? While its appearance remained the same, drastic consequences flowed from a single judgment. There was too much reverence for names, the *Times* argued. A picture or statue sold as the handiwork of a famous artist fetched a big price, and fought its way to a prominent museum. "Suddenly somebody comes along and denies . . . its 'authenticity.'

At once, from being an object of worship by the elect and respect from common folk, it loses all value and is hastily removed to a cellar." Yet whatever beauty the object possessed before the discovery, it retained afterward. This "great mystery" contrasted with literature. Books, suggested the *Times*, "stand on their own merits. They are not liked the better because written by a noted author, or the worse because anonymous."[61]

What was the meaning of genuine? Research revealed that many famous art works emerged from workshops rather than the master's hand. Renaissance geniuses not only copied one another's art, they employed assistants to actually paint, carve, and gild. Was it the age of the copy that made it important? Its quality? The copy's owner? Was the work of art simply a commodity whose cash value (and popularity) varied according to a supply and demand cycle? Reviewing the issues, *The New York Times* decided that the *nouveaux riches* who simply bought what they liked were on safer ground than more ambitious collectors determined to make important purchases. The vulgar might collect bad art but at least they were not victimized. The ambitious collector required expert advice "if not a guardian." The only infallible way to obtain art was to buy directly from its maker.[62] This meant visiting studios and patronizing the living. The alternative was to establish committees of experts who would then pass rulings (by majority rule) on art authenticity.

The discussion was, at a minimum, amusing. "The man in the street," wrote the *Times*, "to whom a picture is good if it appeals to his taste and bad if he does not like it," takes "a deal of enjoyment" in the disputes, particularly when they elevated to sudden glory a picture that had been hanging in relative obscurity for centuries. Paradoxically, its new prominence, by increasing its value, rendered it less accessible to the viewing public.[63]

Two other developments of the day further increased public interest in the cultural significance of art objects. While they testified to a new, more intense consciousness of their social meaning, they were disturbing and threatening to art lovers. The first involved the increased daring of art thievery. This was no new problem. The British crown jewels had been subject to ambitious conspiracies for many years; the nineteenth century had its own startling thefts (including a spectacular seizure of Gainsborough's *Duchess of Devonshire*, purchased by Junius Spencer Morgan and eventually housed in son Pierpont's own collection).

But during the first decade of the twentieth century the number and magnitude of thefts advanced. In France some thieves specialized in church treasures, hauling away reliquaries, monstrances, windows, manuscripts, carvings, statuary, and paintings. Headquartered in Clermont-Ferrand, one gang's technique was to persuade priests that the anticlerical government was about to sell their art. It offered to remove it for "safekeeping."[64] Rumors suggested the loot was then transferred to London before finding its way to American millionaires. The mysterious "anonymous millionaire" was invoked by Europeans on many occasions to explain why famous works of art, apparently unsalable on the open market, were taken. As Americans explained the growth of forgery and fraud, so they were pushed forward as the cause for expanded criminality.

No such exotic reasons were necessary. Much of the art crime was home grown and home inspired. This was never more true than in the single greatest outrage of the early century, one of the most brazen feats of knavery in the history of thievery. This was the August 1911 theft of the *Mona Lisa*, taken by an Italian carpenter in broad daylight right under the noses of Louvre guards, and kept hidden in Paris for more than two years until it was returned to the Louvre (via Florence) in early 1914.[65] No incident dramatized more clearly the ritual significance and singular status accorded to masterpieces in the Western world. "It is shocking to think that a thief could remove a fairly priceless painting from a famous gallery in the heart of a busy city," *The New York Times* editorialized.[66] French papers were less restrained. Noting the scandalous safety conditions of the Louvre, the inattention of the guards, the eating, cooking, and pipe-smoking that took place in the galleries, a writer in the *Revue Bleu* charged that the museum had earned the world's contempt. "France is responsible in the eyes of every person of culture for this irreparable loss," he cried, and "the soul of the universe mourns and will mourn evermore." The theft had become the "crime of 21st August."[67]

Inevitably enough, stories appeared that Morgan had been offered the painting (which he angrily denied). According to the American press, the thief alleged he had tried to sell the painting to one of Morgan's representatives, as well as to dealers in several European cities.[68] Another rumor suggested that the theft merely disguised a transfer; the real *Mona Lisa* had already been sold to some American millionaire for a fabulous sum, and a reproduction had been hung in its place.

The fame of this painting, the length of time it was gone, and the size and reputation of the Louvre, all focused attention on the larger phenomenon of art thefts. A vague sense of danger and intrigue now hung over the collecting drama. Like his colleague the second-story man, then getting attention from elegant detective writers, the art thief became something of a romantic figure, stealing only from the rich (or the well-stocked) before facing his special problems of divestiture.[69] And accompanying his adventures ran the complexities of improved forgery and reproduction techniques, granting the successful collector a special note of triumph as he threaded his way amid criminals and impostors.

A second threat to the masterpiece also focused attention on its role as cultural icon. And this was the relatively recent device of attacking an art work to express some personal or social grievance. In the summer of 1907 a young man with a knife slashed a Poussin canvas hanging in the Louvre. He explained afterwards that he did it to shame his parents, prosperous farmers refusing him financial aid.[70] Two months later an Ingres portrait was cut by a girl with a scissors. Inspired by the earlier slashing, she turned herself in to bring attention to the fact that so much money was "invested in dead things like those at the Louvre collections when so many poor devils like myself starve because they cannot find work."[71] In 1911 Rembrandt's *Night Watch* was badly damaged by a discharged naval cook, angry at the State because he had been dismissed by the Dutch Navy.[72]

Such attacks provoked a series of responses. Some museums, like the Louvre, began to place valuable paintings under glass. This produced new complaints. Sticks and umbrellas (still carried into galleries) could break the glass, critics argued, and the reflecting surfaces now deprived students of effective study. Some suggested that admission to public collections be more carefully controlled, by instituting charges in previously free museums or by creating special galleries (of inexpensive objects) for more casual and potentially dangerous visitors.[73] Guard forces were enlarged, and greater vigilance preached. But there were no absolutely foolproof methods of protection, only a series of interim measures. For art works, so prized a badge of culture, had also assumed other metaphorical burdens. They symbolized the margin, the surplus of wealth modern industrialization had achieved, now being applied to the purchase, display, and cataloguing of history's treasures. Alienation, quite properly, addressed these icons. Where else could civilization be wounded more cruelly? The attacks added to the glamour and notoriety the art enjoyed.

Through this extensive set of transactions, amid the fraud, the thefts, the great auctions, the happy meetings of impoverished

Europeans and wealthy Americans, spreading rumors, making deals, granting interviews, wandered the dealers. This was, if not their greatest age, perhaps their most creative one. Wealthy English, German, and French collectors, assembling objects with feverish intensity, also needed dealers. But they were rarely as dependent on them as were the Americans. Linguistically, intellectually, even socially, American buyers relied on the dealers: to introduce them to artists, collectors, museums, and curators; to refine (or simply to change) their tastes; to stimulate their personal competition; to broaden their areas of interest and knowledgeability; even to correct their appearance and table manners. By the early twentieth century, the traveling agents of European houses had invaded eastern (and occasionally midwestern) cities, impressing the public with their cosmopolitanism, their aesthetic judgment, their claims to infallibility. They whetted appetites, nurtured egos, soothed hurt feelings, and established the rules of the hunt. Through dealers Americans discovered they could own masterpieces thought a few years earlier to be forever out of reach. Through dealers they were led backward in time from their own nineteenth-century favorites, and to regions of the world far beyond Western Europe. Both the older American firms and the Europeans — Scott & Fowles, Knoedler, Duveen Brothers, Durand-Ruel, Seligmann, Berolzheimer, Agnew — provided guidance, encouragement, and merchandise.[74]

Although dealers attracted less attention than did their clients or their art, they helped represent official opinion. At a time when museums had small staffs, when university trained specialists were rare, when curators were just learning how to manage, dealers had the urbanity, articulateness, experience, and self-confidence to permit generalization about the art market. Museum directors like Wilhelm von Bode, his envy and outrage notwithstanding, paid them their due. Dealers, he admitted, had become "bearers of culture." "They are to thank that the American collectors seek only the best; that their sense of quality has developed in a measure quite unknown with us." As "pathfinders" dealers ensured that collecting implied the same high standards from coast to coast.[75] They were agents of high European culture, recreating its world. Museums were still too poor to constitute their principal customers. If art was bought at all it was bought by individuals. And here the affectations and performance techniques, the flattery, promises, threats, and melodrama that some dealers employed, served as instruments in a good cause. To a large extent they were as much taste makers as their clients.

The dealers had much more than the egos of their customers working for them. In early twentieth-century America they could exploit a powerful and competitive struggle for cultural dignity ranging among the country's large cities.[76] The millionaires spoke not simply for themselves nor even for their personal reputations. All assumed they would be handing on their collections to public institutions. The private act of purchase was thus invested with public significance. The collectors had become spokesmen for their communities, already at work planning the civic monuments to announce their arrival on the world scene. Opera houses, orchestra halls, theaters, plazas, boulevards, statuary squares, universities, zoos, park systems, fairs, all testified to municipal grandeur. But the art museum was certainly a principal source of local pride. Ordering a great building and filling it with beautiful objects became a civic obligation. In Chicago, Boston, Philadelphia, and Cincinnati, in St. Louis, Pittsburgh, Baltimore, and Cleveland the collecting passion attracted popular support.

But while there was competition there was also dominance. Grand collecting coincided with the powerful claims of New York City, not simply to American metropolitan sovereignty but to rivalry with London, Paris, and Berlin as a center of learning and culture. Greater New York was created in 1898. During the next

fifteen years the city's architecture, institutional growth, and financial power reflected a special surge of confidence and imperial desire. Millionaires flocked there from the countryside and from rival cities. On the boards of institutions like the Metropolitan, the New York Public Library, and the American Museum of Natural History, they protected the city's honor in the quest for treasure.[77]

Local pride and civic patriotism, at least on the part of the rich, seemed relatively new to New York. The *Times* observed in 1902 that it was traditional to think of this city as simply a camp to make money. Things, however, had changed. Once a desirable possession came on the market, some "public-spirited citizen" managed to secure it. "It was only the other day that Mr. Pierpont Morgan came forward to secure for the Metropolitan Museum the Garland collection, which it seemed in danger of losing. And now Mr. James Henry Smith comes forward to save for the city the famous Rubens which we were in danger of losing to Chicago."[78]

Vigilance was necessary, even for New York's magnificent future. The following month the *Times* struck a different, more petulant tone when it learned that Henry Walters of Baltimore was about to buy the Masaranti Collection in Rome. "New York has lost the chance of a generation and at one blow Baltimore has raised herself far above all other American cities," mourned the *Times*. No New Yorker had bothered to go to Rome and buy these canvases and antiquities "like a sensible businessman." It was too bad, the *Times* concluded, that so little public spirit existed in the city. It made the Metropolitan "look silly" and placed the Walters Museum "on a level with the great public museums of London, Paris, and Berlin."[79] Sparring with other newspapers who warned about the collection's authenticity, harangued by readers who thought New York deserved a change of diet and a greater emphasis on modern art, the *Times* grieved to the last for the collection's loss, one which modern appraisers have found to be a mixed blessing for Baltimore.[80]

New York, however, was not to suffer many such losses. The wealth of Metropolitan trustees, the city's energy, its growth and development made it the drainage point for the siphon diverting so much European art. Stuffed with objects, by 1914 museums like the Metropolitan were being criticized as mausoleums, magnificent monuments crammed with a mass of objects, too many of them mediocre. The chief task of museums like the Met, warned Wilhelm Bode in 1912, was the disposition of superfluous possessions.[81] Describing the "Land of Sunday Afternoon" in 1914, designer Lee Simonson condemned the "unending accumulation" making museums into caves in which "successive Niebelungen hoards recovered from a disintegrating past are accumulated in exactly the piles in which they were originally heaped."[82] The "aesthetic furniture of a plutocracy," Simonson wrote elsewhere, was poor building material for a civic institution.[83] The business of a museum was "not to store the past but to restore it, to restore to the scattered fragments of a dismembered age their meaning."[84]

Within a generation American collectors and the museums they stocked had grown from the weak and dependent children of European parents to so concentrated a level of wealth that plenitude was itself a problem. It had taken only twenty-five years (and several times that many millions of dollars) for the transformation. The celebration of collectors, the transformation of art objects into social talismans, and the consecration of museums as hallowed receptacles had aided the process. In the 1920s the art flow would expand and prices rise still further, but the pattern was now set.

And the pattern maker, the figure bringing together the trends and the paradoxes, the *beau idéal* of the private collector was Pierpont Morgan himself. As trustee and then president of the Metropolitan, as a benefactor of dealers and a patron of cataloguers, a focus for expert consultants, a bidder of huge sums at private sales and public auctions, as the recipient and then the restorer of stolen objects, as donor and preserver as well as pirate raider, Morgan the collector stayed continually in the public eye. When he outbid emperors other Americans rejoiced; when he entertained kings, queens, sultans, and pashas, the American press exulted. His lengthy campaigns against the art tariff — revised in 1909 and basically abandoned some years later — brought enthusiastic appreciation. His name figured in almost every major art rumor of the day and his travel plans received the attention today accorded only rock stars and royalty.[85]

Enhancing Morgan's capacity for fascination was, of course, his own personal collection, a fabulous assemblage of objects on display at the South Kensington Museum and his English houses. Its fate would become an international question, involving governmental figures as well as connoisseurs. It had been an obvious weapon in his war against the art tariff, but more than that it symbolized, to many of his countrymen, the larger transfer of treasure. When, in 1912, he announced he would transport his collection back to New York (some suggested to avoid the English death duties), it was front page news. This "amazing collector," gushed *The New York Times*, who "picks the fruit of European art from its parent tree with the zest and ease of a boy in an apple orchard," had shown the world what can be achieved by "the union of a genius for business with a taste for art."[86] When David Lloyd-George assured Morgan that his art would not be taxed if it remained (unsold) in England, alarmed Americans cried foul. "London museums have been enriched long enough," warned the *Times*, jealous for New York's reputation. And the inheritance tax was not the reason for Morgan's decision, it continued. He had always intended to bring the objects to America. New York was their destined home and "no promises to withhold taxation will serve to keep them on the other side of the Atlantic."[87]

Fears of the Exchequer's designs on his estate may have been a factor, but the *Times* had a point. Morgan's philanthropic career suggested an abiding intention to place his art objects in his native country, although for some time it was not clear just where they would go (Figure 2). But despite the spasmodic flamboyance of his many purchasing gestures, Morgan's civic interests were carefully thought out and directed toward national objectives. As with many other millionaires his passion for ownership was fed partly by the sheer pleasure of obtaining what was difficult to obtain. If the objects were rare or unique, if they were beautiful, and if they were important representatives of a style, a skill, or a civilization, Morgan could become aroused. He admired workmanship, valued associations, enjoyed precious materials, and had his particular aesthetic preferences.

But Morgan's buying transcended issues of taste or personal favor to assume, at moments, something of a military campaign. It was his single-minded pursuit of the priceless, his constancy in the hunt, and his willingness to commit fabulous sums which brought him contemporary fame. But it is the deeper ambitions and the institutional impact which deserve renewed attention today.

The adjectives "collected" and "possessed" conjure up contrasting sets of meanings. To be collected implies a state of calmness, composure, tranquillity, and placidity. Being possessed, on the other hand, insinuates a form of seizure, derangement, sorcery, or maniacal infatuation. Yet in the art world the two words frequently intertwine. Morgan's energy, his zeal, his compulsive fascination with objects suggest a degree of possession. His youthful fascination with bits of stained glass, a boyish obsession which eventually found expression in the windows of his library, was one small indication. His compulsive, lifelong pursuit of individual objects was another. But his philanthropic activities, his support of scholarship and cultural organizations, his larger

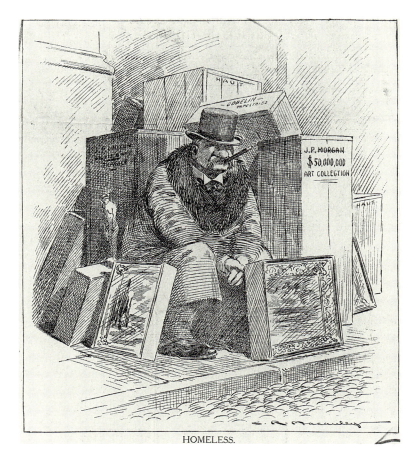

HOMELESS.

2: "Homeless," from *World*, 26 November 1912. Courtesy of The Pierpont Morgan Library, New York.

collecting ambitions argue for something else. In those activities falling beyond either art or business, Morgan united elements of sentimentality, nostalgia, and personal conservatism. He was a devoted clubman, a breeder of dogs and cattle, a yachtsman, and something of a country gentleman. He delighted in his English stays and the great houses he visited might well have inspired some of his own collecting goals. His travels beyond England did not, as with so many Americans, emphasize France and Germany, sophisticated, modern, up-to-date, but Rome and Egypt. He hired scholars to produce careful and lavishly printed catalogues, which he distributed among research libraries. He was a generous contributor to the American Academy in Rome, a patron of neoclassical architecture, an active subscriber to many cultural associations. Finally, he was the most prominent lay member of the Episcopal Church of America, an enthusiastic participant at triennial conventions, the friend and host of prominent bishops, the warden of his own church vestry. Some of these activities reflected Morgan's own sense of self and position. His wealth and pride demanded that he contribute appropriately to various causes, that he be represented, handsomely, in the lists of purchasers and donors. His own taste for good things — to eat, to drink, to sail on — was fed by a lifetime of organized self-indulgence.

But beyond this Morgan pursued a larger task, one well adapted to his conservative values. By his purchases, his patronage, and his various gifts he was, in effect, preparing an historical record, shaping a research industry and stocking the cultural institutions that would dominate high scholarship and many forms of intellectual discourse for the rest of the century. At a time when many of these institutions were still plastic, Morgan's involvement stamped their future course of development.

This aspect of his influence received some comment. As he moved to the conclusion of his father-in-law's biography (despite its obvious bias, the best source for Morgan's life), Herbert L. Satterlee portrayed his subject at ease within the West Room of his famous library, surrounded by its Memlings, its Italian furniture, its Etruscan and Roman antiquities, its priceless books and manuscripts. "As Mr. Morgan sat among these ageless examples of the culture of past centuries," Satterlee wrote reverently, "he must have thought, not of the years of work and the money that he had put into them, but of the artists, authors, and students of future years who would be helped by them to create cultural standards that would give America a place of honor in the world of art and letters."[88] Such sentiments, fitting easily within a book of piety, can be dismissed as banal rather than revelatory.

But Satterlee had a point. Morgan's quest ensured impressive continuity between the connoisseurship and antiquarian traditions of Europe and the growing world of art history and scholarship in America. Noting the clamor for legislative protection against art exports in 1912, the London *Daily News* acknowledged the logic of the danger while it voiced its anxiety. "The American springs from the old civilization as truly as the European," it explained, "and can claim as authoritative [a] right as the European to share in its glories."[89] But it was really Morgan, with a few others, who made the connection so irresistible. The Anglo-American establishment, then forming and shaping the art museums and academies, saw the Morgan touch as ultimately reassuring.

Reassuring, because during the later years of Morgan's life two challenges to extant high culture were arousing some alarm. One was the enormous influx of tens of millions of European immigrants, workers and peasants for the most part, bearing popular tastes, social ideas, and folk memories that diverged from the gentilities that Morgan's class accepted as their standards. Fear of immigrants took many forms and had many sources. There is little

evidence that Morgan absorbed any hysteria, though he undoubtedly held the prevailing bigotries of his friends.

But the task of educating, assimilating, and adapting immigrants to specific values, and transmitting to them certain aesthetic ideals, commanded considerable attention. For several generations the public schools, the newspapers, the stage, the saloon, the library, and more recently vaudeville and movies had been scrutinized as arenas of vice or theaters of virtue. Behind debates about school curricula and Sunday closings, comic supplements and newspaper sensationalism, spectator sports and pernicious advertising lay the sense that a war was raging for the hearts and minds of the new Americans.[90] This was often expressed in terms of shared behavioral norms, standards of political expectation, and adherence to economic values fundamental to a democratic and capitalist society. But there were issues of high culture at stake as well. Would this influx accept or reject the inheritance so cherished by the intellectual elites of Anglo-America? Would traditional taste as well as traditional learning find an acquiescent audience? What would be the venerated texts and valued icons of the next generations? It was not altogether clear in 1912.

A second threat was quite different and more muted. Within Europe itself the forces of modernism had been mounting their own assault on tradition, challenging the criteria used to champion works of art, literature, and architecture, redefining the nature of narration, representation, and dramatic expression. The artistic version of this revolt may well have reached America later than its literary expression, but it did arrive. Several months after Morgan's death in the spring of 1913, and some months before his great loan exhibition went on display at the Metropolitan in February, 1914, the Society of Independent Artists launched its memorable Armory Show, introducing many Americans to post-Impressionism. The art establishment reacted with hostility; the popular press provided extensive coverage and a certain level of derision.[91]

Morgan showed little interest in contemporary art, to judge from his buying habits. But his collecting and administrative instincts helped set the Metropolitan (and other great museums) on a course which would distance them from the protean character of twentieth-century arts for some time to come. Morgan allied himself with the most valued art traditions of the past. He deliberately undertook to represent them to best advantage. Thus his strong personal response to individual art works lay hidden within his larger collections.

Reviewing the Morgan Loan Exhibition in 1914, Frank Jewett Mather, Jr. described its effect as "wholly impersonal," lacking either adventurousness or individualism. Admitting the high quality everywhere, Mather argued in the *Nation* that the objects suggested "a standardization alien to the finest processes of artistic appreciation." The Morgan materials consisted of objects "which, by common consent of international dealers and their clients, are brevetted as of highest rarity." They formed an assemblage, not a true collection, dominated by pieces of curiosity rather than art.[92]

Such reactions helped establish a Morgan who seemed colder, more clinical, less involved in his treasures than he actually was. But the impersonality can be explained by the errand Morgan had undertaken. He was offering his countrymen an armory of standards, a series of sources, a group of canons to keep critics, connoisseurs, and museum visitors busy for generations.

Such didacticism enjoyed occasional notice. In an obituary editorial, the *Nation* described Morgan's distance from contemporary art, but in terms more positive than Mather's critical review suggested. Modern art — and here the *Nation* included both Impressionism and the Barbizon School — seemed too specialized, esoteric, and above all private to appeal to "so potent,

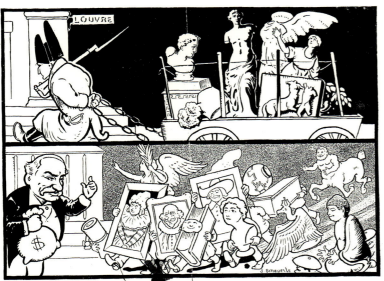

THE FRENCH AND THE AMERICAN NAPOLEONS OF ART.
Filling museums with art treasures one hundred years ago and to-day.

3 : J. Schuerle, "The French and the American Napoleons of Art," source unknown. Courtesy of The Pierpont Morgan Library, New York.

public, and essentially simple a character as was Mr. Morgan's." A few critics attacked the Medici mantel cast over Morgan's shoulders by admiring friends, pointing out that the Medici patronized the living. But, said the *Nation*, transported to the twentieth century Medici patrons would have liked contemporary art no better than Morgan did. "It is the defect of our art . . . that its appeal to those who robustly do the world's work is so small."[93] Blame the artist, not the collector, for the failure.

The Morgan objects, then, projected a sense of obligation, appearing in the service of principles rather than in the grip of grand passions. Obituary editorials stressed again and again the benefits to a larger public which far outweighed any loss of visible personality. In art as in commerce, the similes in favor were military and imperial. Morgan was likened to Napoleon, to Caesar, to Bismarck, to Renaissance princes (Figure 3). His love of art came accompanied by strategic brilliance. "Mr. Morgan was no selfish collector of art merely for the gratification of his sense of that power which unlimited wealth supplies," wrote the *Philadelphia Evening Telegraph*. He had " a much broader and more unselfish object in view," to bring Americans the greatest, most comprehensive set of art objects so that her aesthetic and educational ideals "might be built upon the true and lasting foundations of absolute finality."[94] There has been "no greater or more valuable achievement for the benefit of this nation in modern times," wrote the *New York American* in 1913 about the assembling of the Morgan collection.[95] And the *New York Mail*, while warning that transferring the entire collection to the Metropolitan might endanger the "just proportion" between past and present its exhibits represented, nonetheless admired it. Possession of the Morgan treasures "will do more to put the old world and the new upon an equality than all the trade balances that ever were written or even can be written."[96]

Morgan's death and the subsequent distribution of his art thus climaxed public approval of the collecting passion. The glamorous booty gained acceptance as an appropriate tribute to American economic growth. Art objects and the buildings enclosing them became the shrines for a secular religion that identified itself with the very pith of civilization. This was true in both Europe and America. Englishmen, Frenchmen, Germans, and Spaniards began to speak of what was "due to the nation" in possessing their art. Who is England "unless *I* am?" a bewildered Lord Theign asked those who insisted, in James's *Outcry*, that he keep his painting — done by an Italian several centuries earlier — for England rather than sell it to a Yankee. It had become a "national treasure" whose departure could be "dangerous to the . . . common weal."[97]

The union of high culture with nationalist ideals was clearly flourishing. Aided in the nineteenth century by bourgeois collectors and ruling houses, it was furthered in the twentieth by business corporations and public authorities. Possession of art became a national touchstone in a world where tourism had begun to measure many of the qualities of civilization. As the United States acquired the institutional expressions of older societies, so also the physical evidences of continuity became increasingly valued. In supporting this transit of art objects Morgan and his fellow collectors, acting from many motives and many needs, served as popularizers as well as underwriters. Even the flamboyance, the dramatic exaggeration, the bidding wars, and the dealer manipulations thus acquired some use, heroicizing the art conquests of the day. As feeders and shapers of this high culture, the tycoons had an influence that went almost as far as the effects of their financial transactions. If it has not purchased them a serene immortality, at least to generations trained to scrutinize the meanings of personal display, it has added to their mystery. And this, the millionaires, Morgan particularly, would certainly have enjoyed.

Notes:

[1]There are a number of biographies of Morgan, dozens of essays and articles, and an enormous literature of observation and retrospection. No convincing, comprehensive, modern biography exists. Several of the books tend to repeat one another's anecdotes, albeit in some repackaged form. The first biography, Carl Hovey, *The Life Story of J. Pierpont Morgan: A Biography* (New York, 1912), takes a middle ground between adulation and condemnation, and traces Morgan's love for art and collecting to his father. John K. Winkler, *Morgan The Magnificent: The Life of J. Pierpont Morgan* (New York, 1930), relies heavily on Hovey, is melodramatic, overwritten, and worshipful, although occasionally critical, presenting Morgan as a colossal adventurer, a genius, gifted with "incredible audacity, sublime self-confidence, unqualified courage." Lewis Corey, *The House of Morgan* (New York, 1930), and Frederick Lewis Allen, *The Great Pierpont Morgan* (New York, 1949), are the favored texts, better documented, although I have found them less helpful than the detailed study by Morgan's son-in-law, Herbert L. Satterlee, *J. Pierpont Morgan: An Intimate Portrait* (New York, 1939). Francis Taylor, *Pierpont Morgan as Collector and Patron: 1837–1913* (New York, 1970), is probably the most convincing picture of the man as a collector. Contemporary articles, cartoons, a still unpublished recollection by Bishop Lawrence of Massachusetts (much cited by Taylor), are available at the archives of the Morgan Library in New York. I am grateful to archivist David Wright for making scrapbooks and other materials available to me, and for many helpful suggestions.

[2]For a summary of such generalizations see Neil Harris, "The Gilded Age Reconsidered Once Again," *Archives of American Art Journal* 23, no. 4 (1983), pp. 9–18. Sigmund Diamond, *The Reputation of the American Businessman* (Cambridge, Mass., 1955), devotes a chapter to Morgan's obituary notices, but concentrates on things other than his art collecting.

[3]Taylor, *Pierpont Morgan as Collector*, p. 39. Edward P. Mitchell, *Memoirs of An Editor: Fifty Years of American Journalism* (New York and London, 1924), contains an interesting interpretation of Morgan as collector, pp. 366–368, while also describing William Mackay Laffan, a journalist and specialist on oriental ceramics who often advised Morgan. The chapter on Morgan in Aline B. Saarinen, *The Proud Possessors: The Lives, Times and Tastes of Some Adventurous American Art Collectors* (New York, 1958), is also very useful.

[4]The collecting patterns of this period, as they interact with patronage, are best summarized in Lillian B. Miller, *Patrons and Patriotism: The Encouragement of the Fine Arts in the United States 1790–1860* (Chicago, 1966). The social setting for the art communities is examined in Neil Harris, *The Artist in American Society: The Formative Years, 1790–1860* (New York, 1966).

[5]Francis Steegmuller, *The Two Lives of James Jackson Jarves* (New Haven, 1951), offers the fullest picture of Jarves's life. Saarinen and W. G. Constable, *Art Collecting in the United States of America: An Outline of a History* (Toronto and New York, 1964), describe Bryan's attempts to create a comprehensive gallery.

[6]For this later era see René Brimo, *L'Évolution du goût aux États-Unis* (Paris, 1938); and Wesley Towner, *The Elegant Auctioneers* (New York, 1970), alas entirely unannotated. For collecting and the art market on a worldwide basis see the volumes by Gerald Reitlinger, *The Rise and Fall of Picture Prices, 1760–1960* (London, 1961), and *The Rise and Fall of Objets d'Art Prices Since 1750* (London, 1963), vols. I and II of *The Economics of Taste.*

[7]For Avery and the development of American dealers see the introduction to *The Diaries 1871–1882 of Samuel P. Avery, Art Dealer*, ed. Madeleine Fidell Beaufort, Herbert L. Kleinfield and Jeanne K. Welcher (New York, 1979), vii–lxvii.

[8]Towner, *The Elegant Auctioneers*, passim, describes these sales.

[9]Several of these museums have their own historical monographs. For general overviews see Nathaniel Burt, *Palaces for the People: A Social History of the American Art Museum* (Boston and Toronto, 1977); Daniel M. Fox, *Engines of Culture: Philanthropy and Art Museums* (Madison, Wis., 1963); and Karl E. Meyer, *The Art Museum: Power, Money, Ethics* (New York, 1979), chapter 1. See also Walter M. Whitehill, *Museum of Fine Arts, Boston* (Cambridge, Mass., 1970), 2 vols; and Calvin Tomkins, *Merchants and Masterpieces* (New York, 1970), the last of which contains a good deal of material on Morgan's role in creating the Metropolitan.

[10]Collecting as a literary theme has recently been examined in Rémy G. Saisselin, *The Bourgeois and the Bibelot* (New Brunswick, N.J., 1984), passim, but particularly chapters 4–6.

[11]Henry James, *Roderick Hudson* (London, 1879; Harmondsworth, 1969), p. 26.

[12]*Ibid.*, pp. 32–33.

[13][Finley Peter Dunne] "Art Patronage," *Observations by Mr. Dooley* (New York, 1902), pp. 42–43, 45.

[14]Henry B. Fuller, *With the Procession* (New York, 1895; Chicago, 1965), p. 57.

[15]Richard Harding Davis, "A Patron of Art," *Van Bibber and Others* (New York and London, 1892), p. 151.

[16]Robert Herrick, *The Gospel of Freedom* (New York, 1898), p. 221. Interesting themes raised by collecting are featured in the group of short stories by the art critic Frank Jewett Mather, Jr., *The Collectors: Being Cases Mostly under the Ninth and Tenth Commandments* (New York, 1912).

[17]Theodore Dreiser, *The Financier* (New York and London, 1912), pp. 115, 120. See also p. 187.

[18]*Ibid.*, p. 287.

[19]Theodore Dreiser, *The Titan* (New York and London, 1914; New York, 1959), p. 378. This theme is addressed in Carl Smith, *Chicago and the American Literary Imagination, 1880–1920* (Chicago, 1984), chapters 2–4.

[20]There is an enormous literature of commentary on James's views of art, artists, and collectors. I have found Viola Hopkins Winner, *Henry James and the Visual Arts* (Charlottesville, Va., 1970), particularly chapter 8, especially helpful.

[21]Henry James, *The American* (Boston, 1877; New York, 1963), p. 15.

[22]*Ibid.*, p. 91.

[23]Henry James, *The Princess Casamassima* (London and New York, 1886; Harmondsworth, 1977), p. 352. These words are taken from the letter Hyacinth Robinson writes the Princess from Venice, revealing his weakened attachment to the revolutionary cause.

[24]Henry James, *The Spoils of Poynton* (London, 1897; Harmondsworth, 1983), p. 20. This novella itself contains a spectrum of collectors, ranging from Mrs. Gereth to Mona Vetch's father, an accumulator whose "old brandy-flasks and match boxes, old calendars and hand-books . . . pen-wipers and ashtrays," foreshadow the "collectible" crazes of the mid-twentieth century.

[25]Henry James, *The Golden Bowl* (New York, 1904; Harmondsworth, 1966), p. 160.

[26]Henry James, *The Outcry* (New York, 1911), pp. 78, 131.

[27]Mrs. Gardner's story is told in Morris Carter, *Isabella Stewart Gardner and Fenway Court* (Boston and New York, 1925); and Louise Hall Tharp, *Mrs. Jack: a Biography of Isabella Stewart Gardner* (Boston, 1965). For Mrs. Gardner's involvement with smuggling see *New York Times*, 20 August 1908, p. 9; and an editorial in the same newspaper, "Art and The Customs," 21 August, 1908, p. 6.

[28]Several of these collectors are described in Saarinen, *The Proud Possessors*, and in separate biographies as well as in institutional histories. David Alan Brown, *Raphael and America* (Washington, D.C., 1983), contains an excellent discussion of the rise of this generation of old master collectors in America. Gerald Reitlinger, *The Economics of Taste*, vols. I and II, is also invaluable on collecting tastes. For English collectors see the fascinating anthology compiled by Frank Herrmann, *The English as Collectors: A Documentary Chrestomathy* (New York, 1972). For the French see Albert Boime, "Entrepreneurial Patronage in Nineteenth Century France," in *Enterprise and Entrepreneurs in Nineteenth and Twentieth-Century France*, ed. Edward C. Carter II, Robert Forster, and Joseph N. L. Moody (Baltimore and London, 1976), pp. 137–207, which is both thorough and suggestive.

[29]See for example, "How We Strip Europe of Her Treasures of Art," *New York Times*, 19 February 1911, part V, p. 9. The *Times* had long been vigorously campaigning against the art tariff. It argued that the liberalization of the tariff schedules accomplished in 1909 would enormously increase art imports. See also "$50,000,000 Worth of Art Treasures for America in a Year," *New York Times*, 23 January 1910, part V, p. 2. I have drawn extensively on the *Times* to represent journalistic reaction during this period in large part because its subject index permits effective access to its coverage.

[30]Comments on the huge inflation of this period, as well as the anticipations evidenced during the 1880s when the Rothschilds bought so lavishly at the Blenheim sales of the Marlboroughs, can be found in Gerald Reitlinger, *The Economics of Taste*, vol. I, chapter 7: "The Treasures Depart"; and vol. II, chapter 8: "The Apogee and Decline of Ritzy Taste." The *New York Times* not only covered great American purchases but did stories on major foreign sales of the day like the Doucet sale in Paris and the Weber sale in Hamburg. For typical comments on the price inflation see "Paintings Bought for a Song, Sold for Fortunes," *New York Times*, 18 June 1911, part V, p. 1.

[31]"Topics of the Times," *New York Times*, 14 March 1904, p. 8.

[32]"The Half-Million Tapestry," *New York Times*, 27 July 1902, part II, p. 6. This editorial was occasioned by the Morgan purchase.

[33]"The Price of Pictures," *New York Times*, 20 March 1910, p. 10. See also "Comparative Values in Art," 9 April 1910, p. 10.

[34]This topic was debated in *Century* 35 (April, 1888), pp. 963–964. See also E. L. Godkin, "The Expenditure of Rich Men," *Scribner's* 20 (October, 1896), pp. 495–501; "The Point of View," *Scribner's* 47 (April, 1910), pp. 379–380; and Edward Chase Kirkland, *Dream and Thought in The Business Community, 1860–1900* (Ithaca, 1956), chapter 2.

[35]"The Museum's New President," *New York Times*, 24 November 1904, p. 8.

[36]"New York the Art Market," *New York Times*, 21 October 1906, p. 8.

[37]*New York Times*, 16 January 1910, part III, p. 3.

[38]"The Discovery of Artistic America," *Nation* 90 (27 January 1910), p. 96.
[39]*New York Times*, 13 November 1904, p. 5.
[40]"New York the Art Market," *New York Times*, 21 October 1906, p. 8.
[41]*New York Times*, 19 February 1911, part V, p. 9.
[42]The *New York Times* followed closely the campaign to save the Duke of Norfolk's Holbein in May and June of 1909. See 3 May 1909, p. 1; "Holbein's Christina," 5 May 1909, p. 10; 30 May 1909, part III, p. 3; 31 May 1909, p. 4; "That Arundel Holbein," 1 June 1909, p. 8; "The Fate of That Holbein," 5 June 1909, p. 8.
[43]*New York Times*, 11 May 1911, p. 1. By 1912 the Earl of Carlisle, Lord Ashburton, Lord Ilchester, Lord Warwick, The Marquis of Lansdowne, the Duke of Rutland, and the Duke of Sutherland had all sold art to Americans.
[44]*New York Times*, 20 February 1911, part III, p. 2. Later that year Bode, making one of his American visits, paid tribute to American collectors. "I saw quite enough this time to explode the myth cherished so commonly in Europe that Americans are actuated by sheer snobbery in seeking to possess themselves of old masters." *New York Times*, 10 December 1911, part V, p. 2. For more on Bode, an extremely influential figure in the European museum world, see Edward P. Alexander, *Museum Masters: Their Museums and Their Influence* (Nashville, 1983), chapter 8.
[45]*New York Times*, 27 February 1910, part III, p. 1.
[46]*New York Times*, 13 December 1908, part IV, p. 2.
[47]Henry James, *The Outcry*, p. 45.
[48]"Planting Art Museums," *New York Times*, 6 July 1902, p. 6.
[49]"The Bogy Man in Art," *New York Times*, 23 December 1906, part II, p. 6.
[50]"The Pride of Burgos," *New York Times*, 3 November 1910, p. 8.
[51]See the editorial attacking the Socialist leader in Belgium's Chamber of Deputies who was concerned that King Leopold's pictures might end up in America, "Meat Packers and Art," *New York Times*, 29 May 1909, p. 8.
[52]*New York Times*, 14 November 1909, part V, p. 7.
[53]*New York Times*, 23 January 1910, part V, p. 2. Professor Justi, the giver of the interview, declared, "I shall long treasure in my memory the picture of Mr. Pierpont Morgan — whom Europe is fond of depicting as a self-centred and dollar-obsessed plutocrat — adjourning each morning to his magnificent library gallery, there to receive his visitors and to commune with art.... No mere materialist could ever assemble the collection over which Mr. Morgan rules in New York."
[54]This suggestion was made by a New Yorker in a letter to the *New York Times*, 9 June 1908, p. 6, who pointed out that the South Kensington Museum put purchase prices on its labels.
[55]Clarke's letter agreeing with the suggestion was published in the *Times* 10 June 1908, p. 6. But Clarke indicated that the South Kensington Museum was gradually abandoning the practice, because of dealer and collector pressure.
[56]*New York Times*, 28 March 1910, p. 4.
[57]*New York Times*, 3 April 1909, p. 1. This lengthy story was titled "Hotel Gotham Ousts a Picture Salesman." During the first decade of the century dozens of newspaper stories on frauds and art impostures appeared. For example see *New York Times*, 16 May 1909, part III, p. 2; "When Art Is Real and When It Masquerades," *New York Times*, 24 May 1908, part V, p. 3; *Chicago Tribune*, 10 October 1912, p. 1; *Chicago Tribune*, 13 October 1912, p. 1; *New York Times*, 5 January 1908, part III, p. 1; *New York Times*, 3 June 1907, p. 3; "Velasquez or Copy?" *New York Times*, 29 January 1905, p. 6; *New York Times*, 29 March 1910, p. 8.
[58]The Paine case was front page news in the spring of 1910. See the stories, *New York Times*, 17–19 April 1910, p. 1.
[59]The Clausen case was another sensation; it stimulated countersuits as well. *The New York Times* asked its question in an editorial, "The Clausen Case," 31 March 1910, p. 10, referring as well to the angry disagreement over Bode's purchase of a supposed Da Vinci bust in England, a debate that involved the Kaiser. Clausen, a picture dealer, was first arrested in the spring of 1908. See *New York Times* 15, 17 May 1908, p. 1. In another editorial the *Times* remarked, "The man in the street, to whom a picture is good if it appeals to his taste and bad if he does not like it, must be pardoned for thinking that the pictures of Inness, Wyant, and Martin were as good pictures when they were painted as they are now." "The Bogus Pictures," *New York Times*, 17 May 1908, part II, p. 8.

[60]David Alan Brown, *Berenson and the Connoisseurship of Italian Painting: A Handbook to the Exhibition* (Washington, D.C. 1979), provides an excellent introduction to the subject; so does Ernest Samuels, *Bernard Berenson: The Making of a Connoisseur* (Cambridge, Mass., 1977). By this time the expert art adviser had already worked his way into fiction. Robert Herrick put a venomous portrait of Berenson, in the form of a character named Simeon Erard, into *The Gospel of Freedom*. In James's *The Outcry* the crisis of the novel is precipitated by a reattribution put forward by Hugh Crimble, who was working at "the wonderful modern science of Connoisseurship — which is upsetting . . . all the old-fashioned canons of art-criticism, everything we've stupidly thought right and held dear," p. 34. Several of the short stories in Frank Jewett Mather's *The Collectors* revolve around scientific experts and their judgments. And see Simeon Strunsky, "The Complete Collector—II," *The Patient Observer and His Friends* (New York, 1911), pp. 189–199, for his sketch of a collector of frauds, who insists that gathering a genuine collection has become impossible. In *Post-Impressions: An Irresponsible Chronicle* (New York, 1914), pp. 53–62, Strunsky reprinted his fascinating essay, "Morgan."
[61]"Topics of the Times," *New York Times*, 21 March 1910, p. 8.
[62]"Bogus Art and Good Taste," *New York Times*, 24 May 1908, part II, p. 8.
[63]*New York Times*, "The Bogus Pictures," 17 May 1908, part II, p. 8. See also Charles De Kay, "Ethics of the Pictorial Mart," *New York Times*, 4 March 1906, part IV, p. 8.
[64]This ring was described in the *New York Times*, 13 October 1907, part III, p. 1. See also "A Long Way Round," *New York Times*, 10 October 1907, p. 8; and *New York Times*, 17 October 1907, p. 5. More on French art thievery can be found in the *New York Times*, 15 December 1905, p. 2.
[65]The *Mona Lisa* theft is recounted in Seymour V. Reit, *The Day They Stole the Mona Lisa* (New York, 1981).
[66]*New York Times*, 23 August 1911, p. 6. The theft stimulated a series of stories on other recent art thefts. See *New York Times*, "Famous Works of Art That Have Been Stolen," 27 August 1911, part V, pp. 1, 14.
[67]Quoted in *New York Times*, 28 January 1912, part V, p. 11.
[68]*New York Times*, 13 April 1912, quoted in Reit, *The Day They Stole the Mona Lisa*, p. 115.
[69]Note the editorial, "The Gentleman Burglar Myth," *New York Times*, 18 September 1912, p. 10, attacking the idea that fictional thieves like Raffles or Arsène Lupin had many real counterparts.
[70]*New York Times*, 8 July 1907, p. 1. See also *New York Times*, 28 July 1907, part III, p. 4.
[71]*New York Times*, 4 September 1907, p. 3.
[72]*New York Times*, 14 January 1911, p. 4. For other acts of vandalism see *New York Times*, 10 October 1909, p. 12; *New York Times*, 10 May 1911, p. 1; and *New York Times*, 23 June 1912. This last involved the ink-splashing of a Boucher portrait. The accused declared she was out of work and maddened by the smiling figure in the picture dressed in "luxurious clothes." "I decided to mutilate her hateful face in the hope that perhaps . . . people would notice me and save me from starving."
[73]*New York Times*, 10 October 1909, p. 12; and 24 October 1909, part III, p. 4.
[74]For dealers, in addition to the redoubtable S. N. Behrman, *Duveen* (New York, 1952), I have relied on Martin Birnbaum, *The Last Romantic: The Story of More Than a Half-Century in the World of Art* (New York, 1960); James Henry Duveen, *The Rise of the House of Duveen* (New York, 1957); Edward Fowles, *Memories of Duveen Brothers* (London, 1976); René Gimpel, *Diary of an Art Dealer* (New York, 1966); and Germain Seligman, *Merchants of Art, 1880–1960: Eighty Years of Professional Collecting* (New York, 1961). Of these the Seligman volume is most informative about Morgan. *Letters of Roger Fry*, ed. Denys Sutton (London, 1972), vol. I, also contains many references to dealers, as well as a hostile portrait of Morgan. For Morgan's relations with dealers in Italy see Salvatore Cortesi, *My Thirty Years of Friendships* (New York and London, 1927), chapter 6. For some rather amusing comments on dealers, American millionaires, and Morgan, see *How I Discovered America: Confessions of the Marquis Boni de Castellane* (New York, 1924), *passim*, but particularly pp. 34, 139–140, 170, 249. Ernest Samuels, *Bernard Berenson*, also contains a good deal of information about contemporary dealers.
[75]*New York Times*, 28 January 1912, part V, p. 12. This was translated from an article in *Die Woche*.

[76]For more on this large subject see, among others, Thomas Bender, "The Cultures of Intellectual Life: The City and the Professions," in *New Directions in American Intellectual History*, ed. John Higham and Paul Conkin (Baltimore, 1979), pp. 181–195; Paul Boyer, *Urban Masses and Moral Order in America, 1820–1920* (Cambridge, Mass. and London, 1978), chapters 16–18; Peter B. Hales, *Silver Cities: The Photography of American Urbanization, 1839–1915* (Philadelphia, 1984), chapters 2–3; Neil Harris, "Four Stages of Cultural Growth: The American City," in Arthur Mann, *et al.*, *History and the Role of the City in American Life* (Indianapolis, 1972), pp. 24–49; Helen Lefkowitz Horowitz, *Culture and the City: Cultural Philanthropy in Chicago from the 1880s to 1917* (Lexington, Ky., 1977); and Robert W. Rydell, *All the World's a Fair: Visions of Empire at American International Expositions, 1876–1916* (Chicago and London, 1985).

[77]For the architectural expression of this surge to civic primacy see Robert A. M. Stern, Gregory Gilmartin, and John Massengale, *New York 1900: Metropolitan Architecture and Urbanism 1890–1915* (New York, 1983).

[78]"Civic Patriotism," *New York Times*, 20 April 1902, p. 6.

[79]"The Masaranti Collection," *New York Times*, 11 May 1902, p. 8.

[80]See "A Chance for New York," *New York Times*, 18 May 1902, p. 8; "Letter from an Art Lover," *New York Times*, 20 May 1902, p. 6; "Sober Second Information," *New York Times*, 31 July 1902, p. 8; "The Last Word Not Said," *New York Times*, 3 August 1902, p. 6. Some dealers suspected the authenticity of much of the collection and refused to become involved with the sale.

[81]*New York Times*, 28 January 1912, part V, p. 12. Bode also criticized the architectural planning of American art museums, which he termed "edifices of empty magnificence with uncomfortable large and high rooms."

[82]L. S., "The Land of Sunday Afternoon," *New Republic* 1 (21 November 1914), pp. 22–23. Simonson was directly critical of the Morgan Collection display: "I had become inevitably as listless as any shopper in a huge showroom where nothing is for sale."

[83]Lee Simonson, "Refugees and Mausoleums," *New Republic* 1 (9 January 1915), p. 24. Simonson did admire the Altman Collection, and the George Gray Barnard museum of Gothic fragments, which would eventually become the basis for The Cloisters.

[84]Simonson, "The Land of Sunday Afternoon," p. 23. For another controversial view of American museums see the letter by John Cotton Dana, Director of the Newark Museum, "Art Museum Palaces," *New York Times*, 31 October 1912, p. 12, and angry responses in the same paper, 4 November 1910, p. 10, and 5 November 1912, p. 12. Dana argued that American museum buildings were too magnificent and intimidating, were located too far from city centers, and thus were poorly attended. For more on Dana see Edward P. Alexander, *Museum Masters*, chapter 13.

[85]It is difficult to transmit a sense of just how closely newspapers like the *New York Times* covered Morgan's movements. He may well have been the most carefully watched private citizen of his day. It was front page news when someone tried to forge his checks, see *New York Times*, 11, 12 February 1903, p. 1. It was also news when his baggage was taken off an ocean liner ahead of passengers, *New York Times* 27 July 1906, p. 2. When his niece, living in St. Louis, had an argument about luncheon guests, the *New York Times*, 19 May 1909, put it on p. 1. But most of all his art buying, rumors of his art buying, his return of famous objects like the Ascoli Cope, his foreign honors, his gifts to American museums, his entertainments for (and by) monarchs and potentates, and his travels, really caught journalistic attention.

[86]"An International Benefit," *New York Times*, 11 February 1912, part V, p. 12. See also the cartoon showing a British guard at the South Kensington Museum, pointing out to visitors the empty spaces where Morgan's tapestries had hung, *New York Times*, 4 February 1912, part V, p. 16.

[87]"Trying to Keep the Treasures," *New York Times*, 31 January 1912, p. 10. The Morgan Collection never came as a whole to the Metropolitan for various reasons, including a delay by the New York City Council in appropriating money for a new wing. The *Times* worried that Hartford might take the whole collection, given Morgan's loyalty to his birthplace and his generosity in funding the memorial to his father. See "Morgan Art May Go to Hartford," 27 November 1912, p. 6.

[88]Satterlee, *J. Pierpont Morgan*, p. 565. For Morgan's support of scholarly catalogues see George C. Williamson, *Behind My Library Door: Some Chapters on Authors, Books and Miniatures* (New York, 1921), pp. 101–116.

[89]Quoted in *New York Times*, 7 May 1912, p. 3. The *Daily News* agreed with Prime Minister Asquith that immediate legislation requiring art owners to give the government an option on the purchase of valuable art was probably unnecessary, but it urged creation of a national art inventory and establishment of some priorities.

[90]The literature on these subjects is vast. But some measure of the discussion can be gained from books like Gunther Barth, *City People: The Rise of Modern City Culture in Nineteenth-Century America* (New York, 1980); Frances G. Couvares, *The Remaking of Pittsburgh: Class and Culture in an Industrializing City, 1877–1919* (Albany, 1984); Lawrence A. Cremin, *American Education: The National Experience, 1783–1876* (New York, 1980); Lewis A. Erenberg, *Steppin' Out: New York Nightlife and the Transformation of American Culture, 1890–1930* (Westport, Conn., 1981); Dee Garrison, *Apostles of Culture: The Public Librarian and American Society, 1876–1920* (New York, 1979); Garth Jowett, *Film: The Democratic Art* (Boston and Toronto, 1976), chapters 1–2; Stephen Hardy, *How Boston Played: Sport, Recreation, and Community, 1865–1915* (Boston, 1982); John F. Kasson, *Amusing the Million: Coney Island at the Turn of the Century* (New York, 1978); Arthur Mann, *The One and the Many: Reflections on the American Identity* (Chicago and London, 1979); Lary May, *Screening Out the Past: The Birth of Mass Culture and the Motion Picture Industry, 1896–1929* (New York, 1980); Michael Schudson, *Discovering the News: A Social History of American Newspapers* (New York, 1978); Alan Trachtenberg, *The Incorporation of America: Culture and Society in the Gilded Age* (New York, 1982); Kermit Vanderbilt, *Charles Eliot Norton: Apostle of Culture in a Democracy* (Cambridge, Mass., 1959); and Robert H. Wiebe, *The Search for Order* (New York, 1967).

[91]For reactions to the Armory Show see Milton W. Brown, *The Story of the Armory Show* (Greenwich, Conn., 1963); and George H. Roeder, Jr., *Forum of Uncertainty: Confrontations with Modern Painting in Twentieth-Century American Thought* (Ann Arbor, 1980). For another view of the connection between the emergence of the avant-garde and Old Master taste see Brown, *Raphael and America*, p. 31.

[92]F. J. M., Jr., "The Morgan Loan Exhibition," *Nation* 98 (26 February 1914), p. 220.

[93]"Mr. Morgan as Art Patron," *Nation* 96 (3 April 1913), pp. 234–235. The amateur, the editorial continued, must regard Morgan's artistic career "with something of awe and misgiving, not unmixed with pity, feeling the disproportion between his unwearied activities as a collector and the personal solace which he got from his royally abundant possessions." See also Gardner Teall, "An American Medici: J. Pierpont Morgan and His Various Collections," *Putnam's* 7 (November 1909), pp. 131–143.

[94]*Philadelphia Evening Telegraph*, 1 April 1913, Scrapbooks, Morgan Library, IV. My characterizations of the obituary editorials come from scanning the collection of Scrapbooks in the Morgan Library.

[95]*New York American*, 21 April 1913, Scrapbooks, II.

[96]*New York Mail*, 2 April 1913, Scrapbooks, IV. The *Evening Transcript* in Boston, 1 April 1913, wrote, "It is the manifest destiny of such art collections . . . to become eventually national or public possessions. . . . No critic would mistake the collection for that of a man who collects exclusively to gratify his own taste. . . . in [W]hat would be a defect in a private collection . . . becomes, in the case of a great public collection, an advantage." Scrapbooks, III. Many editorials, written either on the occasion of the transfer of some of the collection to the Metropolitan or on Morgan's death, stressed the immense national advantages which his privately gathered treasure obtained for the country as a whole.

[97]James, *The Outcry*, pp. 171, 20–21.

Majolica

Jörg Rasmussen†

Among the most appealing of Italian Renaissance decorative arts are the brilliantly colored, tin-glazed ceramics known as *majolica*. The technique of applying a smooth white glaze layer over earthenware pottery was originally developed around the ninth century by Islamic craftsmen in an attempt to imitate fine Chinese porcelain. Later, this technological development was transmitted to Spain, and eventually to Italy, where artisans of the fifteenth and sixteenth centuries produced some of the finest examples ever made in this medium. The opaque white glaze proved to be a highly receptive ground for the intricate polychrome designs of Italian craftsmen, and their rich, jewel-like luxury wares were avidly sought by aristocratic and ecclesiastical patrons.

Some majolica was clearly intended for active use, like the *albarelli* and spouted jars that served as drug containers in the pharmacies of Renaissance Italy. Other pieces — such as the finely painted and highly ornamental plates, dishes, ewers, and wine cisterns — may have seen use on special occasions, although it seems more likely that they were intended primarily as decorative accoutrements, to be displayed on credenzas in the dining rooms of grand palazzos. Majolica can thus be seen in the same context as the other so-called "arti minori" which René Schneider has aptly termed "les arts de la vie,"[1] indicating their place in the everyday lives of the upper classes.

Furniture, metalwork, textiles and tapestries, jewelry, glassware, and ceramics were all essential elements of a well-furnished household. Although a clear demarcation existed in the Renaissance between the fine arts and the decorative arts, the latter were based on many of the same aesthetic and intellectual principles. In addition, majolica painters often drew upon paintings, sculptures, architecture, and especially prints for their inspiration, producing ceramics with narrative scenes, figures, and decorative motifs like the famous "*grottesche*," derived from the works of Raphael, Guilio Romano, and other highly esteemed artists of the time.

Indeed, part of the appeal of Italian Renaissance majolica for later collectors was the connection — erroneously interpreted though it was — with the great master Raphael. In the mid-seventeenth century, Bernini's assistant Mattia de'Rossi was paid for some work with wine, paintings, and "two old majolica plates . . . painted it is thought, by Raphael of Urbino or at least someone of that school."[2] The expression "Raphael-ware" was, in fact, the one by which Italian majolica was most familiarly known in England until the middle of the nineteenth century.

At the same time, several illustrious foreigners were recorded as having majolica among their varied collections: Cardinal Mazarin's inventory of 1661, for example, listed thirteen "faience"

plates painted with religious and mythological subjects, installed in a room devoted primarily to the display of paintings.[3] The more than one hundred pieces of Italian majolica once owned by Queen Christina of Sweden (1626–1689), and now in the National Museum in Stockholm, were "collected" only in the broadest sense, having been seized by Swedish troops during the 1648 sack of a Prague palace.[4] In Germany, Duke Anton Ulrich (1633–1718) may have been the most avid early collector of all, having accumulated about a thousand pieces which now reside in the museum in Brunswick.

Englishmen had also developed a taste for Italian ceramics, and by the eighteenth century an active group of British collectors were acquiring the ware. Sir Andrew Fountaine and Horace Walpole were well-known collectors, drawn to majolica in good part because of its legendary connections to Raphael and other eminent Italian artists. A description of Walpole's famous country house, Strawberry Hill, includes the mention of "a fine ewer of fayence, designed by Julio Romano," and "four chocolate cups of fayence, by Pietro Cortona."[5]

With the nineteenth century came an increase in majolica-collecting, both on the continent and in England. Numerous great private collections were formed, like those of Ralph Bernal and Alessandro Castellani, and museums began to acquire works for their permanent collections.[6] The Berlin Kunstkammer, the Louvre, the Musée de Cluny, the museum at Sèvres, the British Museum, and the South Kensington Museum (later to become the Victoria and Albert) had, by mid-century, begun in earnest to seek out Italian Renaissance majolica.[7]

A flurry of important European sales in the late nineteenth and early twentieth centuries were the means by which American private and public collections of majolica came to be formed. The general upsurge of American art collecting after the 1880s was prompted by the desire to possess tangible symbols of wealth and culture and to imitate the tastes and practices of European aristocrats. Among the most zealous of these acquisitive American art patrons was J. Pierpont Morgan. Although he was often criticized for the voracious and abrupt manner in which he purchased works of art — frequently at extravagant prices — Morgan also possessed a keen sense of quality.

Morgan's love of Reinaissance art has often been noted, and as one author has written, "he felt at home with it and enjoyed the sense of peership with kings and emperors which owning their objects gave to him."[8] In addition, he felt a strong attraction for the decorative arts and the high levels of craftsmanship they displayed.[9] Together, these attitudes made him particularly sensitive to Italian majolica and all it symbolized. These luxurious wares, with their rich palette and decoration, their intricate patterns and designs, and above all, their role in the cultural life of prominent Renaissance patrons, probably appealed to Morgan for many of the same reasons that they had appealed to their original owners.

Morgan bought majolica from various dealers, including Seligmann and Lowengard in Paris and Imbert in Rome. Some of the works he purchased bore the coats of arms of popes and kings, as well as eminent Italian families like the Sforza-Visconti. Many of them had distinguished provenances, having previously belonged to the Spitzer, Castellani, Hainauer, and Fountaine Collections, as well as those of Baron de Rothschild and the Barberini family. One cannot help but think that the cachet of these emblems and lineages must have been particularly appealing to Morgan, who in many ways lived his life in the style of European royalty of the past.

Although Morgan's collection of Italian majolica was dispersed after his death, it is possible today to reconstruct its shape and character. Until the nineteenth century, the major emphasis of majolica collecting was towards the *istoriato*, or narrative wares, that were produced primarily in Urbino and its environs after about 1520. It was these wares, of course, that displayed subjects associated with the High Renaissance imagery of Raphael and his associates. A shift in taste, however, resulted in an increased interest in Italian *quattrocento* painting, and with it, majolica of the fifteenth and early sixteenth centuries.[10] These more "primitive," or "severe" works became increasingly fashionable among collectors, and the trend seems to be reflected in the Morgan holdings as well. A survey of the pieces in the Wadsworth Atheneum, and in other collections where Morgan majolica can be found today, suggests that Morgan was himself affected by this shift, subtly influenced perhaps by the art dealers from whom he bought.

Among the earlier works of the Atheneum's holdings are fine examples of Florentine oak-leaf jars with raised cobalt-blue decoration, and early sixteenth-century plates and *albarelli* with geometric patterns, flowers, portraits, and trophies. The later Urbino wares of the collection featured here are not *istoriato* wares, but the elaborate ceramics for which the Fontana workshop became so renowned in the second half of the sixteenth century. These elegant pieces are characterized by their complex and sometimes bizarre shapes which are overlaid with delicate, whimsical ornamental schemes derived from Roman wall decoration. Morgan's evident preference for these particular varieties of majolica may, once again, reflect his attraction to fine craftsmanship and detail, as opposed to the complex iconographical programs of the *istoriato* wares of Urbino and other centers.

Notes:
[1]Quoted in Paul Grigaut, *Decorative Arts of the Italian Renaissance 1400–1600*, exhibition catalogue, The Detroit Institute of Arts (1958), p. 17.
[2]MSS. in Jesuit Archives: Fondo di Gesu, N. 1017, p. 95, mentioned in Francis Haskell, *Patrons and Painters* (New York, 1971), p. 87.
[3]A. V. B. Norman, *Wallace Collection, Catalogue of Ceramics I* (London, 1976), pp. 19–20.
[4]*Ibid.*, 21.
[5]Quoted in Norman, *op. cit.*, pp. 26–27.
[6]An extensive list of sale catalogues given by Norman (pp. 407–425), serves to trace the activity of majolica-collecting from the late eighteenth century onward.
[7]Timothy Wilson, "The Origins of the Maiolica Collections of the British Museum and the Victoria & Albert Museum 1851–55," *Faenza* 71 (1985), p. 68.
[8]Aline B. Saarinen, *The Proud Possessors* (New York, 1958), p. 76.
[9]*Ibid.*, p. 77.
[10]Norman, *op. cit.*, p. 27.

Wendy M. Watson

MAJOLICA REFERENCES

Giacomotti   Giacomotti, Jeanne. *Catalogue des majoliques des musées nationaux, Musées du Louvre et de Cluny, Musée national de céramique à Sèvres, Musée Adrien-Dubouche à Limoges.* Paris, 1975.

Hausmann   Hausmann, Tjark. *Kataloge des Kunstgewerbemuseums Berlin, Bd. VI. Majolika. Spanische und italienische Keramik vom 14. bis zum 18. Jahrhundert.* Berlin, 1972.

Rackham   Rackham, Bernard. *Catalogue of Italian Maiolica.* London: Victoria and Albert Museum, Department of Ceramics, 1940.

Rasmussen   Rasmussen, Jörg. *Lehman Collection.* Forthcoming.

Spitzer   *Catalogue des objets d'art et de haute curiosité . . . composant l'importante et précieuse Collection Spitzer*, vol. IV. Paris, 1893. (Sale catalogue, Chevalier and Mannheim, 17 April–6 June 1893.)

†Jörg Rasmussen (1944–1986)

I

OAK-LEAF JAR
Florence, probably workshop of Giunta di Tugio, 1431
Tin-glazed earthenware, painted in blue and manganese,
with some green
H. $10\frac{3}{16}$ in. (26 cm.)
Provenance: acquired through Lowengard
1917.416

The first more or less native types of Italian majolica of a high standard
are the big oak-leaf jars made in Florence and environs. In some respects
they still follow the hispano-moresque wares, but the extremely shiny
white or slightly pink glaze in particular makes clear that this is a new
type. Our double-handled jar belongs to the most beautiful and
expressive pieces of the group. Very rare are the two profiles of young
men in fashionable Florentine dress. More usual are animals (such as
lions), birds, and flowers. Both handles bear a green crutch emblem,
which is the sign of Santa Maria Nuova, Florence's oldest and most
distinguished hospital. In the year 1431 the potter Giunta di Tugio
received the commission to execute hundreds of majolica pots for the
hospital. Only seven of these drug-pots with the crutch and the star mark
of Giunta di Tugio have survived. One of them was recently acquired by
the J. Paul Getty Museum, Malibu.

Literature: Rasmussen, no. 2.

OAK-LEAF JAR
Florence, about 1430–50
Tin-glazed earthenware, painted in dark blue and manganese
H. 6¼ in. (16 cm.)
Heavily repaired
Provenance: Imbert Collection, Rome, 1908
1917.433

Small, double-handled jars like this one were made in great numbers by the Florentine workshops. The lion and the lily which decorate the front and back of our little pot prove that it was made in Florence: the two are the emblems of Florence. Jars of this size were used mostly not as drug-pots but as flower vases. Apparently they made their way into northern Europe, for we find many of them in Netherlandish and German paintings, mostly in representations of the Annunciation of the Virgin (for example, in works by the Master of Flémalle, Hans Memling).

3

PLATE
Siena, about 1500–10
Tin-glazed earthenware, the front painted in dark and light greyish-blue, green, orange, yellow, and some dry brownish red and black; the back in blue, green, and orange
D. $9\frac{11}{16}$ in. (24.6 cm.)
Broken across and repaired
Provenance: Gutmann Collection, Berlin;
acquired from Seligmann in 1911
1917.438

The famous frescoes in the Cathedral Library in Siena, the "Libreria Piccolomini," by Pinturicchio and his pupils (1503–08) provided the majolica painters of the city with many brilliant and imaginative motifs for decoration. The frescoes were called "grotteschi," after the antique frescoes in the "grotti" of Roman ruins. The winged putto heads, the flowers and branches, and the cornucopias on the rim of this plate clearly derive from that source. In this rather joyful surrounding, the center creates a macabre effect. A naked putto in a wide open landscape is committing suicide by throwing himself onto a sword, hiding his face with his left arm. There is probably no logical explanation for this *cappricioso mortale*. The figure of the putto is drawn in vivid strong outlines, and yet it is not, as is so often the case, the original invention of the painter. There was until 1945 another plate clearly by the same master in the Berlin Schlossmuseum,[1] with puttos in a vineyard. One of these puttos — climbing on the "roof" of the yard — was almost identical to ours. Therefore the painter must have used this model (at least) twice, with more or less success.

Besides the destroyed Berlin piece, there is at least one other plate apparently by the same painter: in Sèvres, Musée National de Céramique, with "Saint Sebastian."[2]

Notes:
[1] Otto von Falke, "Siena oder Deruta?" *Pantheon* 4, supplement 64–5 (August, 1929), p. 364, illus. 1.
[2] Giacomotti, cat. no. 408.

4

PRESEPIO
Faenza, about 1500
Tin-glazed earthenware, painted in blue, green, orange,
and manganese purple
H. 35$\frac{3}{8}$ in. (90.2 cm.); W. 26$\frac{1}{4}$ in. (67 cm.)
Broken and repaired
Provenance: Alessandro Castellani Collection, exhibited in Rome, 1865;
Alessandro Imbert Collection, 1910
1917.432

Probably inspired by the Florentine majolica sculpture from the Robbia
workshop, the Faenza potters began at the end of the fifteenth century to
produce sculptural majolica. These sculptural groups and figures,
however, are totally different from the Robbia works: they are
"primitive," painted in all colors available to the potters, and have a
sweet, naive charm. Usually they are small, but there also exist groups of
an enormous size. Two types are known: religious representations,
which were used as small house-altars or as decorations of church and
house walls; and funny little inkstands with equestrian figures or with
mythological scenes. Because these sculptural majolica works were never
considered to be "art," they are now rather rare.

Our idyllic relief of the "Birth of Christ and the Annunciation to the
Shepherds," a so-called *presepio* (manger), is rather large; it seems that it
once served as an altar-relief.

Exhibitions: "Life of Christ," Wadsworth Atheneum, Hartford,
Conn. 1948, cat. no. 7.

ALBARELLO
Faenza, about 1500
Tin-glazed earthenware, painted in blue, dark manganese, green,
orange, with some yellow and brown
H. 10 in. (25.7 cm.)
Provenance: Alessandro Imbert Collection, Rome; acquired in 1909
1917.439

The term "*albarello*" is probably of Italian origin (= little tree, from the
segments of bamboo-trunks, which were used as apothecary jars by the
Chinese). Our piece belongs to a set of *albarelli* which are similar in shape
and decoration (others are known in New York, the Metropolitan
Museum of Art; in London, Victoria and Albert Museum;[1] and formerly
in the Beckerath Collection, Berlin). They all have a flower (carnation?)
within a laurel wreath on the front and strong and bold foliage on the
back. This foliage is called "Gothic"; the laurel wreath, on the other
hand, is a typical Renaissance motif. It can be assumed, therefore, that
the jar should be dated around 1500, that is, at the transition from Gothic
to Renaissance.

    The contents of our *albarello* was "ALOE LAVATO" (the London
albarello was destined for "ALOE SVCVTRIO").

Notes:
[1]Rackham, cat. no. 136.

FLOOR TILE
Faenza (?), about 1510 (1503–1513)
Tin-glazed earthenware, painted in blue, yellow, and orange
D. $5\frac{7}{8}$ in. (15 cm.)
Chipped on the edges
Provenance: Imbert Collection, Rome
1917.445

This very fine, octagonal floor tile with its elegantly stylized flower
decoration supposedly comes from the Vatican. This may, however, be a
typical nineteenth-century art dealer's pedigree. The tile is so similar to
the floor tile from Forlì in the Victoria and Albert Museum, London, that
one could think that it came from Forlì as well. At least one thing is sure:
the tile must have been produced during the reign of Pope Julius II della
Rovere. His coat of arms was the golden oak tree (Rovere = oak). It was
so important to him that he virtually covered the church state with
golden oak trees. For instance, when he made his triumphal entrance into
Rome after the siege of Bologna in 1506, the people of Rome erected a
golden oak tree as high as a church. Even more important are the letters
I.II.P.M. This means Julius Secundus Pontifex Maximus. Giuliano della
Rovere (his original name) took the name Julius when he was elected
Pope, in remembrance of Julius Caesar. He saw himself more as *un bravo
Italiano* than as a pope. In many wars he tried to free Italy from foreign
forces. He was so belligerent that Erasmus of Rotterdam could write a
booklet entitled "Julius Excluded from Heaven."

Notes:
[1]Rackham, cat. no. 279.

7

PLATE
Deruta, about 1510
Tin-glazed earthenware, painted in blue and gold luster
Provenance: Imbert Collection, Rome, 1910
D. 14⅛ in. (36 cm.)
1917.452

The small Umbrian town of Deruta produced majolica wares which were distinctively different from those of other production centers. They were made not to be used on the table but rather to decorate the walls. Most of them, including our plate, even have holes in the footring so they can be hung up. They are large, heavy, and rather simple. Their main feature is the sometimes magnificently brilliant golden luster. Deruta majolica almost never has *istoriato* subjects, but rather heads in profile or symbols. Our plate was apparently made for the occasion of a wedding. Two hands hold each other, and the label above has the inscription CO(N) FERMA FEDE ("with firm faith"). The decoration is highly stylized, as with most Deruta majolica. See, for instance, the triangular leaves on the rim. Although the Deruta plates are in some respects what we call folk art, their gold luster must have produced an extremely decorative and brilliant effect. Many similar pieces exist in other collections.

8

ALBARELLO
Faenza, about 1510–20
Tin-glazed earthenware, painted in blue, yellow, green, and orange
H. 12 in. (30.5 cm.)
The glaze is cracked and chipped.
Provenance: acquired from Lowengard in 1906
1917.430

This huge, massive *albarello* (for the meaning of the word see no. 5) was used for CON(FECTVM) DE ZVC(CARO) BVGOLOSSATV(M), which is bugloss sugar. Of course the representation of a rather bizarre, half-roman soldier has nothing to do with the former content. He bears the (unknown) shield of the family to which the whole pharmacy once belonged. The strong, forceful drawing of this knight (see the funny putto heads on the shoulders) makes this majolica one of the most impressive in American collections, although the piece is virtually unknown.

There are several features which we recognize from other majolica wares also ascribed to Faenza: scratched tendrils on the back (also on foot and shoulder); the very pale landscape consisting of low mountains and pearl-chain-like clouds; the strong yellow color. This is one of a large group of *albarelli* (nineteen at least) dispersed all over the world — in America alone are seven pieces — with religious, symbolic, and also with highly obscene paintings.[1] They are not all painted by one man, but the painter who did the best ones must also have executed ours. By the same master is a vase in the Metropolitan Museum of Art in New York.[2]

Formerly it was assumed that the "B" which can be seen on the back of most of the smaller *albarelli* means Benedetto da Siena; but today we think of Faenza as the origin of the whole group.

Notes:
[1] Rasmussen, cat. no. 52.
[2] Inv. no. 46.85.24

9

FLAT PLATE

Faenza, about 1520

Tin-glazed earthenware, painted in blue, copper-green, yellow, and orange

On the back in blue is the letter "F"

D. 8⅝ in. (22 cm.)

Chips in the glaze on the back

Provenance: Alexander Barker Collection, London; Baronde Collection; Theis Collection; Heinrich Wencke Collection, Hamburg; acquired through Seligmann

1917.446

Surprisingly enough there is among the thousands of *istoriato* majolica only a handful of representations of contemporary events; the vast majority shows paintings from Roman history or Greek or Roman mythology. (More than half of the small "contemporary" group is, by the way, in American collections.) This very pretty and charming plate, almost unknown, has not yet been interpreted; the subject — apparently the conquering of a town — remains unclear, the more so since the flag with the "black" lion is too common to be named. The soldiers are dressed in the typical style of the early sixteenth century: more fanciful gentlemen than real soldiers. Their faces, somewhat childish, remind one strongly of the famous tile in the Victoria and Albert Museum, London, of "Christ Washing St. Peter's Feet."[1] This piece, surely made in Faenza, probably comes from the workshop of a certain Master Francesco Torelo in Faenza. His *botega* could also have been responsible for our piece.

Notes:
[1]Rackham, cat. no. 263.

10

PLATE
Faenza, about 1520
Tin-glazed earthenware, painted in blue, yellow, copper-green, orange,
with some olive-grey
D. 10⅔ in. (27.2 cm.)
Chips on the rim
Provenance: Castellani Collection; acquired through Seligmann, 1908
1917.434

The workshops of Faenza produced a wide range of extremely varied majolica-ware: from simple dishes and plates for daily use with no decoration other than some blue floral motifs to highly luxurious and refined pieces like ours.

The Faenza painters developed a very elegant and charming style of decoration with winged putto heads, satyr masks, flowers, and cornucopias. In the well, in a little medallion, one sees a child that seems to be meditating in front of a skull. It is a very strange skull which looks more like a severed child's head. On a long label is written "MEMENTO MEI" (remember me). The subject of a child confronting death was especially popular in the early sixteenth century, both in northern and southern Europe. Nevertheless, the picture creates an awkward effect in combination with the serene ornament on the rim.

LARGE PLATE
Castel Durante, about 1530
Tin-glazed earthenware, painted in blue olive-ochre; opaque white on the rim. The central medallion is yellow, blue, and green with some orange and white (*bianco-sopra-bianco*) on the wall; the glaze is rather greyish.
D. 17$\frac{1}{16}$ in. (43.6 cm.)
Broken
Provenance: Frédéric Spitzer Collection, Paris; Oscar Hainauer Collection, Berlin; acquired from Seligmann in 1909
1917.453

This is apparently the largest plate from what was most likely a family service. It is the only one with *bianco-sopra-bianco* decoration on the wall between center and rim. Only recently have we identified the coat of arms: it is that of the Marquis de'Abon of southern France.[1] The letters NA cannot be connected with a specific individual. The coat of arms with the interlocking points seems to mean indispensable unity. Since one plate from the service is dated 1530, our plate may also have been painted in that year. The highly elaborate and very disciplined composition of no less than eight bundles of trophies and musical instruments (the smaller plates have only four) create a vivid effect. This was the favorite decoration in the later workshops in Castel Durante, combined with the almost monochrome coloring, the blue-greyish glaze, and the refined *bianco-sopra-bianco*. Around 1450 when Italian majolica had not yet

reached its high standard, the de'Abon family ordered plates with their coat of arms in Valencia (the one remaining piece is now in Copenhagen).

The other surviving pieces which belong with our plate are in Berlin, Kunstgewerbemuseum, formerly in Munich; Pringsheim Collection, formerly in Florence; Murray Collection; and on the Paris art market (1962).[2]

Notes:
[1]Hausmann, cat. nos. 182 and 183.
[2]Hausmann, p. 251.

Exhibitions: "Decorative Arts of the Italian Renaissance," Detroit Institute of Arts, Detroit, Mich. 1958–59, cat. no. 121, illus. p. 55.

I 2

PLATE
Deruta, about 1530
Painted in blue, copper-green, yellow, and brownish orange
On the back in blue the letter M
D. 12⅝ in. (32.3 cm.)
The edge chipped
Provenance: acquired through Lowengard, 1907
1917.431

Although Deruta is known for producing luster ware, this was not the only type of glaze used there. There exists an amazing number of plates painted in not very sophisticated colors, but not less decorative than the luster pieces. The shape, the weight, and the motifs of the painting do not differ from the luster ware. Our piece belongs to the large group of so-called Bella-plates; in the center is the profile bust *all'antica* of a beautiful woman, in this case a Lvcia B(ELLA) ("the beautiful Lucia"). We do not know whether these women were honorable or not-so-honorable ladies; their images are often coquettish, reminding one of prostitutes. The M on the back probably refers not to the painter but to the man who gave this charming plate to his beautiful Lucia.

13

VASE
Urbino, about 1560–70
Tin-glazed earthenware, painted in blue, green, yellow, orange, black, brownish-olive, and opaque white
H. 23½ in. (60 cm.)
Damaged and repaired
Provenance: Frédéric Spitzer Collection, Paris; acquired through Lowengard, 1907
1917.407

The later majolica wares of Urbino lack the simple charm of the early majolica: they are bizarre and pompous — and totally impractical (our vase cannot be carried by the handles; they would break off). Vases like this were never meant to be used: they are mainly showpieces for glamorous surroundings, to be displayed on marble columns. They were highly regarded from the seventeenth to the nineteenth century; Queen Christina of Sweden supposedly paid for them their weight in gold.

Our vase is one of the richest pieces of that type. The handles are formed by serpents tied together. The pictorial decoration consists of Raphaelesque grotesques, after the frescoes by Raphael and his pupils in the loggia of the Vatican: with fantastic birds, sea monsters, satyrs, sphinxes, and medallions. The painter, a member of the famous Fontana workshop in Urbino, could have been one of the painters of the large service for Duke Guidobaldo II of Urbino.

14

BASIN
Urbino, about 1570–80
Tin-glazed earthenware, painted in blue, green, yellow, orange, manganese, brown, black, turquoise, opaque white, and greyish green
W. 18¼ in. (46.6 cm.)
Broken and repaired
Provenance: Frédéric Spitzer Collection, Paris; Heinrich Wencke Collection, Hamburg; acquired through Lowengard, 1907
1917.409

The interior of this strange piece has the typical decoration of the Raphaelesque wares: the sphinxes, sea monsters, winged terminal-figures, and little cameo-like medallions. The large medallion in the center shows an unidentified scene from antiquity or from the Bible. Very unusual, however, is the back of the basin (it would have been accompanied by a ewer, now missing): three pairs of sculptural swans with horse legs, each pair symmetrically arranged. This decoration is to my knowledge unique, with one exception: there is a basin in the Louvre in Paris of the same size and clearly from the same model;[1] however, the grotesques are less elegant. Since we know the Paris piece comes from the Patanazzi workshop, our basin could have been painted in the Fontana workshop which developed the highest quality in this type of majolica.

Notes:
[1]Giacomotti, cat. no. 1081.

Literature: Spitzer, no. 53.

AUTOMATIC CLOCK WITH PACING LION
Augsburg, about 1619
Silver, partly gilded: embossed, cast, chased; enamel, ebony, bronze
Marks: Maker's mark of Daniel Lotter (Seling no. 1160),
    Master 1602, died 1619;
    Augsburg hall mark, about 1620 (similar to Seling no. 50)
H. 10⅜ in. (26.4 cm.); L. 11¾ in. (29.8 cm.)
Provenance: Gutmann Collection, Berlin; acquired through
J. S. Goldschmidt, Frankfurt am Main, 1902
1917.254

Three metal-work artists belonging to different specialized crafts contributed to this work: a goldsmith, a watchmaker, and a chestmaker. Often in the city of Augsburg craftsmen from several fields would collaborate in the completion of a commission; it was only thus that it was possible to create in a relatively short time cabinets, altars, and cupboards with elaborate metal applications and inlay work, and automatic clocks — works which have made Augsburg world famous.[1]

The goldsmith contributed the lion's figure. He also decorated the six-framed socle panels with enameled scallop-work ornaments with birds. The chestmaker was responsible for the ebony base. Here, various dials, starting mechanisms, and the pendulum have been placed on both long sides of the sarcophagus-like housing. The twelve-cornered support for the housing rests on four claw feet, made of bronze. The simple, clear architecture is differentiated and accentuated by means of various graded profiles. The clockmaker was responsible for the production of the clockwork and the complicated automatic devices. The lion could roll his eyes, open his jaws, and stick out his tongue.

In the seventeenth century, ebony was very expensive and thus its use was subject to the same control by the chestmaker's guild as the use of silver was governed by that of the goldsmiths. The quality of the materials used is guaranteed by two stamps, "*Eben*" for the wood and the pine cone of Augsburg for the silver.[2] Unfortunately, it is possible to identify only the goldsmith by name.

Notes:
[1] See Klaus Maurice, *Die deutsche Räderuhr* (Munich, 1976), *passim*, especially vol. 2, cat. no. 315–329.
[2] EBEN

17

LARGE DISH
Augsburg, about 1652
Silver, partly gilded: embossed, chased, stamped
Marks: Maker's mark of David Bessmann (Seling no. 1502), Ⓑ
   Master 1640, died 1677;
   Augsburg hall mark, about 1652 (Seling no. 78) 🍐
L. 26 in. (66.4 cm.); W. 22 in. (56 cm.)
Provenance: Gutmann Collection, Berlin; acquired through
J. S. Goldschmidt, Frankfurt am Main, 1902
1917.255

In the oval of the plate's center we recognize the relief of Alexander the
Great before the body of Darius. The dead King of the Persians is lying on
his battle chariot, pulled by three horses. Alexander, in medieval armor
with helmet and helmet-plume, bows in his saddle before his dead
opponent, holding the shroud in his hand. To the left and right of this
central scene appear warriors from both armies.

The wide and arched rim of the display plate is decorated with highly
sculptural scroll work, richly nuanced in repoussé technique. The
ornament enables us to recognize a Dutch influence, especially that of the
Utrecht goldsmith family Vianen.

From the hand of David Bessmann there is also a whole series of other
significant works — of prime importance are tankards which are in the
Kremlin Museum in Moscow. Also by Bessmann is another display plate
in the Kremlin Museum with the relief "Diogenes in the Tub,"[1] which
was made only slightly earlier than the work in Hartford.

Notes:
[1]Seling 3, no. 1502b.

Literature: A. Jones Catalogue, 1907, pp. xvi, 32, plate XXXIII.

18

SNAIL WITH NAUTILUS SHELL
Nuremberg, about 1630
Shell with cut out decoration; silver-gilt mount: embossed, cast, engraved, and stamped. The figure of the Moor and clasp are decorated with red, green, and black enamel painting
Marks: Maker's mark of Jeremias Ritter (Rosenberg³ no. 3882), Master 1605–06, died 1646; Nuremberg hall mark, about 1630 (Rosenberg³ no. 3761)
H. 7¾ in. (19.7 cm.); L. 10½ in. (26.7 cm.)
Provenance: Heinrich Seckel Collection, Frankfurt am Main; Gutmann Collection, Berlin; acquired through J. S. Goldschmidt, Frankfurt am Main, 1902
1917.260

The work of Jeremias Ritter, born in 1582, who became a Master in 1605–06 and died in 1646, is often difficult to distinguish from the work of his son Christoph III Ritter, born in 1610, who was apprenticed to his father and became a Master in 1633. It is assumed that Christoph III used, for a period of time, the maker's mark of his father.[1]

The snail's shell is formed from a nautilus, the back part of which has a pattern of cut out stripes. From the top down to the snail's neck there runs a red and green enameled clasp of scallop work. Lateral bands with small shells connect the nautilus with the snail's body. On top is a riding Moor, his arrow-case slung around his shoulder. In his right hand he is holding a bow and in the left the reins, which are wound around the frontal horns of the snail. The realistically shaped snail's body seems to be gliding along in a wave-like motion.

Notes:
[1]Jamnitzer, cat. no. 151, as well as cat. nos. 92, 106, 242, 243; Schürer, pp. 491–509, and especially p. 202, no. 549.

Literature: A. Jones Catalogue, 1907, p. ix–x, plate XIX; Morgan Exhibition, 1914, p. 84; Rosenberg³, vol. 3, no. 3882r; *Wadsworth Atheneum Handbook* (Hartford, 1958), p. 81.

LARGE CUP (GOBLET) IN LION'S SHAPE
Augsburg, about 1670–1675
Silver, partly gilded: embossed, cast, chased
Marks: Maker's mark of Matthäus Schmidt (Seling no. 1621), **MS**
    Master about 1659, died 1696;
    Augsburg hall mark, 1670–1675 (Seling no. 119) ✿
H. 11½ in. (29.2 cm.)
Provenance: Gutmann Collection, Berlin; acquired through
J. S. Goldschmidt, Frankfurt am Main, 1902
1917.265

The lion, with his double tail upturned, stands as if reaching out to take a
long step. He stands on a low pedestal, the surface of which is embossed
in relief to represent stones, earth, and plants. The beast holds in its front
claws a shell-like bowl from which one could drink. The head with
protruding tongue is detachable, enabling the body to be filled with
wine. When the beast was inclined appropriately the drink poured from
a small tube in its jaws into the basin.

Lion's goblets of this type were very popular. A similar Augsburg
example by Johann Caspar Wagner is owned by the Kremlin Museum in
Moscow.[1]

On the lion's breast the coat of arms of the city of Bozen has been
inserted, indicating that the goblet is a city welcome commissioned by
that town.

Notes:
[1]Seling 3, illus. 460.

Literature: A. Jones Catalogue, 1907, pp. xiii, 26, plate XXVII; Morgan
Exhibition, 1914, p. 89.

Exhibitions: Glasgow Art Gallery, Glasgow 1903; "Art of the Renaissance
Craftsman," Fogg Art Museum, Cambridge, Mass. 1937; "Animals in the
Arts," Museum of Fine Arts, Boston, Mass. 1946.

NAUTILUS GOBLET
Dresden, about 1620
Shell engraved and blackened; silver-gilt mount: embossed, cast, chased; foot and carrier figure: silver-gilt: embossed, cast, chased; amethyst crystals
Marks: Maker's mark of Georg Mond (Rosenberg[3] no. 1739); (M)
    Dresden hall mark, about 1620 (Rosenberg[3] no. 1658) (D)
H. 12 13/16 in. (32.5 cm.); L. 7 1/2 in. (19.1 cm.); D. 3 3/4 in. (9.5 cm.)
Provenance: Baron Albert von Oppenheim Collection
1917.269

The goblet consists of two parts which originally did not belong together. The foot was done about 1620, while the rounded top, for stylistic reasons, cannot have been decorated before 1710.

The goblet rests on four round "feet" which have been modeled after sepia (squid) heads. Above the base ring is a wavy water zone which symbolizes the sea habitat of the mussel. On it lie amethyst crystals on which one can see a turtle. A Triton sitting on the turtle serves as bearer figure. With his right hand the Triton supports the rounded top; in his left hand he holds a "mussel-horn" into which he blows with cheeks filled with air.

On one side of the shell a boating party has been finely, subtly engraved, an elegant lady in its center. Moors are rowing the boat and a trumpeter standing in the bow is blowing a signal. The opposite side is decorated with a landscape with buildings in the background, while in the front a huge elephant is stalking along, a crane flying over him. The upper edge of the shell is framed by lambrequins.

Crowning the shell is a silver-gilt figure of a winged frog, which almost certainly was placed there only in the nineteenth century. The silver setting of the shell's rim is turned upward, and ends frontally in the sculptural mask of a bearded man. Below, a mirror monogram is attached, as yet not identified.

The foot and bearer-figure reveal a striking relationship with the unmarked goblet in the British Museum,[1] the cup of which has been cut out of quartz geode and whose setting has been attributed until now to Augsburg.[2]

Notes:
[1]Hayward, pp. 227 and 381f., plate 464.
[2]Seling 2, illus. 94.

Literature: Jones, 1908, p. 103, plate XCIII; Hugh and Marguerite Stix and R. Tucker Abbot, *The Shell: Five Hundred Million Years of Inspired Designs* (New York, 1968), figs. 6 and 7.

FIGURE ON HORSEBACK
Augsburg, about 1670
Silver, partly gilded: embossed, cast, chased, stamped
Marks: Maker's mark of Johann I Scheppich (Seling no. 1564), **⑮**
   Master 1650, died 1701;
   Augsburg hall mark, about 1670
   (punch somewhat distorted, probably Seling no. 105) 🌰
H. 15 in. (38.1 cm.)
Provenance: Gutmann Collection, Berlin; acquired through
J. S. Goldschmidt, Frankfurt am Main, 1902
1917.271

Over a flat base ring the arched foot with sculptural, blossoming acanthus leaves extends into a smooth, vertically rising neck. Above it, surrounded by a curving and wavy border, is a base representing rocky terrain with a tree stump, on which a climbing horse is standing on his rear hooves. The courtier, attired in a magnificent costume of the Louis XIV period, is sitting upright in the saddle and turned to the left.

Horse and rider are executed with the greatest precision, right down to the details of the fashionable attire and the bridle. The coat of the horse, for example, is characterized as that of a dapple-gray horse by shining circles before a background of matt punching.

Figures on horseback of this type have a lengthy tradition in seventeenth-century Augsburg, probably initiated by the goblet in the shape of King Gustav Adolf II of Sweden, which David I Schwestermüller created around 1645–1650.[1]

Notes:
[1] Seling 2, illus. 587.

Literature: A. Jones Catalogue, 1907, p. xv, plate XXXVII; Morgan Exhibition, 1914, p. 90.

Exhibitions: "The Art of the Baroque," Lyman Allyn Museum, New London, Conn. 1954.

NAUTILUS GOBLET WITH FOUR SEASONS
Vienna, 1680
Shell engraved, carved, blackened; silver-gilt mount: embossed, cast, chased, engraved
Marks: Maker's mark of Christoff Neumayr (Reitzner no. 370),[1] **CN**
   working in Vienna 1668–1683
H. 18 in. (45.9 cm.)
Provenance: Count of Nostitz (according to dealer); acquired through
J. S. Goldschmidt, Frankfurt am Main, 1899
1917.277

The arched foot of the goblet is adorned by embossed acanthus ornaments. A circular inscription with the date 1680 is engraved on the base ring. The display side of the foot shows a cartouche with a coat of arms probably of the person who commissioned the work.

A turtle serves as basis for the tall, erect bearer-figure, a slender man wearing only a loincloth, who carries the cup on his head with both hands. This motif has been known since the sixteenth century and is traceable to the inventions of Cornelis Floris. Clasps with smallish leaf patterns enclose the shell in front, on top and on the sides, here sculpted as sea-nymphs. Four silver figures, sculpted independently, represent allegories of the seasons: winter in the middle on top, summer and spring to the left and right one step below, and finally Bacchus as the personification of fall, engraved below winter in the upper part of the shell.

The rear part of the nautilus is decorated with carved ornamental tendrils which contrast in their relief character and color to the mother-of-pearl background. The front part of the shell is adorned by engraved and blackened representations of the gods of the sea, Poseidon and Amphitrite, with their train of tritons and sea monsters.

Notes:
[1]Viktor Reitzner, *Alt-Wien-Lexikon für Österreichische und Süddeutsche Kunst und Kunstgewerbe*, vol. 3; *Edelmetalle und deren Punzen* (Vienna, 1952), p. 157, no 370 (with thanks to Mr. Franz Wagner, Salzburg, for the kind reference).

Literature: Jones, 1908, p. 104, plate XCIV.

Exhibitions: "Art of the Renaissance Craftsman," Fogg Art Museum, Cambridge, Mass. 1937; "Animals in the Arts," Museum of Fine Arts, Boston, Mass. 1946.

A PAIR OF TUB CARRIERS
Frankfurt am Main?, about 1600
Figures and tubs in wood, carved, mount partly colored; silver
mounts: embossed, cast, engraved
Marks: Maker's mark NR, not identifiable;
    hall mark about 1600, an eagle, debatably Frankfurt am Main;
    French and Dutch control marks of the nineteenth century
H. 11¾ in. (29.9 cm.)
Provenance: Acquired through Durlacher Brothers, London, 1902
1917.280–281

Wolfgang Scheffler has not accepted Rosenberg's vague attribution of
this hall mark to Frankfurt am Main, since even after the latest research,
an identification is not possible.[1] Thus, on the basis of current
knowledge, the goldsmith cannot be identified nor can Frankfurt be
confirmed as the origin.

Both figures are seen in walking motion with their silver shoes fitted
into wooden plinths which, held by gothic-style prongs, stand on silver
bases. The finely embossed relief representations on the bases show
hunting scenes which seem incongruous with the peddler couple.

The peddler figures are abundantly equipped with silver bags, purses,
baskets, and knives. Their canes have tendrils wound around them, and
rogues' heads. The woman is wearing a silver apron and on her head is a
scarf and a smooth cap. The man is wearing a hat with a feather and is
carrying a duck in his arms. With them they have dogs on chains; behind
them are blooming bushes. On their backs both are carrying wooden
tubs, the bottoms, lids, and ribbons of which are worked out in silver.
Through the holes in the tub-walls appear the heads of chickens, ducks,
and rogues. We are obviously confronted with a couple of poultry dealers.

The *Grünes Gewölbe* (Green Vault) in Dresden owns a pair of tub-
carrying figures[2] which are very similar to the pieces in Hartford; even
the hall and maker's marks are identical. From the same source we have a
pair of tub carriers from the Mentmore Collections;[3] the latter, however,
show some variants in the motif. It is evident that there was
collaboration between a wood sculptor and a goldsmith who jointly
produced a whole series of these popular figures of the seventeenth
century.

Notes:
[1] Wolfgang Scheffler, *Goldschmiede Hessens* (Berlin and New York, 1976);
Rosenberg[3], vol. 2, nos. 1996 and 2028.
[2] Rosenberg[3], vol. 2, no. 2029a–b.
[3] Auction, Sotheby Parke Bernet & Co., Mentmore, Buckinghamshire, 18–23
May 1977, catalogue, vol. 2: *Works of Art and Silver*, no. 656.

LION'S JUG
Rapperswil, 1688
Silver-gilt: embossed, cast, engraved, chased
Marks: Maker's mark of Heinrich Dumeisen,[1] born 1653,
   Master before 1680, died 1723; Rapperswil hall mark[2]
   Signature: H. Thvmysen 1688
H. $17\frac{1}{2}$ in. (44.5 cm.)
Provenance: From the estate of the descendants of Silberysen;
Gutmann Collection, Berlin; acquired through J. S. Goldschmidt,
Frankfurt am Main, 1902
1917.283

This impressive jug was the gift of the city of Baden (Switzerland) to its mayor, Johann Bernhard Silberysen, who, since 1661, had been Director-in-Chief of castle construction and of town fortifications.

The foot of the jug faithfully reproduces the panorama of the town of Baden after completion of the constructions in 1688. The neck of the base shows an encircling cloud band with half-figures of Christ, Mary, and the Saints; above it are engraved scrolls which implore God to protect the town.

The lion sits erect on a platform with a wavy border which has *à jour*-worked (pierced) acanthus leaves. Around the lion's seat measuring tools and arms are spread; they are clearly allusions to the construction assignment which Silberysen had taken on for the town of Baden. The lion holds in his left claw a palm leaf. His head can be taken off in order to pour wine.

This goblet, which reproduces accurately the panoramic appearance of Baden at the end of the seventeenth century, is to be viewed not only for its high quality as a work of the goldsmith's art, but also as an historic document.

Notes:
[1]Dora Fanny Rittmeyer, *Rapperswilder Goldschmiede* (Zurich, 1949), pp. 36 and 147, plate 31.
[2]*Idem.*

Literature: A. Jones Catalogue, 1907, p. xiv, plate XXXV; Morgan Exhibition, 1914, p. 89; Hugo W. Doppler, "Aus dem Historischen Museum der Stadt Baden im Landvogteischloss," *Badener Neujahrsblätter* 55 (1980), pp. 92–99.

Exhibitions: "Animals in the Arts," Museum of Fine Arts, Boston, Mass. 1946; on loan to the Historisches Museum im Landvogteischloss, Baden, Switzerland, 1978–1986.

TANKARD
Danzig, before 1702
Silver, partly gilded: embossed, cast, engraved, chased
Marks: Maker's mark of Andreas Haidt,[1] Master 1686,
   provable until 1735;
   Danzig hall mark, before 1702[2]
   Austrian control mark of 1807
H. 8⅞ in. (22.6 cm.)
Provenance: Gutmann Collection, Berlin; acquired through
J. S. Goldschmidt, Frankfurt am Main, 1902
1917.285

The foot of the tankard consists of a plain outer ring and an arched inner zone decorated with embossed weapons and arms emblems. The entire surface of the tankard is covered with a single, many-figured, embossed relief. A few of the protruding warrior- and horse-heads are cast separately and soldered on. A clothed female herm forms the curved handle with thumb rest.

The multi-figured relief represents Alexander the Great as victor among his richly armed attendants and army, and his magnanimity toward the defeated. The masterful embossing work is that of a highly gifted goldsmith, Andreas Haidt, also known as a graphic artist, who succeeded in achieving a marvelous illusion of depth. We can discern in the main scene of Alexander no fewer than four different levels of space that flow — without interruption — into one another.

The embossed edge of the lid corresponds, in terms of motif, to that of the foot. The center of the lid is covered by a boldly foreshortened relief of Alexander on horseback galloping toward the viewer. Here, too, the goldsmith has abandoned the actual relief level and soldered on cast, sculptural parts.

Attached to the inside of the lid is the coat of arms of Christoph Kochen (born Reval, Estonia, 1637, died Stockholm, Sweden, 1711), a coat of arms chosen after his elevation to the Swedish nobility in 1683. Christoph Kochen served as Swedish commercial attaché-consultant in Moscow, and since 1686 as Baron of Narva (Estonia); evidently it was he who commissioned this tankard.[3]

Andreas Haidt almost certainly regarded this tankard as his masterpiece and therefore signed it repeatedly with his maker's mark, one time engraving his name as Haidt in the manner of an artist's signature. This goldsmith born in Augsburg was admitted as Master in Danzig. In 1702 the Berlin Academy of the Arts invited him to become a member; it is reasonable to assume that he met the famous sculptor Andreas Schlüter. He received several commissions from King Frederic I of Prussia. In 1713 he moved to the court at Dresden and became an honorary member of that city's academy. He returned to Danzig in 1721.

Notes:
[1] E. von Czihak, *Die Edelschmiedekunst früherer Zeiten in Preussen*, part 2 (Leipzig, 1908), p. 67f., no. 388; Rosenberg[3], nos. 1578 and 1579.
[2] Czihak, p. 44, no. 6; Rosenberg[3], no. 1500.
[3] For the explanation of the coat of arms I am indebted to Dr. Ottfried Neubecker, Stuttgart.

Ivory

Christian Theuerkauff

Who once possessed the masterly carved high-relief group of the *Fall of Man* (cat. no. 27), so impressive both pictorially and sculpturally? Who commissioned such a "*Kunststück*" (an ingenious work) in the seventeenth century? By 1866 this theatrical scene was to be found in Vienna in Baron Anselm von Rothschild's collection, which was extremely rich in baroque ivory works. It could have been made in Vienna, the imperial capital of the German Empire, perhaps for the court of Ferdinand II or III or Leopold I, for one of the princes of Liechtenstein, or for one of the art-loving Austrian monasteries such as Kremsmünster, Göttweig, or Klosterneuburg, between 1620–30 and 1660(?).

Ivory was used in ancient Egypt and elsewhere for the construction of luxury items of furniture and for implements, and was used, in combination with gold, by the Greek sculptors Phidias and Polyclitus for larger-than-life cult statues. It was employed in the late ancient period and in the early and high medieval periods for making writing tablets (diptychs), costly book covers, pyxidia, and liturgical display utensils. However, its use reached an artistic high point in the Gothic period, especially in fourteenth-century Paris. The variety of uses to which it was put was unequaled: small altars, single reliefs, crucifixes, freely sculpted representations of the Mother of God, and, in the area of the profane, elaborate, many-figured mirror cases and splendid combs (today the proud possessions of large collections such as that of the Musée du Louvre and the Musée de Cluny in Paris).

In the Renaissance period in Italy and in the north, ivory as a material for sculpture and household utensils took a back seat to stone, wood, and especially bronze. Not until the advent of the mannerist style at the end of the sixteenth century did a new golden age of ivory carving begin, as seen in the masterly technique of fantastically complicated lathe work (*Contrefaitkugel* or Passig-Turning, that is, decorative pieces made of concentric spheres all carved from the same piece of ivory). Princes, wealthy patricians in south German trade centers (Augsburg, Nuremberg with its famous Zick family of turners who were active into the eighteenth century, and Ulm and Strassburg), and numerous religious and lay dignitaries, collected these turned, ingeniously carved ivory works in their "cabinets of curiosities" (*Raritätenkabinetten*) and "art and curiosity chambers" (*Kunst- und Wunderkammern*). Ivory, fine and firm in its natural structure and highly rated for its color, costliness, and symbolic value, appeared artfully fashioned next to art objects, scientific-technical objects, and natural forms and materials (for example, in the Prague *Kunstkammer* of Emperor Rudolph II [1552–1612] as well as in the display cabinets of Archduke Leopold Wilhelm [1614–1662] of Tirol).

The importation of African and Asiatic (Indian) hard-elastic raw material which was easy to work, cut, and polish, increased in the seventeenth century. It came to Europe via Genoa, Venice, Lisbon, but particularly via Dieppe (see cat. no. 34), London, Antwerp, Amsterdam, and Hamburg. Centers of baroque ivory art developed in these cities, especially in Dieppe, the southern Netherlands (Antwerp, Mecheln, Brussels) and South Germany-Austria (see cat. nos. 27–33). The artistic production of these centers was related to the representational and stylistic tendencies of Europe's large courts — for example, Paris and Versailles under Louis XIV of France, Emperor Leopold I's court in Vienna, and that of the Elector Johann Wilhelm von der Pfalz around 1700 in Düsseldorf. Ivory carvers in these centers were profoundly influenced by significant artists such as Peter Paul Rubens — for example in the work of Lucas Faydherbe and Artus Quellinus the Elder in Antwerp, and Georg Petel in Augsburg. Above all, the art and graphic work and also the large sculptures of artists such as Giovanni Bologna, François Duquesnoy, and Gianlorenzo Bernini in Florence and Rome afforded stimulus and set standards into the early eighteenth century. These influences can be seen in relief scenes with allegories and themes from the Bible, mythology, and history, in countless crucifixes, individual figures, figural groups, and above all, in the display vessels and implements so favored as collectors' pieces, often decorated with bacchanalian representations, such as covered goblets and tankards, boxes, display dishes, and tankards. These influences can also be discerned in inlays on weapons, pistols, powder horns, miniature furniture, and silverware handles. Other forms, such as standardized portrait medallions as produced by artists such as the itinerant Jean Cavalier (active till 1699), are not represented in the Morgan collection.

Ivories were often mounted in rich settings by gold- and silversmiths, or combined with dark ebony or semi-precious stones. By these means the artist heightened the effects achieved by means of graining and the play of light and shadow on the highly polished or matte, sensuously soft surface areas.

It was the ambition and intention of princely collectors such as Rudolph II to unite as many areas of creation as possible from art and nature into a microcosm in the *Kunstkammer*. This notion of a "universal" collection comprised of a variety of objects is mirrored in the "cabinet" pictures of the Hamburg painter Georg Hinz (1630/31–1688), where muscles are found next to weapons, a coral branch next to a clock, glass and semi-precious vessels next to chains of pearls, gold medallions, and ivory, all combined and arranged to evoke the transitoriness of beautiful things (pointedly symbolized by the glass, clock, and skull).

Collections such as those of the Hapsburgs in Vienna (Kunsthistorisches Museum, Schatzkammern; with works of the *Hofpainstecher* [court ivory engravers] Johann Caspar Schenck and Matthias Steinl), treasure rooms like those of the Electors of Saxony and Kings of Poland in the *Grünes Gewölbe* at Dresden (with works by Balthasar Permoser in ivory), the rich resources of the Pfalzers and Wittelsbachers in Munich (Bayerisches Nationalmuseum; see the outstanding ivory catalogue of R. Berliner, 1926), of the Danish kings at Castle Rosenborg and in the Nationalmuseum in Copenhagen, and of the Medici in the Museo degli Argenti in Florence likewise mirror these various aspects of ivory production and point to the high status of this material among collectors in the seventeenth and eighteenth centuries. So also do the "bourgeois" *Kunstkammern* (which disappeared by the late eighteenth century), such as that of the Strassburg patrician Elias Brackenhoffer of 1672, which contained many works by the Kern family (cf. cat. no. 32).

In the nineteenth century, public repositories such as the British Museum, the Victoria and Albert Museum in London, the Metropolitan Museum of Art in New York, the Hermitage in Leningrad, the Walters Art Gallery in Baltimore, and many others acquired their ivory treasures from diverse sources in Europe, and only to a lesser extent *en bloc*. In these collections are also to be found many of the "devotional images" (cf. cat. no. 37) produced and imported in the seventeenth and eighteenth centuries by Jesuit settlements in Portuguese Goa or the Spanish Philippines and shaped by the art of the Iberian peninsula.

The golden age of baroque ivory art ended soon after the invention of porcelain at Meissen, although individual important masters such as the itinerant Johann Christoph Ludwig Lücke (died 1777) in Dresden, Hamburg, London, and Danzig, Joseph Teutschmann in Passau, and Simon Troger's great workshop in Munich-Haidhausen continued to create images and virtuoso pieces of ivory (and wood) until after 1750, when porcelain figures were more esteemed.

In the latter part of the eighteenth century, ivory production was limited — for example in St. Claude or Dieppe — to hand-crafted "microcarvings," souvenirs, anatomical models, and similar things. Little success with regard to artistic effect was achieved during the revival of ivory carving in the nineteenth century, among other places in Erbach and Michelstadt in the Odenwald/Southwest Germany. One finds increased copying and historicism, especially from 1830–40 (seen for example in works in the Spitzer Collection, Paris). Later, art nouveau artists used ivory in combination with metal and wood, especially in France, but also in Belgium and Germany.

The small collection of postmedieval ivories in Hartford reflects, even counting the display vessels and the *Fall of Man* relief, only a few important aspects of the golden age of ivory production and collecting in the seventeenth and eighteenth centuries.

IVORY REFERENCES

Berliner, 1926 — Berliner, R. *Die Bildwerke in Elfenbein, Knochen, Hirsch- und Steinbockhorn.* Catalogues of the Bayerischen Nationalmuseums, Part IV. Augsburg, 1926.

Ermitage, 1974 — Exhibition catalogue, *Westeuropäische Elfenbeinarbeiten aus der Ermitage Leningrad, XI.–XIX. Jahrhundert.* Staatliche Museen zu Berlin, Kunstgewerbemuseum Berlin, in Schloß Köpenick, 1974/75. Berlin, 1974.

Grünenwald, Kern, 1969 — Grünenwald, E. *Leonhard Kern, ein Bildhauer des Barock.* Schwäbisch Hall, 1969.

A. Jones Catalog, 1907 — Jones, E..A. *Catalogue of the Gutmann Collection of Plate, now the property of J. Pierpont Morgan, Esquire.* London, 1907.

Longhurst, II, 1929 — Longhurst, M. H. *Catalogue of Carvings in Ivory, Victoria and Albert Museum,* vol. 2. London, 1929.

Von Philippovich, 1982² — Von Philippovich, E. *Elfenbein.* Bibliothek für Kunst- und Antiquitätenfreunde XVII. 2d ed., revised and enlarged. Munich, 1982.

Rosenberg³ — Rosenberg, R. M. *Der Goldschmiede Merkzeichen,* vols. 1–4. 3rd ed. Frankfurt am Main, 1922–28.

Scherer, 1931 — Scherer, C. *Die Braunschweiger Elfenbeinsammlung.* Leipzig, 1931.

Seling, 1, 2, or 3 — Seling, H. *Die Kunst der Augsburger Goldschmiede 1529–1868,* vols. 1–3. Munich, 1980.

Sponsel, 1932 — Sponsel, J. L., and E. Haenel. *Das Grüne Gewölbe zu Dresden, IV, Gefäße und Bildwerke aus Elfenbein, Horn und anderen Werkstoffen.* Leipzig, 1932.

Tardy, Les Ivoires — Tardy. *Les Ivoires: evolution décorative du Iᵉʳ siècle à nos jours.* Paris, [1966].

Theuerkauff, Collection — Winkler 1984 Theuerkauff, C. *Elfenbein, Sammlung Reiner Winkler.* Munich, 1984.

Volbach, 1923 — Volbach, W. F. *Die Elfenbeinbildwerke.* (Die Bildwerke des Deutschen Museums I). Berlin and Leipzig, 1923.

THE FALL OF MAN
South Germany-Austria: circle or workshop of the "Master of the St. Sebastian's Martyrdoms." Second third of the seventeenth century (before 1650?)
Relief group carved as silhouettes, flat on the back side, of a whitish to brownish-ivory to yellowish-brown color. The surfaces are finely differentiated and nuanced: the tree trunk, the fur of the hare, the hide and ear of the elephant, and the lion's head and mane are engraved in various zigzag patterns.

At the bottom right of the semicircular base there is a crack, the fragment pasted back on. At the bottom left, there is a piece approximately 3 in. long, placed below the base, as an equalizer to the slant of the piece. There are numerous other cracks and repairs. The piece was perhaps originally placed, and probably also framed, on a dark background — for example, slate or ebony. The mount is modern.
H. $12\frac{11}{16}$ in. (32.3 cm.); W. $6\frac{3}{4}$ in. (17.2–17.3 cm.);
Depth below, in the middle, about $3\frac{1}{8}$ in. (8 cm.);
greatest "relief height" about $3\frac{5}{16}$ in. (8.4 cm.).
1917.303[1]

While Eve appears to be almost staring at Adam over the apple, his eyes are lowered; his almost closed right hand seems to be shoving the forbidden fruit aside in a gesture of refusal, while his left hand is clenched in a fist. The expression of the figures and the way they and the animals are differentiated from each other and from the background are extraordinary. Conspicuous, too, are the large hands and feet of the first human couple, as are their poses, and their intense, almost desperate, gesticulations (especially Adam's). The humanized traits of the animals are noteworthy — the "smile" of the hind, the "faithful" look of the horse, the dull expression of the hare.

Based on the general figure style, one is inclined to date this grand scene as mid-seventeenth century, most probably carved in South Germany-Austria, where similar figure types, similar modeling, and at times striking convergences of details and technical traits can be found. These similarities arise in, among others, the work of three ivory sculptors: Matthias Rauchmüller (1645–86), Johann Caspar Schenck (known to have worked from 1650–60, died in 1674) and his circle, and the monogrammist B. G. (active before 1662 until after 1680) in Vienna (?).

For the total composition and the two main figures, no precise prototypes have been discovered, neither in the sixteenth century[2] nor in the seventeenth century. Details, such as the way Adam's leg is extended so markedly, remind one of a Virgil Solis Bible illustration:[3] Eve's right hand holding the apple is reminiscent of the gesture of a figure by Sebald Beham; and Eve's bearing suggests a thematically similar representation by Matthäus Merian the Elder (1625).[4] There is also an unidentified drawing in the Küpferstichkabinett, Berlin, DDR, which corresponds rather accurately to our ivory. Its identification as a preliminary sketch for or copy after the ivory or another (painted?) composition is open to question.[5]

There is a silhouetted ivory relief of the *Fall of Man* in the Kunstsammlungen, Weimar, also with numerous animals, of almost the same period as ours — with Eve borrowed from the B1 engraving by Albrecht Dürer — whose central German origin (possibly from the circle of E. F. Bezold) has probably, though not definitely, been established.[6]

In the types of figures, in the highly sculptural treatment of the anatomy, and in the differentiation of the surfaces, as well as in the very individual character of the expressions, the comparison with the one, established ivory sculpture of Matthias Rauchmüller (the tankard dated 1676 in the collection of the ruling Prince of Liechtenstein at Vaduz[7]), reveals certain similarities. These can most clearly be seen in the putto and in the distinctive style of modeling. In other respects, however, the comparison is hardly convincing. The whirling, gliding rhythm of Rauchmüller's total composition, and that of the individual figures, points to an earlier period for the origin of our work. (Rauchmüller, like the unknown sculptor of our relief, occasionally transforms prototypes of the mannerist period.)

In the monogrammist B. G.'s *Fall of Man*,[8] the conception also differs from the conception of our group. This artist's group has a soothing, calming effect, is devoid of any drama, and reminds one of still life in its detail — notably foliage, hair treatment, and base formation — although in technical details, such as the head of the snake putto, amazingly similar traits may be observed. The posture of the animals also is comparable to other works of the monogrammist B. G.

Comparison with the more lively, more expressive, but also more decorative ivory works of Johann Caspar Schenck, *hofpainstecher* (court ivory sculptor) in Vienna and of his circle[9] also fails to carry our study forward.

Our relief group seems most closely related to work from the circle of the so-called "Master of the St. Sebastian's Martyrdoms," who probably worked in Austria (in Vienna?) about the middle of the seventeenth century.[10] This is suggested by the conception of the moving body which is both sculpturally firm and tautly, precisely modeled; by the emphasis on expressiveness, which includes such characteristic details as the large hands and feet; by the tenseness of the composition; by the contrast between the main figures and the silhouetted, multilayered background scenery; as well as by the relief's technical execution. In the workshop of this "Master of the St. Sebastian's Martyrdoms," there were obviously several other artists at work,[11] as is demonstrated by the differences of the main figures in two reliefs in Linz and Vienna dated 1657 and 1655,

after which this master has been named (see note 10). Moreover, the workshop had a close working relationship with Johann Caspar Schenck and with Master B. G., and seems to have been of significance in Rauchmüller's development.

After all these admittedly less than conclusive comparisons, one can most readily accept the origin of the Adam and Eve Group as being closest to the immediate circle around — or in the Workshop itself — the "Master of the St. Sebastian's Martyrdoms" in Vienna (?), and date it even before 1650.[12] In any case, the *Fall of Man* relief is by far the most significant postmedieval ivory work in this portion of the Pierpont Morgan collection.

Notes:

[1] Most likely identical with cat. no. 151 of the collection of Anselm Freiherr von Rothschild, Vienna (F. Schestag, *Katalog der Kunstsammlung des Freiherrn Anselm von Rothschild in Wien* [Vienna, 1866], I, p. 22, no. 151, without illustration).

[2] Cf. Lucas van Leyden or Hendrick Goltzius (E. K. J. Reznicek, *Die Zeichnungen von Hendrick Goltzius* [Utrecht, 1961], p. 238, no. 9, cat. no. U9, fig. 417; W. L. Strauss, *Hendrick Goltzius, 1588–1617: The Complete Engravings and Woodcuts* [New York, 1977], I, p. 356f., no. 217).

[3] Sigmund Feyerabend, 1560. See P. Strieder, "Copies et interprétations du cuivre d'Albrecht Dürer 'Adam et Eve,'" *Revue de l'Art* 21 (1973), p. 47, note 18, illus. 7.

[4] *Ibid.*, p. 47, notes 16, 199; illus. 6, 8.

[5] Küpferstichkabinett, Staatliche Museen Berlin, DDR, washed pen and ink drawing on yellow-brown paper (inv. no. 625-1980 [ON 454, no. 166]). The paper at Adam's right knee is squeezed so that the proportions are distorted.

It is impossible to determine with certainty the style and date of the drawing, nor its function. The deviations from the ivory relief, a certain spontaneity (the clear details of the feet, for example), and the ostensible autonomy of the drawing could argue for its being a preliminary sketch for the relief. (This according to Werner Schade, Küpferstichkabinett, Staatliche Museen Berlin, DDR and — with reservations — Heinrich Geissler, Stuttgart. To both I owe many thanks for their kind assistance.)

The same differences from the ivory — weaknesses such as Adam's extended left leg, the less than sculptural total conception, and the all too summary treatment of the hands, feet, and other details — can also be interpreted as arguments for a relatively free copy of a specific composition (or as the cleaned-up drawing of a spontaneous first draft?). Rolf Biedermann, Augsburg, among others, argues for a copy, as does Hans Mielke, Berlin, with some reservation. In either case, the relief in all its forms and qualities of expression creates the impression of distinct richness and realism, certainly in comparison with the qualities in the drawing, which reflect the baroque of the mid-century. Does the conception of the drawing, in spite of its wash-painting quality, lean toward two-dimensionality, and thus point to a draft for a graphic work, an engraving or a painting? Or does the drawing reproduce a finished, sculptural composition? For this hypothesis — that the drawing was done *after* and *according to* a preconceived composition — another ivory group lost for a time could serve as proof. In 1953, this group was in the London collection of Mayer (from the Silten Collection, Berlin; however not mentioned in the Catalogue of 1923). In its proportions and style, if it was authentic, it would have to be placed earlier in time than our ivory relief (I would not exclude a nineteenth-century dating).

These questions are not fully answered either by the inscription, address, or signature (?) found at the bottom right, since it is only partly legible: "Jo:I(?)rberg(er) Streituéld(er)," with the possibility that the first letter of the second word could also be an H, F, D, or B! Johannes (?) Herberger, Irberger or (Johannes=Hans) Freyberger would seem to be possibilities, with the word Streituéld = Streitveld = Streitfeld being a place name. The locality near Lauba in the Oberlausitz seems to be eliminated, however, from consideration. (W. Schade made this suggestion.)

Nor are we able to determine whether it was part of a family album (in spite of its relatively large size) similar to the thematically related representation by the Ulm goldsmith Melchior Gelb, who lived in the third quarter of the seventeenth century. (Galerie G. Bassenge, Berlin, Auction 42, II, 2./3. XII, 1983, catalogue p. 35, no. 4630, illus. p. 36. Cf. H. Geissler, *Zeichnung in Deutschland: Deutsche Zeichner 1540–1640.* Exhibition catalogue, Staatsgalerie Stuttgart, Graphische Sammlung, 1979, II, p. 211ff. [P. Amelung, Stammbucher].)

The style of the drawing does *not* exclude an origin either in Central, Northern, or Southern Germany, especially not Augsburg. For the site in the North, the drawings, for example, of Christoph Gertner (among others H. Geissler, *Zeichnung . . .*, 1979, II, p. 118ff., cat. no. N1ff., illus.), born in Arnstadt, Thüringen, whose workshop was in Wolfenbüttel (1604–1621) need to be compared, as do those, though less so, of Daniel Kellerthaler who was active as a goldsmith and sculptor in Dresden (H. Geissler, *Zeichnung . . .*, 1979, II, p. 102, no. M.8, illus.). For the argument of an Augsburg origin one needs to consider the group around Hans Freyberger (about 1572–1632) of Kärnten (Austria) who was influenced by Matthäus Kager (and other works in the style of Rubens). (Cf. H. Geissler, *Zeichnung . . .*, 1979, I, p. 254, no. F22f. illus., and exhibition catalogue *Augsburger Barock*, [Augsburg, 1968], p. 106f., 187, cat. no. 106, 220, illus. 123. Regarding Kager, cf. H. Geissler, *Zeichnung . . .*, 1979, I, p. 256ff., cat. no. F27, illus.)

[6] Inv. no. A 29. In a rich ivory frame, adorned with precious stones and silver-gilded appliqué work. The frame should be examined to determine date of origin. There are additional ivory works in the same collection (tankards, goblets, covered boxes), signed by E. F. Bezold (Petzoldt), that differ in part in their personal style and technique. E. F. Bezold, who (according to Thieme, Becker, *Allgemeines Künstlerlexikon* 26 [1932], p. 517) worked in the sixteenth century, was probably a member of the sculptor family Bezold, of Schneeberg, known there in the sixteenth to eighteenth centuries. Two members of the Bezold-Petzoldt family, Johann IV (1659–1726) and Andreas (1628–1703), presumably also did work in ivory.

In its composition as in its expressions, this Weimar relief on the whole appears more weary, less vigorous, and diffuse in its picturesqueness, without showing the drama, sharpness, and effectiveness all discernible in the Wadsworth Atheneum ivory.

[7] J. Hecht, *Liechtenstein: The Princely Collections* (New York, 1985), pp. 100ff., cat. no. 67, illustrations, fig. 20. According to a note in the museum file in Hartford, Olga Raggio was already thinking of Rauchmüller in connection with the Adam-Eve Group.

[8] For example, in his *Fall of Man* group in the former collection of Alphonse de Rothschild in Vienna, datable about 1660–70. C. Theuerkauff, "Zum Werk des Monogrammisten B. G. (vor 1662 — nach 1680)," *Aachener Kunstblätter* 44 (1973), p. 245ff., especially p. 249, illus. 5; p. 280, cat. no. 7.

[9] See among others von Philippovich, 1982², illus. 143f. Theuerkauff, *op. cit.*, p. 250f., illus. 13f. Theuerkauff, Coll. Winkler, 1984, p. 121f., cat. no. 65, illus. 65.

[10] Of the numerous works of the Workshop of the "Master of the St. Sebastian's Martyrdoms" — reliefs, statuettes, groups, tankards and cups, socle reliefs — let us mention here two tableau-like reliefs of the torment of St. Sebastian of 1657 in the Oberösterreiches Landesmuseum in Linz, and above all the relief of 1655 in the Kunsthistorisches Museum, Vienna (cf. note 11). In particular I would like to refer to the sharply drawn figure of the archer to the left, which is, however, exaggerated almost to the point of caricature; also to the formation of the foliage, tree trunk, and child figures. Strikingly similar to our relief is the relationship of the figures in front to the graded background and the detail of the ringlike, drilled eyes inside the pronouncedly sculptural lid-edges. In addition to the pedestal group of a cup in the Kunsthistorisches Museum in Vienna (with counterpart, or copy, see Theuerkauff, B. G. [1973], illus. 16, p. 253, note 20; von Philippovich, 1982², illus. 145 — inv. no. 4530 and 4531) — whose relief on the domed cover makes us think of Rauchmüller's *Rape of the Sabine Women* — let us mention the group with little Hercules in the De Young Memorial Museum in San Francisco (inv. no. 52, 64. C. Theuerkauff, Jacob Auer, "Bildhauer in Grins," *Pantheon* 41, no. 3 [1983], p. 195, note 16.). It is labeled there as the work of Gerard van Opstal, whose physiognomies, however, create a considerably more distorted effect.

[11] Von Philippovich, 1982², illus. 145f., 255ff. (as works by J. C. Schenck!). Regarding the whole problem, see Theuerkauff, *B.G.* [1973], p. 251f., illus. 15a–b, 16; see also Theuerkauff, Auer, *op. cit.*, p. 195f., note 13ff., illus. 5; J. Hecht, *The Princely Collections* (New York, 1985), p. 97ff., cat. no. 65f. with illustrations.

[12] In favor of this dating is also the striking comparison of the snake putto with the child figures on the privately owned ivory goblet signed by Marcus Heiden (working between 1618 and 1633) in Coburg. Theuerkauff, Auer, *op. cit.*, p. 195, note 18. Von Phillipovich, 1982², p. 422, illus. 372. Whether M. Heiden, previously known only as a turner, really produced the quality figures on parts of the goblet strikes me as very doubtful.

Literature: C. Theuerkauff, "An Ivory Carving of Judith and Holofernes and the Work of the Master B. G.," *The Register of the Museum of Art,* The University of Kansas, Lawrence, Kansas, II, 5–6, 1966, p. 2, 10f., note 2; *Wadsworth Atheneum Handbook* (Hartford, Conn., 1958), p. 77.

Exhibitions: The Hebrew Bible in Christian, Jewish and Muslim Art, The Jewish Museum, 1963, no. 9.

COVERED TANKARD WITH THE QUEEN OF SHEBA BEFORE SOLOMON
North Germany, Danzig. Most probably Christoph Maucher
(1642–after 1705). 1692?
The silver-gilt mounting is probably by Johann Ernst Kadau, son of
Ernst II Kadau (died 1690), after 1690 (1692?).

High and bas-relief of yellowish, heavily grained ivory that in the
background is carved very thin in places and has become brownish on
the raised portions. At the foot of the Negro with cap is a defect; there
is a fissure to the left of the handle. On the cover is a cast, silver-gilt
equestrian statuette on a six-cornered, steplike base. Its right hand is
missing.

The silver mounting is gilded (reddish inside the cover), with a
repoussé, acanthus flower frieze on top of the broad rim of the cover,
a laurel wreath on the roll of the pedestal, and engraved abstract flower
leaves outside on the base. Two cast bird heads and acanthus serve as a
thumb rest; the three-jointed handle with dolphin is cast as well.
Out of the dolphin's open mouth a tongue motif arranged in tiers leads
into the lower part to a C-arch.

Marks: Danzig hall mark (Rosenberg[3], no. 1497) appears three times:
to the left on the rim of the cover, on the rim of the pedestal,
and under the base. Maker's mark IEK appears as well
(in a circle, the I raised — Rosenberg[3], 1567, and Czihak, no. 371).
Rosenberg[3] and Czihak have assigned this mark to Ernst II Kadau, while
we ascribe it to his son Johann Ernst; Dutch import mark from before
1909 appears twice (Rosenberg IV[3], p. 394, no. 7666); on a chest to the
left of the handle, engraved in the ivory, a (house?) mark in the form of
a cross over an angle and the numbers ?92 (= 1692?).
H. 8$\frac{1}{2}$ in. (21.6 cm.); H. of the ivory cylinder 4$\frac{11}{16}$ in. (12–12.1 cm.);
H. of the cover figure 2$\frac{5}{16}$ in. (5.9 cm.); W. with handle 7$\frac{7}{8}$ in. (20 cm.);
diameter of the vessel 5$\frac{11}{16}$ in. (14.4–14.5 cm.)
Provenance: Gutmann Collection; acquired through J. S. Goldschmidt,
Frankfurt am Main, 1902
1917.308

The representation is not Esther before Ahasuerus; rather — according
to the text in 1 Kings 10: 1–13 — the Queen of Sheba, who "with many
people, with camels carrying spices and much gold and precious stones"
came from Arabia to pay homage to King Solomon. The ivory artist
apparently utilized here a (graphic?) pattern similar to the relief on the
basin of a tazza by an unknown, but perhaps also North German master,
around 1660, at Rosenborg Castle in Copenhagen.[1] The Copenhagen
basin made use of the same prototype in reverse.

Based on the gold mounting with the characteristic dolphin handle,
bird-head grip, acanthus and laurel frieze, and cover plate, as well as the
style of ivory carving, this splendid tankard belongs with two others by
the Danzig goldsmith Ernst II Kadau or Johann Ernst Kadau: the tankard
with Moses and the iron snake in the Kunsthistorisches Museum in
Vienna[2] and the one with Jeroboam's sacrifice in the Wawel at Crakow.[3]
If one compares the established works — the "miniature" monument to
Leopold I as victor over the Turks in Vienna[4] (from 1700) and the large,
sumptuous platter with scenes of Moses, formerly in the Berlin
Schloßmuseum[5] — all three tankard reliefs seem to have their origin in
the workshop of Christoph Maucher, who was working in Danzig from
about 1670, and who was also famous as an amber artist.[6] Typical of his
work are the broad, female physiognomies; the old male figures
appearing weary and twisted in strangely complicated positions; and the
graphic modeling method and predilection for precise details. These
tendencies are shown — to be sure, designed with a stronger linear
emphasis — in an ivory pitcher (also designated to be by Johann Ernst
Kadau rather than by his father Ernst II Kadau) with the subject of wine,
found in the Staatliche Kunstsammlungen, Kassel.[7]

Judging from the carving technique and conception of the reliefs, our
tankard as well as the one from Crakow, and to a certain extent also the
Viennese one, may have belonged to a "series" of vessels with Old
Testament subjects. Since Ernst II Kadau (Master 1674) died in Danzig
in 1690, and since the house mark with the numbers [16]92 can very
probably designate the date of the ivory cylinder of our tankard, his son

Johann Ernst Kadau could be indicated by the maker's mark IEK[8] (which
also appears on the Berlin large platter and other vessels). To be sure, the
son does not appear up to this point in the Danzig records,[9] but very
likely can have carried on his father's workshop (and sometimes his
mark?).

The "socled" statuette of the Roman rider on top of the lid could
theoretically have replaced an ivory figure, perhaps a Cupid putto figure
(cf. the Viennese or Crakow tankard).

Notes:
[1]E. von Philippovich, 1982[2], illus. 163f.
[2]Inv. no. 4492, H. 8$\frac{7}{8}$ in. (22.5 cm.) (R II[3], no. 1567, unambiguously J.EK in
the trefoil, hall mark 1498).
[3]A. Fischinger, *Gdansk [Danzig] Silver, Wawel State Collections of Art* (Warsaw,
1981), frontispiece, inv. no. 1295, H. 9$\frac{5}{8}$ in. (24.5 cm.). Also the maker's mark
of the Crakow tankard appears several times: among other places, on the lid,
on the edge of the vessel, and on the base, and shows unambiguously a "J/EK"
in a field similar to a trefoil. Marjorie Trusted, London, pointed this piece out
to me.
[4]C. Theuerkauff, "Kaiser Leopold, im Triumph wider die Turken . . .,"
Hamburger Mittel- und ostdeutsche Forschungen 4 (1963), p. 60ff., illus. pp. 61, 69,
80. E. von Philippovich, 1982[2], illus. 297.
[5]Volbach, 1923, p. 80f., catalogue no. 3141, plate 85 (maker's mark I/EK).
R. Verres, "Der Elfenbein und Bernstein Schnitzer Christoph Maucher,"
Pantheon 12, no. 2 (1933), p. 244ff., illus. pp. 245, 747.
[6]Last publication, M. Trusted, "Four Amber Statuettes by Christoph
Maucher," *Pantheon* 41, no. 3 (1984), p. 245ff., cf. illus. 5, 9.
[7]Inv. no. vol. II 65. H. 19$\frac{5}{8}$ in. (50 cm.). The maker's mark on top, on the rim
of the pitcher, a "J/EK" in a field similar to a trefoil, probably stands for
Johann Ernst Kadau; another pitcher (or a tankard) with cover figure of
Aaron, formerly in the Schloß-museum in Gotha. This "aus Helfenbein
gearbeitete Kanne, woran die Historie der Kinder Israel da sie sich bey dem
güldenen Kalbe frölich bezeugen zu sehen, . . . silbernen verguldeten Deckel,
auf welchem der Priester Aron mit dem Opferlamb beede von Helfenbein, . . .
ist dem höchstseel. Herzog Friedrich an Sr. hochfürstl. Durchl. Geburtstag a o
1689(!) von Herrn Herzog Johann Adolphen zu Sachsen Weißenfels verehret
worden." (pitcher fashioned out of ivory, on which can be seen the history of
the children of Israel as they happily bear witness at the golden calf, . . . silver
gilded cover, on which the priest Aaron with the sacrificial lamb, both of
ivory, . . . was presented to the late Duke Friedrich on his Serene Highness's
birthday in the year 1689 [!] by Duke Johann Adolph zu Sachsen Weißenfels.
[our translation]) (Inventory of works of art from 1721, Gotha, p. 12; friendly
communication from Dr. W. Steguweit). The mounting could have been by
Ernst II Kadau or his son Johann Ernst.
[8]Also the opinion of H. Seling, letter of 2 October 1984.
[9]A. R. Chodyński, "Uwagi o złotnikach i srebrnikach Działajacych w Gdańskù"
[Essays on Gold- and Silversmiths Working in Danzig], *Biuletyn Histori
Sztuki* 38, no. 2 [1976], p. 109ff., names only Ernst I Kadau (1643), Ernst II
Kadau (Master 1674) and his brothers Benjamin (1680) and Natanael (1678).
The son of Ernst II Kadau, Johann Ernst, seems to have achieved his master
status outside of Danzig. I thank Magister Chodyński for his friendly help.

Literature: A. Jones Catalogue, 1907, p. 48, no. 3, plate XLIX, 3; Rosenberg,
II[3], p. 9, no. 1567, c.

Exhibitions: Glasgow Art Gallery, 1903.

COVERED GOBLET WITH DANCING PUTTOS
South Germany, most probably Augsburg (follower of Johann Bernhard Strauss?). Late seventeenth, early eighteenth century. Silver, regilded mounting by Albrecht Biller (1653–1720), Augsburg.

Ivory cylinder with protruding, partially engraved base area in high relief, in places almost sculptured free-hand, areas of yellowish-brown color, giving the effect almost of wax, but with easily visible grain. The very thin relief ground shows a greenish discoloration in spots. There are some cracks; for example, on the putto with grapes in his lowered left hand.

The cover, the broad upper part, the base of the cylinder, and the domed foot — with its wavy edges with acanthus leaves, fruit, and foliage bunches — are repoussé silver, partly embossed. The drumming cover putto and the upright, supporting figure of Cupid — formerly holding a bow and arrow (there is a hole in his right hand) — are cast; neither is gilded.

Marks: Augsburg hall mark — probably for 1710–1712 ✹
(Seling 169) — is hard to identify, but it appears twice on the narrow side of the edge of the cover and foot. In addition, the maker's mark of Albrecht Biller appears ▣
(Master around 1681; Seling 1778).
Total H. 14¼ in. (36.3 cm.); H. to edge above 11 9/16 in. (29.4 cm.);
H. of the ivory cylinder 3 7/16 in. (8.8–8.9 cm.);
H. of the cover figure 1¾ in. (4.6 cm.);
greatest diameter on edge of cover 6⅛ × 5⅜ in. (15.6 × 13.7 cm.)
Provenance: Gutmann Collection; acquired through J. S. Goldschmidt, Frankfurt am Main, 1902
1917.300

The slight size and daintiness of the actual ivory cylinder is relatively rare. It is especially striking in relation to the strongly accentuated, jointed silver mounting, which seems to make direct reference in its decoration of fruit bundles to the four relatively elongated, thin-limbed puttos. The latter are holding grapes or else little gourds (or apples from the Garden of Eden) in their hands; their dance movements on the leaf-covered base area, standing out clearly in relief, become especially conspicuous on the completely smooth relief ground.

The conception of the relief, the figures in their disposition and their physiognomies, the foliate plants on the base, and the modeling style of body and hair point to an origin in Augsburg in the late seventeenth century. The origin is in the vicinity or among the immediate followers and imitators of Johann Bernhard Strauss (1611 — probably active until 1677; died after 1681), who immigrated from Markdorf on Lake Constance and was also trained as a goldsmith. He was also a carver of mother of pearl.[1]

Apart from the Netherlandish sources (for example Peter Paul Rubens as a model for the "Drunken Silenus" of an ivory cylinder dated 1656 or 1666, today in Karlsruhe[2]), Strauss and the makers of our goblet seem to have utilized, for the puttos, prototypes by François Duquesnoy which were distributed in countless bronze statuettes. Thus, in the final analysis, not only the ivory putto with the gourds in his hand — in mirror image — but also the cupid pedestal figure go back to the cupid of Duquesnoy's bronze Apollo group or to its variants as a single figure (sometimes shown balancing on a sphere, alluding to the reign of love over the world) with bow and/or arrow.[3]

Given the fruits and the poppy plants of the mounting at the top and the bundles of blossoms and foliage, the use of the Cupid statuette seems limited not only formally, but also as to content — that is, a reference to love and the enjoyment of wine — for after all the poppy is one of the attributes of Venus and Bacchus.[4]

Stylistic prototypes for the ivory figures are found not only on Strauss's ivory tankard, dated 1651, in the Victoria and Albert Museum, London,[5] but also on the pedestal part of Strauss's later goblet, originating before 1677, in the Kunsthistorisches Museum, Vienna.[6]

One would almost like to think the same sculptor or carver who created the dance of the four ivory figures had also supplied the goldsmith with the models for the figures. A similar relationship applies to the puttos of four silver display vases by Albrecht Biller of around 1700

in the Staatliche Kunstsammlungen, Kassel,[7] which also make use of various prototypes — with a narrow, high forehead-temple region, or a broad physiognomy such as in the case of the drummer statuette on the lid.

The form of this goblet is very rare; more frequent are goblets fashioned entirely of ivory, from the second half of the seventeenth century. These have more emphatic cover domes and more massive pedestals, as for example Johann Bernhard Strauss's abovementioned Viennese goblet, or two stylistically comparable examples with Augsburg mounting by Hans Jakob Mair in Dresden[8] and Berlin[9] from before 1689.

Notes:
[1] C. Scherer, "Der Augsburger Goldschmied Bernhard Strauss," *Der Kunstwanderer* (1920), p. 463ff., illustrations.
[2] The Hever Castle Collection, Sotheby's, London, 6 May 1983, II, p. 88f., no. 312, 4 illustrations. *Jahrbuch der Kunstsammlungen in Baden-Württemberg* 21 (1984), p. 184, illustrations p. 184.
[3] M. Fransolet, *François du Quesnoy* (Brussels, 1942), plate XII, b. Theuerkauff, Winkler Collection, 1984, cat. no. 100 (mirror image). O. Raggio, in *Liechtenstein: The Princely Collections*, The Metropolitan Museum of Art (New York, 1985), cat. no. 49, illus.
[4] A. Henkel, A. Schöne, *Emblemata* (Stuttgart, 1978) (Special issue), among others nos. 1752, 1831.
[5] Longhurst, II, 1929, p. 90f., no. 4529-1858, plate LXXVII and fig. 7. E. von Philippovich, 1982², illus. 182f.
[6] Von Philippovich, 1982², illus. 182f.
[7] Seling, I, p. 297; II, illus. 473, illus. 600–603; III, p. 248.
[8] Sponsel, 1932, p. 68, Plate 14b.
[9] C. Theuerkauff, in *Die Brandenburgisch-Preußische Kunstkammer*, exhibition catalogue (Berlin, 1981), p. 187f., cat. no. 102, illus. Volbach, 1923, p. 81, no. K 3115, illus. pp. 80, 81.

Literature: A. Jones Catalogue, 1907, p. 49, no. 2, plate L, 2.

Exhibitions: Glasgow Art Gallery, 1903.

FIGURED HANDLE, MOST PROBABLY FROM A DISPLAY PITCHER OR
EWER
South Germany, Johann Michael Maucher (1645—around 1700) and
workshop, Schwäbisch-Gmünd? Late seventeenth century
Carved freehand from one piece of light yellowish, partly brownish,
partly heavily grained ivory. Underneath on the narrow side there is a
rectangular opening and diagonal drill-hole. There is another hole
above, under the male figure, recently filled in with wood-filler.
These holes and the dent on the volute below indicate that the handle
was mounted on the body or neck of the vessel. Scarcely any cracks.
H. $6\frac{5}{16}$ in. (16.1 cm.); greatest W. $2\frac{9}{16}$ in. (6.6 cm.)
1917.313

This is an exceptionally high-quality fragment, successfully combining
ornament and figure into a functional form. It is not related in type to the
so-called hunting tankards in Dresden or Munich[1] or in Bologna,[2] but
rather to the one in Braunschweig[3] and the one signed "MM" (ligatured,
for Michael Maucher), consisting entirely of ivory, in the Hohenlohe-
Museum at Schloß Neuenstein.[4] In comparison with the Braunschweig
ewer, which totals $13\frac{1}{4}$ in. in height, the one to fit our handle would have
to have been about $13\frac{3}{4}$-15 in. high.

In style as well as in the finely carved, expressive faces, bodies, and
ornamental elements, an origin in the immediate vicinity of Johann
Michael Maucher is possible. Maucher was also a skilled gunmaker, who
delivered — in Schwäbisch-Gmünd and, beginning about 1692, also in
Würzburg — magnificent weapons, richly decorated in relief, to
princely courts. The numerous display pitchers/ewers of parallel origin
and the often accompanying platters — for example, the one in Bologna
from 1672 or one formerly in Berlin[5] — show another hand in style
and technique than our handle. The handle, to be sure, admittedly
deviates also from the ewer signed by Maucher, formerly in the
Kunstgewerbemuseum, Berlin (from Ansbach in South Germany).[6] The
goblet with pedestal group in Neuenstein,[7] which dispenses with
ornamentation to a great extent, lends itself to comparison. In comparing
the style of our handle with the $19\frac{3}{4}$ in.-high covered pitcher with nearly
circular handle in the Staatliche Kunstsammlungen, Kassel[8] (which was
conceived in Danzig by Ernst II or Johann Ernst Kadau), Christoph
Maucher as the carver seems to be ruled out. However, he and Johann
Michael probably often worked together until around 1670. A definitive
interpretation of the iconography — "salvation" of woman by man
above the allegorical Invidia and Furor? — would probably only be
possible if one knew what was represented on the receptacle body and
stand.

Notes:
[1]Sponsel, 1932, p. 150, plate 55. Berliner, 1926, page 63, cat. no. 222, plate 134.
[2]Exhibition catalogue, Museo Civico, Bologna, *Lavori in osso e avorio dalla
preistoria al rococo* (Bologna, 1959), 60ff., nos. 148, 150, plate 35.
[3]Scherer, 1931, p. 130f., cat. no. 407, plate 66.
[4]Exhibition catalogue, *Barock in Baden-Württemberg*, Badisches Landesmuseum,
Karlsruhe, Schloß Bruchsal, 27 June to 25 October 1981, p. 478, cat. no. H 7,
illus. (platter). W. Klein, 1920.
[5]Volbach, 1923, p. 88, cat. no. 3137, plate 82.
[6]Volbach, 1923, p. 88, cat. no. 3139, plate 84.
[7]W. Klein, *Johann Michael und Christoph Maucher* (Schwäbisch-Gmünd, 1920),
p. 12, no. 12, plate V.
[8]Inv. no. vol. II.65. Cf. here cat. no. 28, note 7.

COVERED TANKARD WITH SYMBOLS OF THE FIVE SENSES
South Germany, Augsburg, early eighteenth century
Silver-gilt mount by Philipp Stenglin (1667–1744), Augsburg, 1717–18

Carved ivory cylinder with slightly protruding base region and smooth background, in high and flat relief. The material is whitish with light brown places; above all in the thin ground above, the grain is strongly visible. There are two cracks over the putto with cornucopia, and others above to the right of the handle on the putto with mirror and the putto with lute.

The relatively delicate cover statuette of Cupid with bow (without string) lacks fingers and parts of the left hand, which at one time probably held an arrow. He is attached with metal pins to the base plate, which is in turn screwed onto the cover.

The edges above and below are profiled. The narrow, rimmed cover and base ring are of gilded silver, embossed with ribbon work, acanthus, flower baskets, and bundles of leaves, and engraved in places. A cast Negro herm serves as handle, which is attached with two blossom-shaped nuts above a leaf mask. In the base below are two other blossom-like nuts, screws, and chevrons.

Marks: Augsburg hall mark for 1717–18 (Seling 178)
and maker's mark of Philipp Stenglin (Seling 1880)
appear twice: on the edge of the cover and on the base. In addition, there are Austrian control marks (R³, 7876) for 1806–07.

Total H. with cover statuette 9⁷⁄₁₆ in. (24 cm.); H. of the cylinder 5³⁄₈ in. (13.8 cm.); H. of the Cupid figure 2³⁄₁₆ in. (5.6 cm.); greatest W. with handle 7¼ in. (18.2 cm.); diameter below 5 × 4⁵⁄₁₆ in. (12.8 × 11.1 cm.).

Provenance: Gutmann Collection; acquired through J. S. Goldschmidt, Frankfurt am Main, 1902

1917.309

The male and female puttos, nine all together, are mostly unclothed or only sparsely draped and can be recognized by their attributes and activities as symbols of the five senses. To the right of the handle is a boy with spectacles in his left hand and a hand mirror in his right. He is beside a girl crowned with a wreath who is holding an extended telescope in front of her: the sense of sight. The adjacent putto — a girl? — singing to the accompaniment of the lute with the little male companion holding the sheet of music represent the sense of hearing. To the right of them one putto is carrying roses in a basket on his head, and holding a lemon in his right hand; a second figure is smelling a rose blossom and holding a cornucopia with roses, leaves, and lemons: obviously the sense of smell.

Another pair symbolizes the sense of taste: a boy crowned with grapes and vine leaves is pouring wine out of a pitcher down the throat of a putto seen from the back. The sense of touch is designated by a female putto in front of the handle who is touching the figures standing next to her on their cheeks and shoulders. Her left hand is on her own body.

Stylistically, the crowning Cupid figure with the bow seems strikingly small in relation to the vessel and relief frieze, carved by another hand. Perhaps there was originally a silver statuette in its place.

The raised relief frieze of the figures is in front of an otherwise smooth background, with a slightly protruding base on which the puttos stand (unlike, for example, the goblet mounted by Albrecht Biller, no. 29). But the type and stylistic formation of the figures are conceivable only against the backdrop of the ivory sculptures made by the goldsmith Johann Bernhard Strauss, active in Augsburg (mentioned in documents from 1640 to 1681), and of his successors. One can compare among others his Viennese and London goblet and tankard of 1670–80 or 1651.[1]

Perhaps the workshop which delivered this impressive relief to the silversmith Philipp Stenglin (who had been active as master in Augsburg since 1697, and by whom there is a tankard from around 1712–15 representing the Four Seasons[2]) can be sought in Augsburg. The relief may have been made by a follower of the woodcutters, painters, and copperplate engravers Johann Philipp and Daniel Steudner, Jr., and especially of the sculptor Marc Christoph Steudner, Sr. (died 1704). Less likely is the circle of the much younger Esais Philipp Steudner (1691–1760).[3] The etchings of Daniel, Jr. often duplicate thematically similar compositions of allegorical putto representations (after, among others, Matthias Scheits).[4] The tankard is the only ivory sculpture known to be mounted by Philipp Stenglin.

Notes:
[1] Cf. E. von Philippovich, 1982², illus. 182ff., 181.
[2] Seling, 2, p. 278f.
[3] Scherer, 1931, p. 59ff., cat. no. 109f., plate 23.
[4] A. Hämmerle, "Die Familie Steudner," Das Schwäbische Museum (Augsburg, 1926), p. 97ff., especially p. 102ff., illus. 5f, p. 110ff., nos. 7–10, 11–14.

Literature: Wadsworth Atheneum Handbook (Hartford, Conn., 1958), p. 110.

Exhibitions: Glasgow Art Gallery, 1903; Dwight Art Gallery, Mount Holyoke College, "The Eye Listens: Music in the Visual Arts," 23 October–15 November, 1950, cat. no. 40.

COVERED TANKARD WITH ALLEGORICAL REPRESENTATIONS, AMONG
OTHERS THE FOUR ELEMENTS
South Germany, under the immediate influence of Leonhard Kern
(1588–1662) and his workshop; possibly Augsburg, about 1650–60
Silver-gilt mounts by Hans Jakob Mair (about 1641–1719), Augsburg,
1665–70; regilded

Ivory cylinder with high and bas relief, engraved in places, white to
yellowish in color, in some places light brown. Under the handle there
is a prominent crack and a smaller one above the flute player.
The round base for the surmounting ivory figure of the Bacchus boy is
separately carved; his left arm is pegged on, as are parts of the left leg,
and both feet.

The cover, upper rim, and foot of the silver setting are decorated
with repoussé tulips and acanthus foliage. There is a partially tooled
leaf frieze as well, along with undulating rims. The cast handle is in the
form of a female herm and fruits, the upper part with a double claw
thumb rest.

Marks: Augsburg hall mark 1665–70 (Seling 101) and maker's mark of
Hans Jakob Mair (Seling 1657), appear three times: on the cover;
on the upper rim (near the base of the handle); and under
the bottom.
H. 13 in. (33 cm.); H. of the ivory cylinder about $5\frac{1}{2}$ in. (14 cm.);
H. of the surmounting figure 4 in. (10.3 cm.); W. (with handle) $9\frac{7}{16}$ in.
(24.1 cm.); diameters of lower rim $7\frac{1}{16} \times 6\frac{7}{16}$ in. (18 × 16.5 cm.)
Provenance: Gutmann Collection; acquired through J. S. Goldschmidt,
Frankfurt am Main, 1902
1917.306

It is not possible to determine unequivocally what the seven — almost
exclusively male — puttos are intended to represent. In this group, the
one who is digging with the spade could symbolize the element earth; the
female putto with the sail-like, fluttering cloth the air; the torchbearer
fire; and the putto to the left of the handle, who is pouring water out of a
vase on his shoulder, water. It is possible the male figure blowing the
woven horn personifies music, and the impressive figure seen from the
back holding fruits and grapes the abundance of nature (the Bacchic
element?). That this putto is stepping emphatically on a gourd seems to
be an allusion to fecundity and at the same time a symbol of love.[1]

The content, composition (treating the individual figures in diverse
positions and views, and from high to the finest bas relief), as well as the
partly elongated figures and their head types, point to a workshop which
operated under the influence of Leonhard Kern in Schwäbisch-Hall. This
sculptor and ivory carver also attempted to reproduce basic positions of
the human body in his numerous representations of children — as
individual figures, groups, or reliefs; of alabaster, stone, boxwood, or
ivory. Especially noteworthy is the clothed recumbent figure: Baroque
artists in general, and especially Kern, delighted in the apparent
contradiction presented by placing a figure normally used as an allegory
of sleep or *memento mori* into such a lighthearted scene (to be sure without
attributes such as skulls or hour glass). The contrast of this putto to the
musician (who, curiously, is holding the flute with only one hand, while
the left one is making a gesture that could be construed as erotic — if he
is not simply keeping time), suggests an interpretation of the clothed
putto as a symbol of pensiveness, and thus of Vanitas. The pendant to the
musician would be, then, the girl holding the cloth; she is connected to
him by means of the torchbearer of love, and the large gourd at his feet.

Kern's prototypes were influential well into the eighteenth century.
They were used as models for ivory cylinders of quite varied quality, and
almost always represent putto friezes with Bacchus, Amor, and similar
concepts.[2]

In contrast to the special quality of the cylinder relief, and on the basis
of the style and carving technique (for example, the hair), the very
differently proportioned finial statue of Bacchus holding the long-stalked
grapevine and the remarkable footed basin (*tazza*) seems to be a
relatively late addition (probably from the nineteenth century). Instead
of an ivory figure (cf. here nos. 31, 33), it is possible to imagine as the
original surmounting figure a silver statuette (cf. no. 29), thematically
related to the representation of the main relief. This thematic
relationship is evident in many ivories, among them a tankard with sea
puttos, partly of Kern's type, whose horn-blowing putto on the lid is
riding on a dolphin. Its Nuremberg mounting is by Andreas Bergemann.
It is in the possession of the city of St. Gallen, Switzerland.[3]

Notes:
[1] The fruits — both of which are love symbols but which are too big to be
either quinces or pomegranates — are probably to be interpreted as acorn
squash, known everywhere since the sixteenth century, and also known,
because of the many seeds, as symbols of love and fecundity. Cf. *Ullstein-
Lexikon der Pflanzenwelt* (Frankfurt am Main, Berlin, and Vienna, 1973). I thank
Dr. H. Zepernik, Botanisches Museum, Berlin, for a clarifying conversation.
[2] Compare the above tankard to the following ivory cylinders: a. a covered
tankard with grape-eating putto as finial figure, which was acquired by the
Brandenburgische Kunstkammer in Berlin in 1689, also mounted by Hans
Jakob Mair, in the Kunstgewerbemuseum, Stiftung Preußischer Kulturbesitz,
Berlin, whose handle corresponds almost exactly to the present one [Volbach,
1923, p. 85, inv. no. K 3121, illus. p. 86. Seling, 3, p. 218f., no. 131]; b. a
second, though unmarked tankard in the same place [Volbach, 1923, p. 85,
inv. no. K 3122]; c. a third, unmounted ivory cylinder, also in Berlin, which
shows, among other things, the recumbent figure [Volbach, 1923, p. 85f.,
inv. no. K 3123, plates 78, 85. Grünenwald, Kern, 1969, p. 48, no. 132];
d. in large degree corresponding to an unmounted cylinder in the Bayerisches
Nationalmuseum, Munich [Berliner, 1926, cat. no. 203, plate 111 a–d.
Grünenwald, Kern, 1969, p. 49, no. 162] is the figure composition of e. the
likewise unmounted piece in the Hessisches Landesmuseum, at Darmstadt
[inv. no. Kg. 63; 415. Grünenwald, Kern, 1969, p. 48, no. 145]. Here, as in our
relief, are the recumbent figure, the boy carrying grapes, who is seen from
behind, and the girl holding the cloth; f. an unmounted cylinder in the Herzog
Anton Ulrich-Museum, Braunschweig [Scherer, 1931, cat. no. 358, plate 55.
Grünenwald, Kern, 1969, p. 48, no. 142]; g. another one in the
Württembergisches Landesmuseum, Stuttgart [Grünenwald, Kern, 1969,
p. 50, no. 178]; and h. a tankard in the possession of the Earl of Mansfield,
Scone Palace, Scotland, which was quite obviously not mounted at least until
the nineteenth century.
[3] H. W. Seling, *Katalog der Silbersammlung, Museen der Staat St. Gallen*
(St. Gallen, 1965), p. 18, no. 23, plate 8.

Literature: A. Jones Catalogue, 1907, p. 39, plate XLI.

Exhibitions: Glasgow Art Gallery, 1903.

COVERED GOBLET WITH DIANA, GODDESS OF THE HUNT,
AND HER COMPANIONS

North Germany or the Netherlands? End of seventeenth century
Silver-gilt mounting, its enamel influenced by France, created in the
Netherlands? High and flat relief with free-sculptured parts,
statuettes, and groups of ivory carved very thinly in places. The ivory
is partially heavily grained and yellowish in color. The figured foot
ring, pedestal group, cylinder, cover ring, and cover statuette are
fashioned individually.

The silver-gilt setting is richly enameled with flowers — including
tulips and poppies — and tendrils not exactly suited to the ivory
vessel; there are restorations to the enamel. There is a wide crack in
the ivory casing. Simple profiles border the enameled areas, above a
serrated edge.

Total H. $12\frac{3}{8}$ in. (31.6 cm.); H. of the ivory cylinder $3\frac{5}{16}$ in.
(8.5–8.6 cm.); H. of the cover statuette $1\frac{15}{16}$ in. (5 cm.);
diameter of the vessel $3\frac{5}{16} \times 3\frac{9}{16}$ in. (8.5 × 9.1 cm.)
1917.297 a–b

On the vessel relief itself is an escort of the hunting goddess Diana with
bow, quiver, and line, turning around. In front of her is a female escort
who is disemboweling a hind or a roe, and in front of them is a slain
chamois (kind of goat). The goddess Diana is recognizable by her
crescent moon; she is wearing a goat skin and is carrying a staff in her left
hand. She is accompanied by other female hunting figures.

In view of its glorious enameled flowers and tendrils — in red, wine
red, orange, pink, and green on a turquoise-blue background — the
unmarked mounting (from about 1670–80) could have originated in
France, or earlier still in the northern Netherlands (?), but was not likely
made in Northern Germany.[1]

In the final analysis, South German works (for example, the entirely
ivory Augsburg goblet by Johann Bernhard Strauss in Vienna, from
about 1670–80 [?][2]), seem to be prototypical for the total vessel
construction as well as for the style of the figures. The figures by Strauss
also seemed to have influenced Joachim Hennen of North Germany/
Denmark, as seen for example, in the so-called Løvenørn goblet,
illustrated in a painting by George Hinz in 1666.[3]

Compared to, for instance, the goblet "Diana with Callisto" in the
Grünes Gewölbe at Dresden,[4] mounted by Hans Jakob Mair around 1670
in Augsburg, the relative simplicity of the three-dimensional construction of the goblet is striking. Again, this simplicity is suggestive of
an Augsburg ivory goblet — also similar in relief style — from around
1670–90, now in the Walters Art Gallery in Baltimore.[5] It suggests even
more the covered goblet with bacchanal mounted around 1665–70 by the
Hamburg goldsmith Friedrich Biesterveld, located in the Museum für
Kunst und Gewerbe in Hamburg.[6] Although certain details, such as the
nymph of the hunt with the dog disemboweling the deer, can be found on
a South German ivory beaker (Bayerisches Nationalmuseum, Munich),[7]
the figure types, style of clothing, and relief projection of our display
goblet are comparable to the frieze on the Hamburg covered cup. Its
pronounced daintiness remains striking; the delicateness, the schematic
repetition of facial types and motifs of movement, and the sharp-edged,
carved individual forms (for example, the clothing) do not make it easy to
date the ivory definitively.

Notes:

[1] The opinion of H. Seling: France or Holland?; in the opinion of B. Heitman,
Hamburg, whom I thank very much for sharing this information, most likely
"Netherlandish"; the red tones point to a French influence.

[2] Von Philippovich, 1982², illus. 182ff.

[3] Last publication, J. Rasmussen, "Joachim Henne, ein höfischer Kleinmeister
des Barock, Jahrbuch der Hamburger Kunstsammlungen 23 (1978), pp. 32, 45,
cat. no. 8, illus. 13ff. U. Bastian, "George Hinz und sein Stillebenwerk,"
phil. dissertation, Hamburg, 1984, p. 114ff., p. 286f., cat. no. 55ff., 56ff.,
illus. 55ff. 67f., 128; cf. also cat. no. 54, illus. 54f.

[4] Sponsel, 1932, p. 68, plate 14 b = Seling no. 1657 i.

[5] Inv. no. 71.470. Last publication, R. H. Randall, Jr., et al., Masterpieces of Ivory
from the Walters Art Gallery (New York, 1985), no. 384, illus.

[6] J. Rasmussen, in exhibition catalogue, Barockplastik in Norddeutschland, Museum
für Kunst und Gewerbe (Hamburg, 1977), p. 404f., cat. no. 127, illus.

[7] Berliner, 1926, cat. no. 189, plate 110.

SEA PUTTO WITH TWO DOLPHINS
Probably France. Late eighteenth or nineteenth century
Partly whitish, partly yellowish ivory with a dull sheen that is
yellowed on the back, cut off flat underneath, and attached with a
metal pin to the base.

There is a small crack under the left eye of the big dolphin,
whose teeth are visible. The slit-shaped eyes of the putto are drilled.
H. 2¾ in. (7.1 cm.)
1917.314

The group was probably not composed as a crowning piece of a goblet,
tankard, or beaker (as, for example, on Georg Petel's Augsburg covered
beaker of around 1628–29),[1] but rather as an independent representation, perhaps originally on a bronze base. It has no parallels in type
or style, either in South German-Austrian or Dutch baroque. Nor are
there thematic connections with baroque Cupid-representations with
dolphins, which have been popular since the inventions of Cornelis Bos
and others from the middle of the sixteenth century.[2] These are in bronze
(Francesco Fanelli) and especially in ivory, for example, as crowning
pieces of richly mounted display vessels.[3]

The childishly soft figure type and full-cheeked facial type — with the
drawn-in area around the temples, the high forehead, and the little
mouth derived ultimately from the prototype of François Duquesnoy —
are somewhat similar to French sculptures of the second third of the
eighteenth century. These include René Frémin's puttos with animals in
La Granja, among others,[4] Edmé Bouchardon's fountain of the rue de
Grenelle, and individual figures by Lambert Sigismund Adam from
1740–50.[5] These similarities could point to an origin in France, as does
also the artificially ingenious composition with the dolphin motif at both
arms. In view of the dry modeling method and the ornamental and
technical details of the carving — rhomboid engraving on the fish tail of
the putto and leaflike, isolated fins and tailfins of the dolphin — the
sculpture most probably may date from the nineteenth century, perhaps
according to an exact prototype in bronze or marble.

Notes:
[1] Among others, illus. p. 166, left, in Tardy, *Les Ivoires*.
[2] Sure Schéle, *Cornelis Bos* (Stockholm, 1965), plate 26, no. 70a, p. 142.
[3] Cf. for example Berliner, 1926, cat. no. 228, plate 142f.
[4] F. Souchal, *French Sculptors of the 17th and 18th Centuries: The Reign of Louis XIV*
(Oxford, 1977), Frémin, no. 64ff., 113ff., 156ff., 170ff., with illus.
[5] Among others, exhibition catalogue, *The French Bronze 1500–1800*,
M. Knoedler & Co. (New York, 1968), cat. no. 64, illus.

Exhibitions: The Art of the Renaissance Craftsman, Fogg Art Museum, Harvard
University (Cambridge, 1937), p. 40, no. 58.

RECLINING FEMALE FIGURE (FRAGMENT)
South Germany (Augsburg?). Second third of the seventeenth century?
Plump figure of whitish ivory polished to a dull finish that has yellowed considerably on the back side, and which in spots has turned to a brownish-yellow color.

Both legs are pegged above the knee (iron dowels visible), as are her left arm from the shoulder down (pin), and her right hand (pin). It is not easy to determine whether the iron pin on her back side is old. There is a diagonal crack over the body, on front and back.
H. 2 9/16 in. (6.5 cm.)
1917.317

The completely naked figure seems to stretch out her left arm horizontally, and is making a protective movement with her right arm in front of her. The hair, parted in the middle, is gathered together on the nape of the neck, partly plaited, and is artistically shaped like a cross.

The figure is perhaps a fragment of a multi-figured group of Diana with her nymphs (and Actaeon?), or of a composition such as Europa on the bull or Dejanira kidnapped by the centaur Nessus, as shown by Giovanni Bologna's bronzes.[1] If this were the case, it would be strange that there is no sign of draping.

Taking into account the loose, full-bodied hair and the soft facial type,[2] striking parallels are found for the sculptural, firmly modeled body, and for the figure style characterized by the crossed arm, in Augsburg silver of the middle of the century,[3] and in comparable ivory sculptures. To this number belong, for example, the splendid Viennese beaker mounted by Wolfgang I. John before 1634 with its "replica,"[4] and the impressive tankard, dated 1651, by the goldsmith Johann Bernhard Strauss (active in Augsburg) in the Victoria and Albert Museum, London.[5] Still, it is not possible to connect a particular workshop with our statuette.

Notes:
[1] Exhibition catalogue, *Giambologna*, Kunsthistorisches Museum, Vienna (Vienna, 1978), p. 147ff., cat. no. 60ff., illus.; 160f., cat. no. 68, illus.
[2] Even considering a relatively late origin, for example soon after 1700, in comparison, for example, with Johann Leonhard Baur's Orpheus-Euridice group, dated 1716, in London. C. Theuerkauff, "'Ein künstlicher Bildschnitzer im kleinen . . .' Auf den Spuren von Johann Leonhard Baur (1682–1760)," *Kunst und Antiquitäten* 3 (1981), p. 24, notes 5, 20, illus. 5f.
[3] Seling, 2, illus. 576, 581, 476, 418.
[4] Exhibition catalogue, *Augsburger Barock* (Augsburg, 1968), p. 321, cat. no. 466, illus. 35 (inv. no. 4480 and 4469).
[5] *Ibid.*, p. 91, cat. no. 94, illus. 36. Von Philippovich, 1982², illus. 181, cf. illus. 182f.

LARGE COVERED BEAKER DEPICTING BOAR AND BEAR HUNT
South Germany, probably Munich, circle of Franz I (1651–1695) and
Dominikus Stainhart (1655–1712). End of the seventeenth, beginning
of the eighteenth century?
The silver-gilt mount is without marks, and originates from the late
nineteenth century; the cover may be of sheet brass.

Ivory cylinder with slightly protruding base region in high relief
and, in places, finest flat relief; occasionally, trees and animals are
sculpted freehand from behind, making them stand out three-
dimensionally. The color of the ivory is yellowish, sometimes almost
brownish, on the projecting parts. A thick crack to the right of the
bear hunt is partly filled; the end of the hunting spear is broken off,
as is the sword blade of the plump cover figure of Mars. This figure is
on a more recent ivory base; there are fractures and cracks in both feet
and elsewhere.

The cover is profiled and tiered, with a bulge on each tier. On the
silver base is a simple acanthus frieze. The ivory itself is not correctly
"mounted," but only set on.
Total H. 11 in. (27.9 cm.); H. of Mars $3\frac{3}{8}$ in. (8.6 cm.);
H. of the cylinder $4\frac{5}{16}$ in. (11 cm.); diameter below $5\frac{11}{16}$ in. (14.5 cm.)
Provenance: Gutmann Collection; acquired through J. S. Goldschmidt,
Frankfurt am Main, 1902
1917.298 a–b

The surmounting Mars figure is probably not by the same person who
made the cylinder relief; it is similar to a figure sold at a 1983 art auction
in Berlin,[1] which was a nineteenth-century copy after a prototype in a
series of representations of the gods in the Staatliche Kunstsammlungen,
Kassel.[2]

The hunting scenes are certainly fashioned after graphic prototypes — compare the hunt and rider representations of Peter Paul
Rubens, and especially those by Antonio Tempesta and Johann
Stradanus, and ivory reliefs adapted from them on platters and tankards
by Johann Michael Maucher (see no. 30) or of Johann Michael Hornung.[3]
The scenes are cleverly inserted into the graduated landscape representation, despite individual distortions (for example, the hindquarters
of the boar).

Judging from the types of figures, the characteristic, short-cropped
heads, the configuration of the root-covered earth, the form of the
irregularly gnarled tree trunks and big-leaved branches, as well as the
surface treatment of the clothes, hides, and hair, the work probably
originated in the circle of the brothers Franz I. and Dominikus Stainhart
in Munich, before 1700 (?).

Several other works can be compared with our tankard: the *Departure
from Noah's Ark* relief by the somewhat older Franz I. Stainhart in the
Bayerisches Nationalmuseum, Munich;[4] two scenes of the rape of the
Sabine women in St. Florian and in Vienna;[5] and an unmounted ivory
cylinder with animal fights in Klosterneuburg.[6] But the closest comparison is the tankard with animal fight scenes in the Schatzkammer of
the Munich Residenz, which J. Anton Kipfinger from Weilheim mounted
and which came to light as a late work of Franz I. before 1695.[7] To be
sure, the tankard cover in Hartford does not attain the precision of the
individual forms found in the Munich Residenz tankard. Much the same
applies to the tankard, mounted by Franz Kessler in Munich (?), of the
battle of Pyrrhus against the Romans in the Hermitage, Leningrad,[8] so
that, in spite of the similarity to the later style of Franz I. Stainhart, an
exact dating of our tankard is not possible.

Notes:
[1] Leo Spik, Auction 526, 13 October 1983, cat. no. 827, plate 94. Last
publication, Theuerkauff, Winkler Collection, p. 162f., under cat. no. 88,
no. 20f., note 19ff.
[2] Idem.
[3] Cf. E. Tietze-Conrat, "Die Erfindung im Relief," *Jahrbuch der Kunsthistorischen
Sammlungen in Wien* 35 (1920), p. 142, fig. 39, p. 175, no. 52. C. Scherer,
"Der Elfenbeinschnitzer Johann Michael Hornung," *Der Kunstwanderer*
(1924–25), p. 4ff., illus.
[4] Berliner, 1926, cat. no. 407, plate 205.
[5] C. Theuerkauff, "'Kunststückhe von Helfenbein': zum Werk der Gebrüder
Stainhart," *Alte und Moderne Kunst* (1972), part II, p. 32, illus. 5f., notes 11f.
[6] C. Theuerkauff, *Elfenbein in Klosterneuburg* (Klosterneuburg, 1961), p. 46f.,
cat. no. 16, illus. 17.
[7] Theuerkauff, *Stainhart* (1972), part II, p. 28, illus. 13, 13 a.
[8] Ermitage, 1974, cat. no. 25, illus.

Literature: A. Jones Catalogue, 1907, p. 48, no. 2, plate XLIX, 2.

Exhibitions: Glasgow Art Gallery, 1903.

ST. SEBASTIAN

South Italy or Spain? Second half of the seventeenth century?
Plump statuette of yellowish ivory, in places brownish and showing
cracks, with brown traces on the arms, right foot, and elsewhere.
On the loincloth are remnants of gold paint. The arms, nose, and feet
are restorations, as is the part of the loincloth behind the right hip.
The arms and corners of the cloth are attached to the body with glue,
and the arrow holes are filled with wood dowels; one arrow, broken off,
has been retained. The statuette is secured to a tree trunk with foliage
and a rock, all of gilt-bronze, by means of pins and twisted wires on the
wrists. The tip of the left index finger is broken off.

   The sculpture is atop an ocatagonal, stair-stepped hardwood base
which is fitted with ebony framing and little ivory tiles. This obviously
new base is cracked and glued in numerous places.
Total H. $13\frac{3}{16}$ in. (33.7 cm.); H. of the figure $9\frac{5}{16}$ in. (23.7 cm.);
diameter of the base $4\frac{3}{4} \times 4\frac{7}{8}$ in. (12.1 × 12.4 cm.)
1917.302

The saint, in type connected to Jusepe Ribera,[1] is represented here in a
powerful pose but with rigidly pathetic movements. It has no real
stylistic parallels in the baroque miniature sculpture of the Netherlands
and Germany. A similar combination with a metal or metal-like tree is
exhibited in the ivory figures from the collection of the reigning prince of
Liechtenstein, Vaduz,[2] or in the Walters Art Gallery, Baltimore;[3] in
type, these deviate completely and are attributed rightly or wrongly to
Adam Lenckhardt. Furthermore, an origin outside Europe — compare
among others the statuette in Medina di Rioseco/Valladolid[4] — seems to
be ruled out. On the other hand, there are representations from South
Italy or Spain which are similar not only for the general type but also for
the stylistics and carving technique. For example, there is an ivory statuette with a coral trunk found in the Museo Duca di Martina, Naples,[5] as
well as several statuettes and groups in Spanish collections which are
more or less connected with Claudio Beissonat (who was actively
working for the court in Naples in the second half of the seventeenth
century) — among others, a dead Christ in Madrid.[6] It is not possible to
attribute our statuette to a certain workshop or to date it more precisely.

Notes:
[1] A. E. Pérez Sanchez, et al., L'opera completa del Ribera (Milan, 1978), no. 203
(mirror image, three-quarter figure); Museo e Gallerie Nazionale di
Capodimonte, Naples, no. 131; Prado, Madrid.
[2] C. Theuerkauff, "Der Elfenbeinbildhauer Adam Lenckhardt," Jahrbuch der
Hamburger Kunstsammlungen 10 (1965), p. 49ff., note 104, fig. 21.
[3] Theuerkauff, "Lenckhardt," p. 50f., fig. 19. Cf. another statuette in
Baltimore, inv. no. 71.1154. Most recently, R. H. Randall, Jr., et al.,
Masterpieces of Ivory from the Walters Art Gallery (New York, 1985), p. 260, cat.
no. 403, illus. 403.
[4] M. M. Estella Marcos, La Escultura Barroca de Marfil en España, Las Escuelas
Europas y las Coloniales (Madrid, 1984), I, fig. 264f.; II, p. 269f., cat. no. 614
(Philippine Spanish).
[5] Exhibition catalogue, Civiltà del Seicento a Napoli, Museo di Capodimonte
(Naples and other places, 1984–85), 1984, p. 452, cat. no. 5.189, illus.
[6] Estella Marcos, I, fig. 113f.; 166ff.; II, p. 69ff., cat. no. 103ff.,
especially cat. no. 114.

Exhibitions: "Baroque Sculpture and the Decorative Arts," Jewett Arts Center,
Wellesley College, March 1965, cat. no. 21.

Meissen

William Hutton

No one was more strongly seized by the baroque period's mania for Far Eastern porcelain than was Augustus the Strong, Elector of Saxony and King of Poland, who backed the experiments that led to the European discovery of the formula for true, or "hard-paste," porcelain. This took place at Dresden in 1708–09, and the following year he established a factory to produce it at Meissen, twelve miles away. For fifty years it had no serious rivals. The King's interest did not slacken, and subsequent exacting patronage from high places was a continuing spur. The factory's history during its great period is further singular for the remarkable talents it enlisted, for Meissen created the subjects and styles of European porcelain art in painted decoration, relief ornament, and figures.

The dominant artistic personality in the Morgan collection is Johann Joachim Kaendler (at Meissen 1731–75), the real creator of the porcelain figure in European art, though his colleagues Johann Friedrich Eberlein (1735–49) and Friedrich Elias Meyer (1748–61) are represented here by characteristic models. Knowledge of who made what when at Meissen during its great period from 1710 to 1760 is incomplete, and the factory's output was perhaps too many-sided ever to be completely known. The situation is further conditioned by the loss from the factory archives of most records from 1749 to 1763. Scholars have only occasionally been able to consult the archives; the only document fully transcribed from them is Kaendler's partial record of his own work from 1740 to 1748 called the *Taxa*, published by Pfeiffer.

With the founding of decorative arts museums in the last half of the nineteenth century, organized knowledge of ceramic art became possible. This impulse was strongest in Germany, where one result was the move in 1876 of the great Dresden porcelain collection to accessible quarters following a century of obscurity in the basements of the Japanese Palace. A generation later, with the great improvement in reproduction techniques, both scholarship and visual images were able to reach a wider audience. Thus, the turn of the century saw early and still fundamental works on the history of the Meissen factory and its productions by Berling (1900, 1911), Sponsel (1900), and Zimmermann (1908). The appearance of monographs by Zimmermann (1926) and Honey (1934) were later landmarks in Meissen studies. Honey's was the first comprehensive book on Meissen in English, and his historical and critical perceptions remain valuable. More recently, an essential contribution to knowledge is Rainer Rückert's catalogue of the 1966 Meissen exhibition at Munich; many of the 1180 entries are documented by previously unpublished extracts from the factory archives. Part of that exhibition was drawn from the great collection of Ernst Schneider, which in 1971 became a separate museum of Meissen at Schloss Lustheim, near Munich.

Only a few Americans seem to have taken much interest in Meissen, or German eighteenth-century porcelain in general, before the 1920s. George B. McClellan, in a charming essay on collecting in the guide to his collection of German and Austrian tablewares given to the Metropolitan Museum of Art, wrote that his father bought German porcelain on visits abroad in the 1860s and 1870s. The nature of that group, destroyed by fire in 1881, is unknown, but it must have been among the first of its kind here. Meissen was well represented in the large collection of European porcelain formed by the New York clergyman Rev. Alfred Duane Pell, part of it going to the Metropolitan Museum as early as 1902, while later gifts were made to other American museums before and after his death in 1924. At that time Ralph and Constance Wark began their notable collection, which came to emphasize painted decoration at Meissen during its first fifty years. Now in the Cummer Gallery of Art, Jacksonville, Florida, its over 700 examples include many exceptional for quality and rarity.

On the whole, however, Americans were more attracted by English and French porcelain. It was only after the 1930s, when many central Europeans familiar with the porcelain art of Germany settled in this country, that a market could develop to attract serious collectors and dealers. The results of this influx of connoisseurship and works of art may be seen in many public collections, nowhere more so than at the Metropolitan Museum, where the R. Thornton Wilson, Untermyer, Sheafer and Linsky collections now enable the Museum to show the most comprehensive view of the Meissen factory's accomplishments to be found in this country. Scholarly catalogues have been published of the Untermyer and Linsky collections, as has one of the Meissen section of the broadly representative collection of German porcelain given by Hans Syz to the Smithsonian Institution's Museum of History and Technology.

Dealers' invoices to Morgan from 1899 to 1910 account for two-thirds of the 362 pieces of Meissen at Hartford. Most of it came from Duveen in London; Morgan bought his first Meissen there in May 1899, four cabinets of "fine old Dresden" containing no less than 161 pieces. These were all figures except for eight lots of vases and candlesticks, and this proportion holds for his Meissen as a whole, as there is almost no tableware. From 1901 to 1910 another seventy-five items came from Duveen, as did three from Julius Goldschmidt in Frankfurt. Brief descriptions in invoices rarely permit identification with specific pieces, and information on provenance is wholly lacking. On the few occasions that Morgan used dealers other than Duveen or Goldschmidt, it was to acquire single works that are both large in scale and of particular interest.

As a whole, the Morgan Meissen reflects fashionable taste at the turn of the century which preferred the factory's interpretations of the rococo. This accorded with the use of "Dresden" as a decorative element of the revived eighteenth-century styles in vogue from the 1870s onward. There was ample precedent for this, as it was just these kinds of *Saxe* figures which the Paris luxury merchants of the 1740s and 1750s had had mounted with gilt-bronze to harmonize them with their settings.

That Morgan did not attach the importance to the Meissen that he did to his French porcelain may be inferred from the fact that he kept it at his country house outside of London rather than in his London residence at Princes Gate, or at the Victoria and Albert Museum. So far as is known, he received no specialist advice on Meissen, and thus his *en bloc* purchases include, as well as some fine pieces, a substantial number that are of slight aesthetic quality, are much restored, or that are defective factory "seconds" with later decoration.

Among Kaendler's most singular creations are figures gently satirizing the vagaries of aristocratic and court society at Dresden. These include the "crinoline groups," so-called because of the great play he made with that curiosity of fashion. The Morgan collection has examples of outstanding quality, and they form the heart of this selection of porcelain sculpture, which also includes religious, mythological, allegorical, pastoral, and chinoiserie subjects, as well as animals and birds.

MEISSEN REFERENCES:

Albiker, 1935/1959	Albiker, Carl. *Die Meissner Porzellantiere im 18. Jahrhundert.* Berlin, 1935. 2d ed. 1959.
Berling, 1900	Berling, Karl. *Das Meissner Porzellan und seine Geschichte.* Leipzig, 1900.
Berling, 1911	*Festive Publication to Commemorate the 200th Jubilee of the Oldest European China Factory, Meissen.* Dresden, 1911. (reprint, New York, 1972).
Boehn	Boehn, Max von. *Modes and Manners, Vol. IV, The Eighteenth Century.* London, 1935.
Bursche	Bursche, Stefan. *Meissen Steinzeug und Porzellan des 18 Jahrhunderts, Kunstgewerbemuseum Berlin.* Berlin, 1980.
Charleston	Charleston, R. J. *Meissen and Other European Porcelain . . . The James A. de Rothschild Collection at Waddesdon Manor.* London, 1971.
Courajod	Courajod, Louis. *Livre-Journal de Lazare Duvaux, marchand-bijoutier ordinaire du Roy, 1748–1758.* Paris, 1873 (reprint, Paris, 1965, 2 vols.).
Gröger	Gröger, Helmuth. *Johann Joachim Kaendler, der Meister des Porzellans.* Dresden, 1956.
Hackenbroch	Hackenbroch, Yvonne. *Meissen and Other Continental Porcelain, Faience and Enamel in the Irwin Untermyer Collection.* London, 1956.
Hofmann, 1932/1980	Hofmann, Friedrich H. *Das Porzellan der Europäischen Manufakturen im XVIII. Jahrhundert.* Berlin, 1932. 2d ed. 1980.
Honey, 1954	Honey, William B. *Dresden China: An Introduction to the Study of Meissen Porcelain.* London, 1934 (reissued, Troy, N. Y., 1946; London, 1954).
Hood, 1964	Hood, Graham. "Meissen from the J. P. Morgan Collection," *Wadsworth Atheneum Bulletin,* 5th ser., no. 17 (Summer, 1964): 1–15.
Hood, 1965	———. "America's Cultural Debt to J. P. Morgan: Meissen Porcelain from His Collection at Wadsworth Atheneum," *Connoisseur* 158 (March, 1965): 195–201.
Jean-Richard	Jean-Richard, Pierrette. *L'oeuvre gravé de François Boucher dans la Collection Edmond de Rothschild (Musée du Louvre, Cabinet des Dessins, Collection Edmond de Rothschild, Inventaire général des gravures, Ecole francaise, I).* Paris, 1978.
Jedding	Jedding, Hermann. *Meissner Porzellan des 18. Jahrhunderts in Hamburger Privatbesitz, Museum für Kunst/und Gewerbe Hamburg.* Hamburg, 1982.
Le Corbeiller	Le Corbeiller, Clare. "Porcelains." *The Jack and Belle Linsky Collection in The Metropolitan Museum of Art.* New York, 1984.
McClellan	McClellan, George B. *A Guide to the McClellan Collection of German and Austrian Porcelain.* New York, 1946.
Pauls	Pauls-Eisenbeiss, Erika. *German Porcelain of the 18th Century: The Pauls-Eisenbeiss Collection, Vol. I, Meissen from the Beginning until 1760.* London, 1972.
Pfeiffer	Pfeiffer, Max Adolf. "Ein Beitrag zur Quellengeschichte des europäischen Porzellans" (transcription of Kaendler's *Taxa,* 1740–48). *Werden und Wirken, ein Festgrüss, Karl W. Hiersemann* (Leipzig, 1924): 267–87.
Rückert	Rückert, Rainer. *Meissener Porzellan: 1710–1810.* Munich, 1966.
Sponsel	Sponsel, Jean Louis. *Kabinettstücke der Meissner Porzellanmanufaktur von Johann Joachim Kandler.* Leipzig, 1900.
Syz	Syz, Hans, J. Jefferson Miller II and Rainer Rückert. *Catalogue of the Hans Syz Collection, Vol. I, Meissen Porcelain and Hausmalerei.* Washington, D.C., 1979.
Zimmermann, 1908	Zimmermann, Ernst. *Die Erfindung und Frühzeit des Meissner Porzellans.* Berlin, 1908.
Zimmermann, 1926	———. *Meissner Porzellan.* Leipzig, 1926.

TWO BUSTS OF SAINTS
German, Meissen, about 1743. Models by
J. J. Kaendler and P. Reinicke, 1743
Hard-paste porcelain, unpainted

38a. Franciscan Saint looking right.
Factory mold no. 14
Marks: faint crossed swords in underglaze blue
(on back edge)
H. 11¾ in. (29.9 cm.) (porcelain only)
Printed paper label: Collezione Sangiorgi
1917.1507

In 1710 Annibale Albani (1682–1751) came to Dresden as papal nuncio in order to prepare the crown prince, later Augustus III, for his conversion to Catholicism; Albani received the Cardinal's hat in 1712 at the successful conclusion of his mission. Two years after succeeding as ruler of Saxony-Poland in 1733, Augustus III comissioned an altar service modeled by Kaendler for his old mentor,[1] now an influential figure at the Vatican, and who had kept closely in touch with the Dresden court, a Catholic enclave in a Protestant country. He must also have been well abreast of artistic projects at Dresden, where many Italian artists were employed, notably on the great new Catholic Court Church by Gaetano Chiaveri, begun in 1738, with sculptural embellishment by Lorenzo Mattielli.

It is plausible that reports of Kaendler's growing reputation would reach Rome as his remarkable versatility constantly widened the repertoire of porcelain. Kaendler was first trained as a sculptor, and a strong sculptural sense informs his best work. Thus it is not surprising that a patron in Italy, the home of a great sculptural tradition, might be attracted by that side of Kaendler's talent where his abilities as a late baroque sculptor were particularly evident. In 1743 Albani ordered a series of papal portrait busts,[2] and in or about the same year Kaendler modeled at least eight busts of religious figures for the cardinal and another member of his family.[3] The Hartford busts were almost certainly among them.[4]

These vigorously modeled busts are of men whose cowled habit terminating in a corded molding identifies them as Franciscans, though there are no further attributes by which to identify them as specific saints.[5] Openings in the back of the heads may have held metal halos as well as acting as firing vents. In a third, similar bust the bearded head is turned right and looking down.[6]

As the porcelain material of the Hartford busts is compatible with an origin about 1743, they may be ones that were sent to Cardinal Albani.

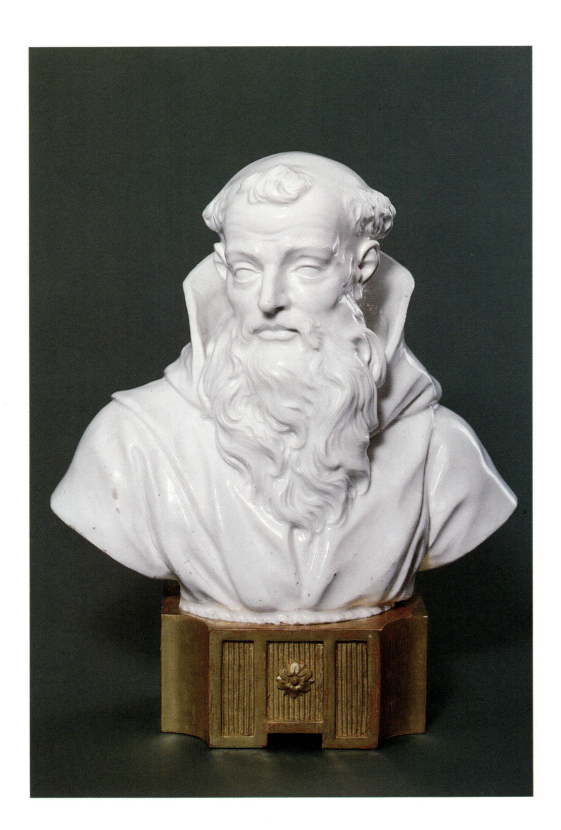

Notes:

[1] Karl Berling, "Altarschmuck aus Meissner Porzellan, ein Geschenk an die verwitwete Kaiserin Amalie," *Kunst und Kunsthandwerk* 16 (1913), pp. 125–135; Rainer Rückert, "Neue Funde zur Wiener Altargarnitur," *Keramos* 50 (1970), pp. 122–129.

[2] Modeled by Kaendler: Berling, 1911, p. 40, fig. 66, as assisted by Eberlein; Zimmermann, p. 175, fig. 50, as assisted by Reinicke.

[3] "*The Mother of God,*" for Prince Albani: Kaendler, *Taxa,* 1740–48 (Pfeiffer, p. 279); Zimmermann, p. 139, plate 34 (incorrectly dated 1738 as the bust is confused with the standing Virgin and Child modeled that year).

"*An old woman in mourning dress*": Kaendler, *Taxa,* 1740–48 (Pfeiffer, p. 280); perhaps the "bust in the form of a woman," for Cardinal Albani, December 1743 (Gröger, p. 83).

"*An old man in antique style,*" for Prince Albani: Kaendler, *Taxa,* 1740–48 (Pfeiffer, p. 280).

St. Sebastian: Berling, 1911, p. 44, fig. 86 (assisted by Reinicke, 1743); as "ordered for Rome," March 1743 (Gröger, p. 83).

St. Rosalia, for Prince Albani: Berling, 1911, p. 44, fig. 85 (assisted by Reinicke, 1743).

[4] These may be among "a large bust for Cardinal Albani," August 1743, or "some busts for the above named Cardinal," about December 1743 (Gröger, p. 83).

[5] The saint looking right: Berling, 1911, p. 44, fig. 82 (by Kaendler and Reinicke, 1743). An example of the saint looking up was in the C. H. Fischer sale, Cologne, 22–25 October 1906, no. 976, repr.

[6] Berling, 1911, p. 44, fig. 81 (by Kaendler and Reinicke, 1743). George Savage, *Eighteenth Century German Porcelain* (New York, 1958), plate 43c (example in the W. S. Stout Collection, Dixon Gallery and Gardens, Memphis).

38b. Franciscan Saint looking up
Marks: faint crossed swords in underglaze blue (on back edge)
H. 12¾ in. (32.4 cm.) (porcelain only)
Printed paper label: Collezione Sangiorgi
1917.1508

Provenance: Bought from Sangiorgi Gallery, Rome, 1911

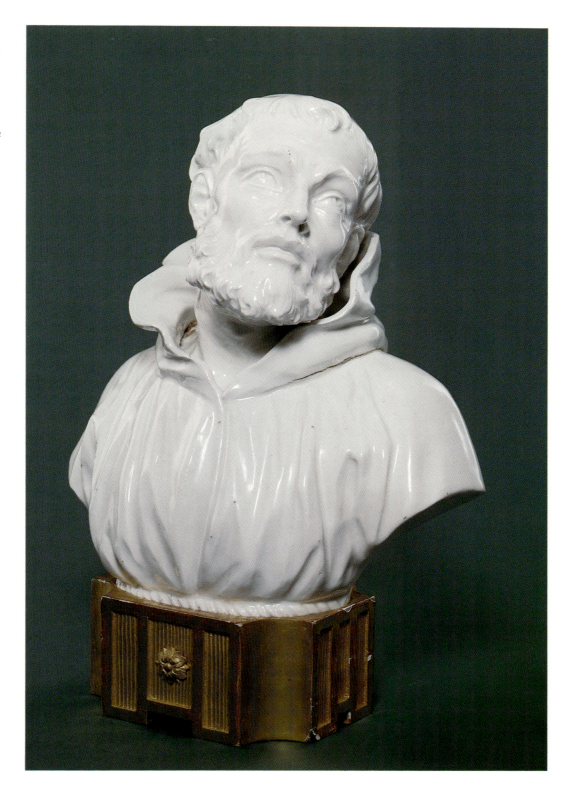

THE JUDGMENT OF PARIS
German, Meissen, about 1762. Model attributed to J. J. Kaendler, about 1762
Hard-paste porcelain painted with enamel colors, gilt and silvered.
In plan the group is an irregular, lobed rhomboid, the edges formed by a series of rococo scrolls. There are ten sections: 1) Paris seated; 2) a rocky mound with oak and palm trees; 3) Juno seated in a chariot resting on clouds and drawn by 4) two peacocks; 5) Venus with doves receiving the apple from Paris; 6) Minerva with helmet, breastplate, and shield, an owl at her feet; 7) a tree; 8) Mercury running and carrying a *caduceus* and bag; 9) two sheep; and 10) oak tree and dog scratching itself. The silvering of Minerva's breastplate and Mercury's helmet has turned black. Factory mold nos. 2906–16.
Marks: crossed swords in underglaze blue beneath the open glazed base of each section. Letters incised on internal opposing faces indicate how sections fit together. Incised in socket on rocky mound: *Paris Platz.*
H. 23 in. (58.4 cm.); L. 26 in. (66 cm.); W. 33 in. (83.8 cm.)
Provenance: Bought from Cartier et Fils, Paris, 22 Nov. 1906
1917.1482 A–K

In Greek mythology, the goddess Eris, or Strife, threw a golden apple inscribed "For the fairest" among the guests at the wedding of Peleus and Thetis. As Juno, Minerva, and Venus all claimed it, Jupiter ordered them to submit the decision to a mortal. After he chose the shepherd Paris, son of King Priam of Troy, Mercury led the goddesses to Mount Ida where Paris was tending his sheep. Juno offered him riches and power, Minerva victory in war, and Venus the fairest of women for his wife. Paris awarded the apple to Venus; she helped him win Helen of Sparta, whose abduction precipitated the Trojan War.

Kaendler and Eberlein are said to have modeled a large *Judgment of Paris* in 1745 for Count Brühl.[1] This may be the group an example of which is in the Pauls collection.[2] Later, when Prussia occupied Saxony during the Seven Years War, an example of Brühl's group was among the vast quantities of Meissen seized from existing stock.[3] Frederick the Great's close interest in porcelain extended much further than booty of war, however. Despite the pressures of campaigning, he repeatedly visited the factory, and issued detailed orders for new designs of all types. On 11 November 1762 the king himself gave an already overwhelmed Kaendler a further long list of entirely new models of figures, table services, and vases to be delivered by the end of April 1763. These specifications included the Judgment of Paris with a base as the centerpiece of an ensemble of eight groups of mythological couples,[4] all nine elements to be "1½ Fuss hoch."[5] The number and large size of the groups must have required assistants, but as work records for this time are missing, attributions are uncertain, though Kaendler's central role may be assumed. The couples have been variously attributed to him, to Friedrich Elias Meyer, and to Carl Christoph Punct.[6] However, while some figures show Meyer's characteristic elongated proportions and small heads, he had left the factory in 1761, Punct succeeding him that year. The date of the king's order is in agreement with dating as estimated from the mold numbers, though work on this ensemble must have continued for several months.[7]

The fine modeling of this complex group make an attribution to Kaendler reasonable. While the slightly grayish paste of some sections appears in other war period productions, the painting is of the factory's highest quality. Colors are brilliant, and applied with restraint. Only one other contemporary, unpainted, example is known.[8]

Notes:
[1] Zimmermann, p. 183.
[2] Pauls, pp. 158–160, H. 33 cm., made in two sections. The figures are Paris, Venus with Cupid, Minerva, and Juno. This group is now in the Historisches Museum, Basel.
[3] Zimmermann, p. 237.
[4] Sponsel, p. 202–203. The couples were: 1) Apollo and Daphne; 2) Pan and Syrinx; 3) Venus and Adonis; 4) Diana and Endymion; 5) Orcus and Cephalus; 6) Bacchus and Ariadne; 7) Jupiter and Semele; and 8) Hercules and Dejanira.
[5] As the *fuss* is roughly equivalent to our foot, this is about 46 cm. *Diana and Endymion* (Hofmann, fig. 164, 46 cm.); *Venus and Adonis* (E. Zimmermann, "Von Friedrich dem Grossen neu in Auftrag gegebene Meissner Porzellane," *Cicerone* 2 [1910], p. 54, fig. 3, 45 cm.)
[6] *Apollo and Daphne* (Berling [1910], pp. 56–57, fig. 115, as Kaendler); *Pan and Syrinx* (ibid., fig. 116, as Meyer); *Diana and Endymion* (Hofmann, fig. 164, as Meyer); *Venus and Adonis* (Zimmermann, p. 241, plate 53, as probably Punct). Apparently, no examples of the other four couples are known.
[7] Factory mold numbers are between 2890 and 2996 (Berling [1911], p. 56 and note 245); for estimated dating from mold numbers see Rückert, p. 42.
[8] Residenzmuseum, Munich (Herbert Brunner, *Die Kunstschätze der Münchner Residenz* [Munich, 1977], p. 231, fig. 256, as incorrectly attributed to M. V. Acier and dated about 1770). Three sections bear mold numbers 2096.143, 2908.43, and 2913. How and when the group came into the possession of the Munich court is not known.

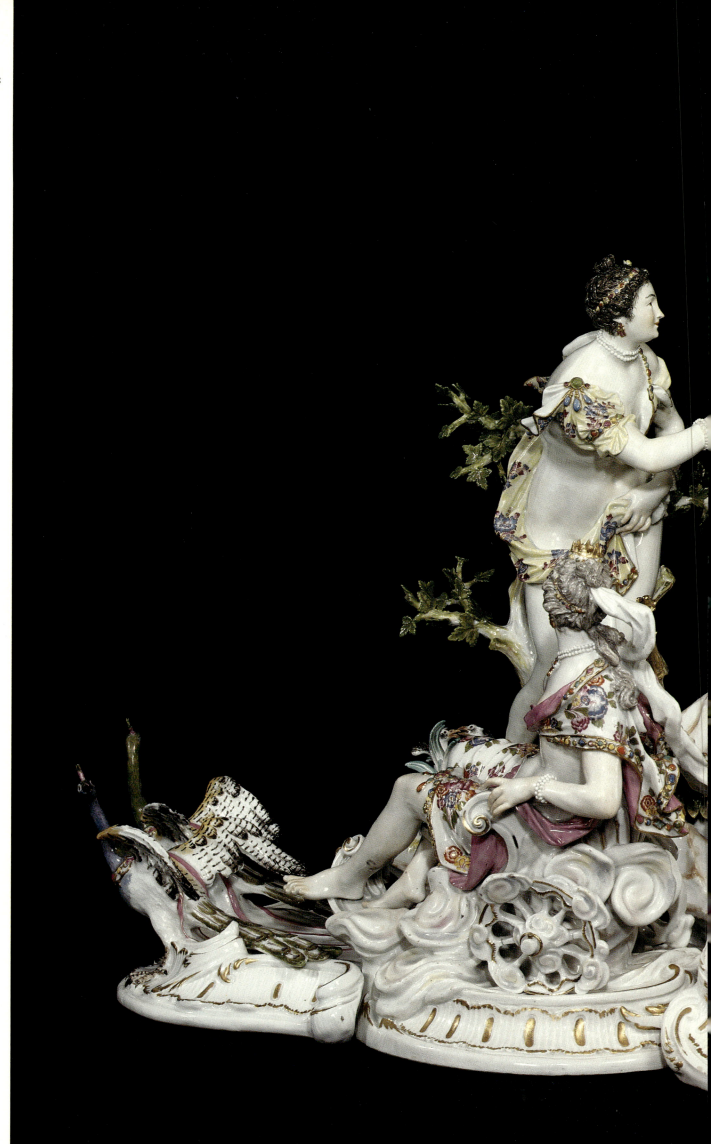

ALLEGORIES OF THE FOUR CONTINENTS
German, Meissen, about 1760
Hard-paste porcelain, painted with enamel colors and gilt.
Mounted on later gilt bronze bases.

40a. *Europe*. Model by J. F. Eberlein, 1746–47. A woman wearing a crown
and robe, and holding an orb and scepter is seated on an architectural
fragment near attributes including a world globe, books, pallet,
and mallet. Factory mold no. 860.
H. 10¼ in. (26 cm.); L. 11¼ in. (28.6 cm.)
1917.1295

40b. *Asia*. Model by J. F. Eberlein, P. Reinicke, and J. J. Kaendler, 1745.
A richly jeweled woman wearing a turban with a crescent and holding
a scepter and a censer is seated on a caparisoned camel by a palm tree.
Factory mold no. 687.
H. 12⅛ in. (30.8 cm.); L. 9¹⁵⁄₁₆in. (25.2 cm.)
1917.1292

40c. *Africa.* Model by J. J. Kaendler, 1745. A woman wearing an elephant-head helmet, robe, feathered girdle, and leggings, and holding a scepter and stalks of wheat is seated on a lion. Factory mold no. 689.
H. 12¼ in. (31.1 cm.); L. 9¼ in. (23.5 cm.)
1917.1293

40d. *America.* Model by J. F. Eberlein, P. Reinicke and J. J. Kaendler, 1745. A woman wearing a feathered headdress, robe, and short skirt is seated on a crocodile. She has a jeweled girdle around her waist and holds a parrot and cornucopia of fruit. Factory mold no. 858.
H. 10¾ in. (27.3 cm.); L. 13⅛ in. (33.3 cm.)
1917.1294
Provenance: Bought from Charles Davis, London, 5 June 1900

These groups were part of a commission from a Russian grand duchess.[1] All were completed in 1745 except *Europe*, delayed by Eberlein's illness.[2]

Complete sets of these large *Continents* are quite rare.[3] The slightly yellow tone of the porcelain and warped bases suggest these examples may be "seconds" taken from storage and decorated at the factory during the Seven Years War.[4]

The *Continents* are better known in the smaller versions Kaendler modeled in 1746.[5]

Notes:
[1]Berling (1911), p. 42.
[2]Albiker (1959), nos. 260–263

Europe: Eberlein, October 1746: "One figure of a continent representing Europe, begun for the Russian order." February 1747: "Worked on the continent representing Europe, the rest of the time was sick." March 1747: "The rest of the time, as much as possible during severe sickness, continued the group of Europe." May 1747: "Finished the continent of Europe, composed of a figure of a queen seated by many instruments of art and science; behind her stands a horse."

Asia: Eberlein, August 1745: "Began a group of one of the four continents representing Asia in the form of a Turkish woman sitting on a camel, in the right hand a scepter, the left holding a censer; belonging to and uniform with the Russian order." Reinicke, September 1745: "Entirely finished neatly modeling in clay Asia, represented by a figure sitting on a camel, with garments richly trimmed with embroidery and precious stones, in one hand holding a scepter, in the other a censer." Kaendler, September 1745: "Divided up in the proper way and prepared for molding the model of a large group representing a continent as a woman sitting on a camel."

Africa: Kaendler, *Taxa*, after 28 September 1745: "One group representing Africa, namely a woman in appropriate garments with an elephant helmet on her head sitting on a lion. 20 Thalers." Kaendler, October 1745: "Divided up and gave over for molding the model of a group of one of the continents representing Africa."

America: Eberlein, September 1745: "One figure of the continents, namely a woman sitting on a crocodile with a parrot on her hand and a cornucopia; uniform with the Russian order; however, not yet finished." Reinicke, October 1745: "One group representing America by a figure sitting on a crocodile, her garb of feathers ornamented with precious stones and pearls; already begun and completely finished." Kaendler, October 1745: "Corrected and then divided up and gave over for molding the model of a group of the continent America, a woman sitting on a crocodile."

[3]Jedding, nos. 238–241, lists examples.
[4]A list of factory "seconds" dated 2 May 1761 includes *Continents*, though whether these were the large or small models is not clear (Sponsel, p. 197).
[5]E.g. Pauls, pp. 134–137; Jedding, nos. 238–241.

BUYING HEART-SHAPED BOXES
German, Meissen, about 1740–45. Model by J. J. Kaendler, about 1738
Hard-paste porcelain, painted with enamel colors and gilt. A woman
wearing a yellow skirt with oriental flowers over a red crinoline,
a green-edged puce robe with gilt flowers, and a short blue cape lined
with ermine is seated in a high-backed baroque chair. She holds up a
heart-shaped box to a gallant; a snuff box is in her other hand. His coat
has a grey diaper pattern, its gilt cuffs with oriental flowers matching
his vest; he also holds up a box. A girl pedlar offers an octagonal box
from her trinket box; her "Tyrolean" garb includes a green hat,
blue-green and black bodice, and skirt having puce stripes incised with
wavy lines. A blackamoor page holding a cup and saucer on a tray
stands at the back. Factory mold no. 100.
H. 8$\frac{1}{16}$ in. (20.4 cm.)
1917.1342

This is one of the earlier crinoline groups,[1] so-called in recent times
because of the extravagant skirt which, from 1736 until nearly 1745,
Kaendler made the leitmotif of figures and groups satirizing the manners
and affectations of court society. They are among his most original
inventions, their wit wholly his own, though some inspiration for figure
types probably came from the factory's large collection of engravings
after Watteau, his followers, Boucher, and other French artists.[2]

As the subject, except for the pedlar, is a variation of Kaendler's
Handkissing Group of 1737,[3] it seems likely to have been modeled soon
after; the fine painting of the Wadsworth example is probably a few years
later than the model date. The page's figure is a later addition to the
Hartford group. It almost certainly replaces a damaged figure, as a page
of this or of another type is a normal element of the group's composition.

Notes:
[1]Rückert, nos. 859, 860.
[2]Other crinoline groups include catalogue nos. 43, 45, 46, 47.
[3]Rückert, no. 857; Bursche, nos. 304, 305.

Literature: Wadsworth Atheneum Handbook (1958), p. 107.

42

TWO FREEMASONS
German, Meissen, soon after 1744. Model by J. J. Kaendler, 1744
Hard-paste porcelain, painted with enamel colors and gilt.
The standing man measuring a globe with dividers wears a puce coat
having gilt cuffs with oriental flowers that match his vest. The seated
man's coat has a grey diaper pattern, also with gilt cuffs and vest.
Both wear yellow and blue Masonic aprons. Behind them is a column
section with base; in front, a Corinthian capital. Factory mold no. 376
Marks: very faint crossed swords in blue under the base.
H. 9$\frac{1}{8}$ in. (23.3 cm.)
1917.1376

In this group,[1] more explicit in its irony than the single *Freemason*
(No. 44), the seated man's rank as a Master is shown by the gilt angle
square worn from his neck and the turned-down apron bib.[2]

Notes:
[1]Kaendler, *Taxa*, 1740–48: "A small group of two Freemasons, one standing
and measuring off a globe, one hand by his mouth; the other sitting and
speculating. Both wear their aprons and orders. 16 thalers" (Pfeiffer, p. 277).
Kaendler, May 1744: "A new small Freemasonry group divided up, etc."
Kaendler, November 1744: "A new small Freemasonry group divided up as
necessary so that it can be executed in porcelain as soon as possible"
(Rückert, no. 872).
[2]Bursche, no. 310. The single *Freemason* also wears Master's insignia.

Literature: Hood, 1964, p. 14, fig. 13; Hood, 1965, p. 200, fig. 12.

43

A LADY OF THE *MOPSORDEN*
German, Meissen, soon after 1744. Model by J. J. Kaendler, 1744
Hard-paste porcelain, painted with enamel colors and gilt.
A woman standing on a pedestal is holding a pug dog, with another
at her feet. She wears a yellow bodice; the black skirt, worn over a red
crinoline, is painted with oriental flowers and has a purple front panel
incised with a feathery leaf pattern. The pedestal has four panels
painted with gallant figures in park landscapes, and gilt ornaments at
the corners.
Marks: faint crossed swords in blue under the base
H. 11³⁄₁₆ in. (28.4 cm.)
1917.1328

The *Mopsorden*, or Order of the Pug, named for a favorite lapdog of the
period reputed for its loyalty and spirit, was a substitute at Catholic
courts in Germany for Freemasonry, prohibited by Pope Clement XII in
1738.[1] Its rituals were lighthearted versions of Masonic ceremonies; but

unlike the Freemasons, the order accepted women. This model,
evidently meant to complement the Freemason (no. 44), was made by
Kaendler for the Princess of Herford, ruler of a small ecclesiastical state.[2]

The figure's broadly treated colorism and the fine delicacy of the
pedestal landscapes are of notable quality.

Notes:
[1] Hackenbroch, fig. 28; E. Kollmann, "Der Mopsorden," *Keramos* 50 (1970),
pp. 71–82.
[2] Joanne Charlotte of Anhalt-Dessau, who governed the prince-bishopric of
Herford from 1729 to 1750 (Pauls, p. 206). Kaendler, *Taxa*, 1740–48: "A lady
of the Order of the Pug standing on a pedestal and holding a pug in the left
hand with another at her feet, for the Princess of Herford. 10 thalers" (Pfeiffer,
p. 280). Kaendler, June 1744: "The model of a well-dressed woman with two
pug dogs properly divided up and readied for making molds" (Rückert,
no. 873).

Literature: Hood, 1964, p. 12, fig. 11; Hood, 1965, p. 199, fig. 9.

44

A FREEMASON

German, Meissen, soon after 1743. Model by J. J. Kaendler, 1743
Hard-paste porcelain, painted with enamel colors and gilt.
Man standing on a pedestal and wearing the Masonic apron and a blue
coat whose gilt cuffs with oriental flowers match his vest; behind him
is a tree stump. One hand held a rolled paper (now missing), the
other rests on a pedestal with Masonic attributes. Both pedestals have
marbleized panels, the large one with gilt leaf ornament at the corners.
Marks: faint crossed swords in blue under the base
H. 11 11/16 in. (29.8 cm.)
1917.1353

In the 1720s the Masonic order spread rapidly within aristocratic circles
from Britain to the Continent, in 1733 reaching Germany. The first
Saxon lodge was founded in 1739,[1] and the enthusiasm there for
Freemasonry is reflected in several figures modeled by Kaendler within a
short period, this being first among them.[2]

Notes:
[1] Jedding, no. 218.
[2] Kaendler, *Taxa*, 1740–48: "A Freemason standing on a pedestal with his apron and other attributes, finely dressed and holding a plan in one hand; lying on another pedestal beside him are a justifier, protractor and plummet, 6 Thalers" (Pfeiffer, p. 276); Zimmermann, p. 190, as 1743. The figure wears the Masonic insignia of a Master (see cat. no. 44).

Literature: Hood, 1964, p. 14, fig. 13; Hood, 1965, p. 200, not illustrated.

45

COURTIER AND LADY
German, Meissen, about 1745–50. Model by J. J. Kaendler, 1744
Hard-paste porcelain, painted with enamel colors and gilt. The man
wears a white coat with a blue sash and vest, the woman a white robe
with oriental flowers over a pink crinoline. Factory mold no. 550.
H. 8¼ in. (21 cm.)
1917.1330

While the man is wearing the Polish Order of the Eagle, Kaendler's
description makes it clear this is not Augustus III and his queen, as has
been supposed.[1] The figure of the woman is similar to the *Lady of the
Mopsorden* modeled the same year (no. 43).

Notes:
[1]Kaendler, *Taxa* (Pfeiffer, p. 280): "One small group of a cavalier wearing a
star on his chest and the Polish Order, and also holding a snuff box, leading a
lady in full dress by the hand. 16 Thalers." Berling (1911), p. 35 gives the date
as 1744.

46

COUPLE KISSING

German, Meissen, about 1745. Model by J. J. Kaendler, about 1743–45
Hard-paste porcelain, painted in enamel colors and gilt. The man's
coat is diaper-patterned in puce; he wears a gold vest with oriental
flowers and blue-green breeches. The woman's yellow robe, with a
black front panel and blue-green lapels and cuffs, is worn over a
crinoline, has oriental flowers, and is edged with a band of leaves,
flowers, and gold strapwork. Factory mold no. 518.
H. 7$\frac{15}{16}$ in. (20.3 cm.)
1917.1343

Kaendler adapted this pose from a print by Laurent Cars after François
Boucher illustrating Molière's comedy *Dom Garcie de Navarre, ou le prince
jaloux*.[1]

The model is a fairly rare one,[2] and the decoration of this example is of
particularly good quality in color and costume patterns.

Notes:
[1] From *Oeuvres de Molière*, new ed. (Paris, 1734) (Jean-Richard, no. 407).
[2] Rückert, no. 874; Bursche, no. 307.

47

FAMILY GROUP
German, Meissen, about 1744; model by J. J. Kaendler, 1744
Hard-paste porcelain painted with enamel colors and gilt. A woman sitting in a rococo chair is wearing a crinoline beneath a peach-color dress painted with oriental flowers. On her lap she holds a small child in a long dress who wears a violet-luster and gilt cap. A man in a white coat with gilt cuffs painted with oriental flowers to match his vest leans over to kiss the woman.
Marks: trace of mark under flat base
H. 6¾ in. (16.2 cm.)
1917.1334

Like cat. nos. 45 and 46, this group has a grace of outline and harmonious rhythm in composition appropriate to the sentiment of these subjects.[1] These groups may be contrasted with the tellingly jagged rhythms of *The Gout Sufferer* (no. 48) or the energetic, thrusting ones of *Shepherd Musicians* (no. 49).

Notes:
[1] Kaendler, *Taxa*, 1740–48: "A group of three figures, namely a very well-dressed lady sitting on a chair and holding a child on her lap wearing a little fur hat and a long robe; a cavalier is near the lady" (Pfeiffer, p. 280). Zimmermann, p. 186 (as 1744); Pauls, pp. 208–209; Bursche, no. 308.

Literature: Siegfried Ducret, *German Porcelain and Faience* (New York, 1962), no. 45, repr.

48

THE GOUT SUFFERER

German, Meissen, about 1745–50. Model by J. J. Kaendler, 1745
Hard-paste porcelain, painted with enamel colors and gilt. A man in a
long white robe and black breeches, his lower legs bare, sits on a bench
and holds a glass. A kneeling woman in a white dress with oriental
flowers holds his foot on a towel; nearby are a footstool and bottles.
Factory mold no. 696.
H. 5⅝ in. (14.3 cm.)
1917.1431

This singular theme was developed by Kaendler from a print after
Boucher of a woman assisting a young man with his stocking, whose
gallant context was transformed into a sharply ironic commentary on
"woman helps man."[1]

    The child mentioned in Kaendler's description is missing from most
examples.[2]

Notes:
[1]Giselda Zick, "Kaendler and Lafontaine," Keramos 53–54 (1971), pp. 97–107.
The print is by Nicolas de Larmessin after Boucher, La courtisane amoureuse,
from Suite d'estampes nouvelles pour les contes de La Fontaine (Jean-Richard,
no. 1252).
[2]Kaendler, Taxa, September 1745: "One group composed of three figures,
namely a gout sufferer seated on a canape and crying out over his pain; near
him a woman is putting a little bed under his leg (Pfeiffer, p. 284). Nearby is a
child eating porridge from a pan. 16 Thalers." Kaendler, October 1745:
"The model for one group divided up and sent to storage; a gout sufferer sits
on a canape and cries out; a woman has various wine bottles nearby." Peter
Reinicke, March 1745: "A figure representing a gout sufferer, 12 Zoll high,
began the modeling in clay" (Rückert no. 880). As Rückert suggests, the
large size mentioned in the last entry probably refers to a preliminary model.

SHEPHERD MUSICIANS
German, Meissen, soon after 1744. Model by J. J. Kaendler, 1744
Hard-paste porcelain, painted in enamel colors and gilt. The woman playing a lute wears a small feathered hat and white cape; her tiered skirt with white, puce, and yellow panels has a stylized floral border. The singing man holds a sheet of music inscribed "Aria." He wears a white cape over a slashed red jacket incised with a floral pattern, black hat and breeches, and red stockings; a sheep is at his feet. The music sheet is partly missing. Factory mold no. 520.
Marks: faint crossed swords in blue and "34" impressed twice under the base
H. 8⅝ in. (22 cm.)
1917.1381

While Kaendler describes the couple as shepherds, his second entry shows their costumes were given a special twist,[1] and their distinctly theatrical flavor recalls his many Italian Comedy figures of this period.[2]

The painting of this example, with several features left white and the man's jacket decorated by drawing on the wet enamel with a sharp point, is particularly attractive.

Notes:
[1]Kaendler, *Taxa:* "A group representing a shepherd and shepherdess, the latter playing the lute, a sheep lying by them. 16 Thalers" (Pfeiffer, p. 279). Kaendler, February 1744: "A very painstaking shepherd group divided up and ready for molding. The shepherdess playing the lute sits under a green tree next to the shepherd, who is singing from sheet music; both are most elegantly tricked out" (Jedding, no. 212).
[2]In a seated group of 1740–41, differently costumed, and with music-making roles reversed, the man is identified as Scaramouche (Rückert, no. 865). Hackenbroch, fig. 45 and Bursche, no. 313 cite the only example known with the tree Kaendler mentions.

SHEPHERD LOVERS
German, Meissen, early 1740s. Model by J. J. Kaendler, early 1740s
Hard-paste porcelain, painted in enamel colors and gilt. The man's
jacket is puce with black and gold oriental flowers, his blouse white,
and breeches blue-green. A dog is at his side. The woman's bodice is
black and red, the skirt yellow with a wide flower, leaf, and lambre-
quin border; her blouse and apron are white. Factory mold no. D 19.
Marks: faint crossed swords in blue under the base
H. 6⅓ in. (16.5 cm.)
1917.1493

For his figures, including the dog and lamb, Kaendler used a pastoral
subject after Boucher, making fewer changes than usual,[1] but character-
istically altering the original's sentimental sweetness in his translation.[2]
"The astringent touch of mockery is seldom absent from these groups:
thus a pair of Shepherd Lovers languidly inclined toward each other are
made absurd by the fixed forward stare of the dog and sheep."[3]

Notes:
[1]Gabriel Huquier the Elder, after Boucher, from *Quatrième livre de sujets et
pastorales* (Pierre-Richard, no. 1156).
[2]Kaendler, *Taxa:* "A group representing a well-dressed woman in an *Andrijan*,
also a well-clad shepherd in his habit; they are embracing one another. A lamb
is also to be found" (Pfeiffer, 276 and Rückert, no. 869). The *Andrienne* was a
long, loose robe brought into fashion by an actress who wore it in Terence's
play *Andria*; the shepherdess here is wearing a more practical apron, however
(Boehn, p. 176).
[3]Honey, p. 112.

PAIR OF MALABAR MUSICIANS
German, Meissen, mid-eighteenth century. Models by F. E. Meyer,
about 1751
Hard-paste porcelain, painted with enamel colors and gilt.

54a. Woman Playing a Hurdy-Gurdy (photo left)
She is standing and singing, wearing a straw hat and fur-lined puce
robe over a pale yellow skirt with oriental flowers. She carries a
lantern on her back. Rococo-scrolled base with an urn.
Factory mold no. 1519.
Marks: crossed swords in underglaze blue (at edge of flat base)
H. 12$\frac{7}{16}$ in. (31.7 cm.)
1917.1315

54b. Man Playing a Guitar (photo right)
He is standing and singing, wearing a straw hat and fur-lined blue robe
over a pale puce gown. Four white mice are on the hat and robe.
Rococo-scrolled base. Factory mold no. 1523.
Marks: crossed swords in underglaze blue (inside open base)
H. 12$\frac{7}{16}$ in. (31.7 cm.)
1917.1314

"Malabars," named for the Malabar coast of India, was the term
Diderot's *Encyclopédie* used for Indians in general. When Friedrich
Eberlein made the first of these exotic types in 1746, he identified it
simply as an "Indian woman,"[1] though by 1749 they were known in Paris
as *Malabares*.[2]

The musician Malabars were done a few years later, almost certainly
by Meyer, who came to Meissen in 1748, and whose gracefully curving
figures with slender proportions and small heads mark a distinctive style
at the factory.[3] The Meyer Malabars were popular for some time, as they
appear in both this and in a smaller size in the factory's 1765 price list.[4]

The Hartford examples were not produced at the same time, as the
bases are made differently.

Notes:
[1] This is a larger figure with baskets (Rückert, no. 985); the companion male
with quiver and shield was presumably made by Eberlein shortly after
(Rückert, no. 984).
[2] The *marchand-mercier* Lazare Duvaux (see cat. no. 58) sold gilt-bronze bases
for a pair of *Malabares* on April 14, 1749 (Courajod, no. 193). These are
probably the Eberlein models, as Meyer did not arrive at Meissen until
1 June 1748.
[3] Berling (1911), plate 17, p. 46 (both); Rückert, no. 987 (man). Mold numbers
give a date about 1751 (Rückert, p. 42). As modeling records for 1748–63 are
missing, Meyer's work is attributed on grounds of style.
[4] Sponsel, p. 208 ("Malabaren, 14 und 8 Zoll hoch."). Examples of the smaller
size (H. 17.1 cm.) were in Christie's, London, sale of 23 May 1967, lot 104.

NESTING PIGEON

German, Meissen, about 1745–50. Model by J. J. Kaendler, 1732
Hard-paste porcelain, painted in enamel colors, the feathers in tones of
black, grey, and brown, the eyes red. The nest is of feathers, twigs, and
yellow and green moss. Factory mold no. 78.
Marks: crossed swords in underglaze blue (on base edge)
H. 5 13/16 in. (14.8 cm.); L. 12 3/16 in. (31 cm.)
1917.1276

Kaendler modeled three pigeon subjects in 1732–33: this nesting
female,[1] the male as a standing figure,[2] and a group of two birds mating.[3]
By 1735 thirteen figures of pigeons were delivered for the Japanese
Palace.[4]

The Japanese Palace housed Augustus the Strong's colossal porcelain
collection. Plans from 1730 for its remodeling included life-size animals
and birds to be made at Meissen, and it was to model these figures that
Kaendler was appointed to the factory in 1731. Before the king died in
1733 a considerable number had been made, and others followed in the
next two years.

These pigeons were more or less remodeled about 1745, judging from
the colors and execution of most examples,[5] including the Hartford one,
whose fine quality is seen in the plumage incised after molding and the
careful, restrained painting.

Notes:
[1]Kaendler, October 1732: "A pigeon sitting and brooding on a nest"
(Albiker [1959], no. 107).
[2]Zimmermann, p. 104; Albiker (1935), p. 108.
[3]Albiker (1959), no. 108.
[4]Sponsel, p. 59, among animals and birds delivered though not ordered.
[5]Female: Rückert, no. 1102. Male: Rückert, no. 1103; Jedding no. 264.
Berling (1911), p. 33 dates the male 1745, and this is in agreement with
its present mold number (827). The female (78) and group (77) kept their
early numbers. For 1740s examples of all three pigeons see 77 *Meissner
Porzellanvögel . . .*, sales catalogue, Ball-Graupe, Berlin, 15 March 1933,
nos. 25, 34, and 36.

PAIR OF SPARROW HAWKS
German, Meissen
Hard-paste porcelain, painted with enamel colors,
the plumage brown and black.

A. Sparrow Hawk Feeding on a Lark (photo right)
Mid-eighteenth century; model by J. J. Kaendler, 1734
The stump has green foliage. Factory mold no. C 127.
Marks: crossed swords in underglaze blue (on base edge)
H. 11 in. (28 cm.)
1917.1283

B. Sparrow Hawk Feeding on a Mouse (photo left)
About 1740–50; model by J. J. Kaendler, 1739
The stump has green and yellow foliage, brown fungi, and a red beetle.
Factory mold no. 196.
Marks: no factory mark; impressed numeral 34
H. 11$\frac{3}{16}$ in. (28.5 cm.)
1917.1284

The 1735 list of animals and birds delivered for the Japanese Palace includes two examples of *Lerchen Stösser* ("lark hawks," or sparrow hawks).[1] This must be the hawk feeding on a lark modeled in 1734,[2] considered by Zimmermann to be among Kaendler's best and most thoroughly realized animal subjects.[3] The mate to it did not appear until 1739–40,[4] at the time Kaendler was also modeling similarly composed "Jays" and "Rollers."[5]

The Hartford examples were not produced at the same time, as the hawk with mouse[6] shows appreciably finer painting than does the other.[7]

Notes:
[1]Sponsel, p. 59; among animals and birds delivered though not ordered.
[2]Albiker (1959), nos. 86–87: Kaendler, April 1734, "1 *Rittelweibgen* or *Lerchengeyer* feeding on a lark, represented life size resting on a decorated base."
[3]Zimmermann, p. 121.
[4]Albiker (1935), p. 110, fig. 103, as Kaendler, October 1739. Kaendler, *Taxa*, 1740–48 (Pfeiffer, p. 270): "A *Rüttel-Weib* or *Lerchen Stösser* sitting on a stick and holding in its claws a mouse on which it is feeding." This entry is near the beginning of the *Taxa*.
[5]Albiker (1959), nos. 88–89; Rückert nos. 1108–1111.
[6]The meaning of the impressed number is not known (Rückert, p. 42).
[7]The figure with a lark's mold number indicates a later remodeling in 1768–70 (Rückert, p. 42). This was probably done to replace a worn or damaged mold.

PAIR OF SQUIRRELS
German, Meissen, about 1750. Models attributed to J. J. Kaendler, about 1749
Hard-paste porcelain, painted with enamel colors; gilt chains hang from the yellow and black collars.

57a. Squirrel facing right and holding a nut, the fur with brown markings (photo left). Factory mold no. 1275.
Marks: crossed swords in underglaze blue (on base edge)
H. 7$\frac{15}{16}$ in. (20.3 cm.)
1917.1269

57b. Squirrel facing left, a nut in his mouth, the fur with black markings (photo right). Factory mold no. 1276.
Marks: faint crossed swords in underglaze blue (on base edge)
H. 8$\frac{7}{16}$ in. (21.5 cm.)
1917.1270

Kaendler modeled two squirrels in 1732,[1] and a single figure the next year.[2] In the 1740s Kaendler and his assistants did many smaller animals and birds,[3] and on the evidence of the factory mold numbers, these squirrels were probably modeled about 1749.[4] The 1753 inventory of Count Brühl's porcelain included squirrels, and those are likely to have been recent models such as these.[5] The Hartford models are described in the factory's price list of 1765 as "squirrel(s), large, with chain."[6] These examples are notable for the way crisp, vigorous finishing after molding and restrained painting set off the white porcelain to particular advantage.

A pair is known having French gilt bronze mounts with the Paris crowned "C" mark used from February 1745 to February 1749.[7]

Notes:
[1]Zimmermann, p. 104, as August 1732. Albiker (1935), p. 111, fig. 164, gives this date in parentheses to indicate uncertainty.
[2]Albiker (1959), nos. 38 and 39, Kaendler, September 1733: "1 small squirrel." Although no mold number is given, the lack of a base agrees with this early date. Confusingly, Albiker did not catalogue the Hartford models in his 1959 edition.
[3]Sponsel, pp. 133–134; Zimmermann, pp. 192, 205.
[4]Rückert, p. 42. The factory records are missing from 1749 to 1763.
[5]Sponsel, p. 139.
[6]Berling (1900), p. 198; Sponsel, p. 208. For the Hartford models see Charleston, no. 56, who also cites other examples.
[7]Sotheby Parke Bernet, New York, 22 October 1974, no. 457. For the crowned "C" see P. Verlet, "A Note on the 'Poinçon' of the Crowned 'C'," *Apollo* 26 (1937), pp. 22–23.

58

OVAL BASKET
German, Meissen, about 1750
Hard-paste porcelain with applied forget-me-nots painted blue and
yellow at the intersections of the evenly pierced sides, the gently
scalloped rim edged with gilding. Mounted with gilt bronze to contain
an arrangement of soft-paste porcelain flowers.
Marks: no mark visible (base covered by mount)
H. $3\frac{3}{8}$ in. (8.6 cm.); W. $11\frac{1}{2}$ in. (29.2 cm.); D. $9\frac{1}{2}$ in. (24.1 cm.);
H. of arrangement $23\frac{15}{16}$ in. (61 cm.)
Provenance: Heirs of Count Rouget, Paris; bought from Jacques
Seligmann, Paris, 14 May 1900.
1917.1234

Baskets of various forms and ornamental complexity were made at
Meissen by 1740 or soon after. Kaendler modeled at least nine by 1744,
though none of those closely corresponds to this relatively simple type.[1]
At the same time he also introduced applied and relief-molded European
flowers as a decoration for tablewares and vases: an "entirely new service
most carefully overlaid with the so-called forget-me-not flower that can
be painted blue as it is in nature" was modeled in June 1740.[2]

The sale records from 1748 to 1758 of the Parisian *marchand-mercier*
Lazare Duvaux, who regularly provided a rich and elegant clientele,
including Mme. de Pompadour and the king, with luxurious furnishings
and ingeniously devised appointments of all sorts, list many entries for
Meissen, particularly in the earlier years of that period.[3] Many of these
show *porcelaine de Saxe*, as it was known in France, imaginatively combined
with Vincennes soft-paste porcelain flowers and other materials in
objects such as chandeliers, candelabra, potpourris, and clock cases. The
refined naturalism and fantasy of these inventions was carried even
further, the beautiful Vincennes flowers being employed in bouquets to
fill baskets, planters, and vases. Courajod believed Duvaux was at the
forefront of fashion not only in devising new ways of using these flowers,
which by 1748 represented five-sixths of the Vincennes production,[4] but
also in making a specialty of associating porcelain of all kinds with gilt
bronze.[5]

The Hartford basket of flowers is a spectacular example of this kind,
and corresponds closely to several entries by Duvaux.[6] The flowers
include carnations, ranunculus, tulips, lilies, cornflowers, convolvulus,
orange blossoms, and lilies of the valley.[7] The excellent quality gilt-
bronze mount in rococo style is French of the same date and is formed as a
strongly scrolled *terrasse* from which rise two upwardly curving handles.

Duvaux's journal shows that by 1754 the fashion for such arrangements was largely past, perhaps owing to their extreme fragility. By that
time he was also handling far less Meissen, undoubtedly because of the
rapidly improving artistic quality and variety of forms produced at
Vincennes, by then under royal patronage.

Notes:
[1]Kaendler, *Taxa*, 1740–44 (Pfeiffer, pp. 272–280).
[2]Rückert, no. 671 (quotes archives).
[3]Courajod, p. 12ff.
[4]W. B. Honey, *French Porcelain of the 18th century* (London, 1950), p. 34.
[5]Courajod, p. lxxv.
[6]Courajod, entry no. 205, 9 May 1749: "A large *Saxe* basket on a chased and
ormolu-gilded bronze *terrasse* and console, embellished with several lacquered
copper plants and very beautiful Vincennes flowers, 1,500 livres." Entry no.
521, 26 May 1750: "A *Saxe* basket mounted in ormolu gilded bronze garnished
with Vincennes flowers worth 35 louis, 840 livres." Arrangements of flowers
in Meissen baskets were sold for a few years more, as entries for November
1751 (no. 941) and December 1753 (no. 1603) show.
Examples of bouquets in the same type of basket are illustrated by
F. H. Hofmann, *Das Porzellan* (Berlin, 1932), plate XXIV (with Meissen
flowers) and Christie's, London sale of 20 June 1985, no. 16 (with Vincennes or
Sèvres flowers). A similar basket but modeled with twig loop-handles as a
potpourri of Meissen flowers was in the C. H. Fischer sale, Cologne,
19–20 October 1906, no. 594.
[7]The metal stems and silk leaves are later replacements.

Sèvres

Sir Geoffrey de Bellaigue

P. Mitchell, editor of the *New York Sun*, discerned in J. Pierpont Morgan's approach to collecting "a genuine affection and hunger for the rarest and finest and most beautiful achievements in the arts."[1] These qualities are not, however, echoed in Roger Fry's vitriolic condemnation of the banker written in 1907: "For a crude historical imagination was the only flaw in his otherwise perfect insensibility."[2] A more balanced assessment is provided by Francis Henry Taylor, who describes Morgan as "primarily a cultivated man of the world with a much better European education than the average antiquary possessed."[3]

Whatever the motives which prompted Morgan to collect, Taylor is in no doubt about his achievement. "Pierpont Morgan was the greatest figure in the art world that America has yet produced, a visionary and a patron such as we never knew before, nor ever shall again."[4]

In monetary terms, Morgan's purchases of French eighteenth-century porcelain (consisting principally of wares from the Vincennes/Sèvres factory) must be regarded as of minor interest when compared with the sums he spent on books, manuscripts, autographs, antiquities, paintings, sculpture, tapestries, enamels, jewelry, gold boxes, and oriental porcelain. In recent biographies of Morgan — F. L. Allen (1949), Cass Canfield (1974), and Stanley Jackson (1984) — Sèvres porcelain hardly rates a mention. Gerald Reitlinger in *The Economies of Taste* (1963) limits himself to a single purchase, the Coventry Sèvres *garniture* bought for about £15,500 in 1908–10. This figure shrinks in importance when it is compared to some of his other purchases, such as the four tapestry panels from the Don Quixote series woven at the Gobelins, for which he paid in excess of £80,000 in 1903.

Though Morgan often bought other people's collections *en bloc*, this does not seem to have been the way he acquired his French porcelain. The collection was built up by individual purchases, principally from dealers in London and Paris, during the last decade of the nineteenth century and the first decade of this century. He no doubt relied on advice from experts and dealers — Jacques Seligmann,[5] for example, or possibly the comte de Chavagnac (see cat. no. 68). Even so, his choice of French porcelain may well reflect his personal taste in a way which his bulk acquisitions in other fields do not. That Morgan himself attached equal importance to this aspect of his collection as to his other more costly interests is evident from the catalogue he commissioned the comte de Chavagnac to write. It was published in a sumptuous limited edition in 1910 on paper specially made in France for this purpose. When the bulk of his collection was shipped to America from his London house, 13 Princes Gate, the Sèvres filled nine of the 351 crates dispatched to the Metropolitan Museum. The

Sèvres was included in the Morgan exhibition staged in 1914, one year after the banker's death. Some two-thirds of the pieces catalogued by Chavagnac eventually came into the possession of the Wadsworth Atheneum.

In his collecting Pierpont Morgan has been described as a traditionalist, a man of conservative tastes who thought in the past tense, not in the future. It would have been surprising for a collector of Sèvres in the late nineteenth and early twentieth centuries to have shown equal interest in hard- and soft-paste porcelain, let alone a preference for the former. In this respect Morgan was a man of his times. Chavagnac is almost apologetic when he admits to a few hard-paste pieces, though he does concede that they are worthy of mention.[6]

In Sèvres porcelain, the *garniture* was what the rich nineteenth-century collectors most prized. Morgan also acquired sets of ornamental vases for display on chests of drawers or mantelpieces, but they were relatively few in relation to his other purchases. Reitlinger has noted that by the turn of the century the *garniture* was no longer regarded as the *ne plus ultra* among porcelain collectors.[7] Perhaps here too Morgan's taste reflects this change of emphasis.

French works of art with distinguished eighteenth-century provenances have always exerted a particular appeal among collectors, and it would be logical to expect that Morgan would have been receptive to such historical associations. Though he did purchase, unwittingly perhaps, a number of pieces which research has revealed belonged to French eighteenth-century figures, Chavagnac's catalogue cites only Madame du Barry and Machault d'Arnouville as previous owners. The acquisition of pieces with a distinguished pedigree was evidently not a governing factor in his collecting of French porcelain.

To the collector or admirer with a catholic taste, the Morgan collection of French porcelain offers a wide range, be it in terms of the type of ware, of shapes, of ground colors, or of decoration. Not for Pierpont Morgan the myopic collecting of Sèvres painted with a single ground color, such as yellow or turquoise blue, as can be found in some North American collections. Nor did he limit his purchases exclusively to tableware or ornamental vases. They covered both and also included sculpture (glazed and biscuit), paintings on porcelain, porcelain-mounted furniture, clocks, inkwells, and boxes.

Pierpont Morgan had a discerning eye for quality and his purchases of French porcelain reveal him to be a connoisseur who was prepared to trust his judgment. Chavagnac, who was a recognized expert and a collector in his own right, had no doubt about Morgan's abilities, a "goût sûr et raffiné."[8]

Notes:
[1]Frederick Lewis Allen, *The Great Pierpont Morgan* (London, 1949), p. 146.
[2]*Ibid.*, p. 145.
[3]Francis Henry Taylor, *Pierpont Morgan as Collector and Patron, 1837–1913* (New York, 1957).
[4]*Ibid.*, p. 39.
[5]Germain Seligman, *Merchants of Art: 1880-1960: Eighty Years of Professional Collecting* (New York, 1961), pp. 1–9, 18–22, 32–34, 69–77.
[6]Chavagnac, *Morgan Cat.*, p. vi.
[7]Gerald Reitlinger, *The Economies of Taste*, vol. II, *The Rise and Fall of Objets d'Art Prices since 1750* (London, 1963), p. 163.
[8]Chavagnac, *Morgan Cat.*, p. v.

The following abbreviations have been used:

AN: *Archives Nationales*
IF: *Institut de France*
MNS: *Manufacture Nationale de Sèvres*

SÈVRES REFERENCES

Bourgeois	Emile Bourgeois. *Le Biscuit de Sèvres au XVIIIᵉ siècle.* 2 vols. Paris, 1909.
Brunet and Préaud, *Sèvres*	Marcelle Brunet and Tamara Préaud. *Sèvres: Des origines à nos jours.* Fribourg, 1978.
Chavagnac, *Morgan Cat.*	Comte Xavier de Chavagnac. *Catalogue des porcelaines françaises de M. J. Pierpont Morgan.* Paris, 1910.
Eriksen, *David Collection*	Svend Eriksen. *The David Collection: French Porcelain.* Copenhagen, 1980.
Eriksen, *Early Neo-Classicism*	Svend Eriksen. *Early Neo-Classicism in France.* London, 1974.
Eriksen, *Pitti Palace Cat.*	Svend Eriksen. *French Porcelain in Palazzo Pitti.* Florence, 1973.
Eriksen, *Waddesdon Cat.*	The James A. de Rothschild Collection at Waddesdon Manor. Svend Eriksen. *Sèvres Porcelain.* Fribourg, 1968.
Eriksen and Bellaigue, *Sèvres Porcelain*	Svend Eriksen and Geoffrey de Bellaigue. *Sèvres Porcelain: Vincennes and Sèvres 1740–1800.* London, 1986
Jean-Richard	Jean-Richard, Pierrette. *L'oeuvre gravé de François Boucher dans la collection Edmond de Rothschild (Musée du Louvre, Cabinet des Dessins, Collection Edmond de Rothschild, Inventaire général des gravures, Ecole francaise, I).* Paris, 1978.
Laking	Guy Francis Laking. *Sèvres Porcelain of Buckingham Palace and Windsor Castle.* London, 1907.
Lazare Duvaux	Courajod, Louis. *Livre-Journal de Lazare Duvaux marchand-bijoutier ordinaire du Roy, 1748–1758.* Paris, 1873 (reprint, Paris, 1965, 2 vols.).
Queen's Gallery, *Sèvres*	Queen's Gallery, Buckingham Palace, 1979–80. Geoffrey de Bellaigue. *Sèvres Porcelain from the Royal Collection.* London, 1979.
Préaud and Faÿ-Hallé	Grand Palais, 14 October 1977–16 January 1978. Tamara Préaud and Antoinette Faÿ-Hallé. *Porcelainiers de Vincennes: Les origines de Sèvres.* Paris, 1977.
Troude	Albert Troude. *Choix de modèles de la manufacture nationale de Sèvres appartenant au Musée Céramique.* Paris, n.d.
Verlet, *Sèvres*	Pierre Verlet. *Sèvres: Le XVIIIᵉ siècle . . .* Paris, 1953.

59

PAIR OF POT-POURRI VASES (*pot-pourri à jour*)
France, Vincennes, about 1751–53
Soft-paste porcelain, white ground, sparingly gilded and painted in strong colors with a bouquet of flowers in each of the four reserves. The flowers and foliage rising up from the scrolled feet are painted naturalistically, as is also the orange blossom forming the knob of the pierced cover.

Marks : on both in blue foliate, interlaced LLs enclosing on one a dot within a circle of smaller dots, and on the other a many-pointed asterisk. Incised marks : none.
H. 10¼ in. (26.1 cm.); W. 6⅝ in. (16.8 cm.)
1917.982 and 983

These four-lobed vases with their spirally pierced covers, scrolled feet, and wind-blown flowers modeled in relief are fine examples of the factory's production in the full Louis XV style. The blue ribbon seemingly threaded through the pierced arcading of the neck recalls the interlacing on the chestnut baskets (see no. 63).

Vases of this shape — the model was almost certainly created by Jean-Claude Duplessis — were probably known at the factory as "*pots-pourris à jour*."[1] They are recorded in the inventory of 1 October 1752 and came in four sizes,[2] the Wadsworth pair being examples of the largest or second size.[3] On some versions the flowers and plant stems in relief are omitted.

The luscious character of the painted bouquets has suggested to Svend Eriksen that the Wadsworth vases date from 1752 or a little earlier.[4] The presence of the dark blue pigment, which Antoine d'Albis defines as *beau bleu*, further limits the probable date of production. He has established that its first use at Vincennes dates from 1751.

The pot-pourri vase, which was introduced into France at the end of the seventeenth century, was regarded in the eighteenth century as an essential part of the furnishings of a fashionable apartment. Recipes for their contents, which distilled the most subtle fragrances through evaporation, were a closely guarded secret. Ladies went to great lengths to find the particular ingredients which set off to best advantage their own type of beauty.

Notes:
[1]Préaud and Faÿ-Hallé, p. 91.
[2]The earliest specific reference to a fourth size occurs in an entry in the Sales Ledger dated 28 June 1756 (MNS, Vy 1 fo. 131).
[3]Marcelle Brunet identifies a pair in the Musée des Arts Décoratifs, Paris, as versions of the third size. They measure 19.5 cm. in height (Brunet and Préaud, *Sèvres*, fig. 46).
[4]Eriksen and Bellaigue, *Sèvres Porcelain*, plate 63.

Literature: Chavagnac, *Morgan Cat.*, no. 74; Graham Hood, "French Porcelain from the J. P. Morgan Collection at the Wadsworth Atheneum," *Connoisseur* 158 (February, 1965), p. 131, fig. 1; Graham Hood, "French Porcelain from the J. P. Morgan Collection at the Wadsworth Atheneum," *Wadsworth Atheneum Bulletin*, sixth series, vol. 1, no. 3 (Winter, 1965), p. 2, fig. 1; Graham Hood, "European Ceramic Masterpieces," *Apollo* 88 (December, 1968), p. 36, fig. 1; Eriksen and Bellaigue, *Sèvres Porcelain*, plate 63.

GROUP OF THREE FIGURES (*groupe de Vandrevole ou le Jaloux*)
France, Vincennes, about 1752
Glazed soft-paste porcelain
H. and W. $9\frac{7}{16}$ in. (24 cm.)
Provenance: Bought from Durlacher Brothers, London, on 8 June 1900, together with two other groups (1917.955-956). At the time all were fitted to "metal mounted tulip wood stands of the period."
1917.954

The plaster model of the group is preserved in the Sèvres Archives and a terra cotta in the Musée National de Céramique, Sèvres. As was first suggested by Emile Bourgeois, the name by which this group was commonly known at the factory in the eighteenth century, *groupe de Vandrevole*, could possibly refer in a corrupted form to Van der Voorst, to whom the model, which is based on a design by François Boucher, is attributed.[1]

The scene represents a jealous father, Mathurin, who is intent on surprising the young lovers, his own son, Corydon, and Lisette, a shepherdess. It is taken from a scene in the ballet pantomime by Charles-Siméon Favart, *La Vallée de Montmorency ou les amours villageois*, first produced at the Paris Opéra-Comique in 1752, which itself was an adaptation of Favart's pantomime, *Les Vendanges de Tempé*, first performed on 28 August 1745 at the fair of Saint Laurent in Paris. Favart's pastoral pantomime was an immediate success and was the inspiration for several compositions by Boucher, which were later reproduced as sculptural groups by the Vincennes/Sèvres factory.[2]

The surviving versions of *Vandrevole ou le Jaloux* are of two different models. One, in biscuit porcelain, which is in the Pitti Palace, Florence, differs from the Wadsworth example in its scale, in the pose of the three figures, and by the omissions of the vase, one of the two sheep, and the lover's hat. It was bought for 300 *livres* from the Sèvres factory by the dealer Testard on 4 February 1769. It is a version of the revised model, of which the first example to be sold was entered in the Sales Ledger on 24 May 1756.[3]

The Wadsworth version is based on the original model. Three glazed groups, each valued at 72 *livres*, are included in the 1752 Stock List, of which one was bought on 30 June 1753 by the factory's principal shareholder, Jean-François Verdun de Montchiroux. Subsequently two other versions, priced at 120 *livres*, were sold on 11 September 1753 and 17 September 1754.[4]

Notes:
[1] Bourgeois, vol. I, p. 17.
[2] *Idem.*
[3] Eriksen, *Pitti Palace Cat.*, no. 44; Eriksen and Bellaigue, *Sèvres Porcelain*, plate 65.
[4] Eriksen and Bellaigue, *op. cit.*

Literature: Chavagnac, *Morgan Cat.*, no. 48; Charles E. Buckley, "Eighteenth-Century French Porcelain in Hartford's Art Museum," *The Connoisseur Year Book* (1956), p. 48; *Wadsworth Atheneum Handbook* (Hartford, Conn., 1958), p. 96; Graham Hood, "French Porcelain from the J. P. Morgan Collection at the Wadsworth Atheneum," *Connoisseur* 158 (February, 1965), p. 132, fig. 4; Graham Hood, "French Porcelain from the J. P. Morgan Collection at the Wadsworth Atheneum," *Wadsworth Atheneum Bulletin* 1, no. 3 (Winter, 1965), p. 4, fig. 3; Eriksen and Bellaigue, *Sèvres Porcelain*, plate 65.

WATER CISTERN AND BASIN (*fontaine unie et cuvette*)
France, cistern, Vincennes, 1755; basin, Sèvres, 1786
Soft-paste porcelain painted in monochrome blue with flowers, putti and figure scenes (flesh tones on the figures), and elaborately gilded
Marks: Cistern — in blue, interlaced LLs enclosing the date-letter C for 1755. Incised mark: ᒾ
Basin — in blue, interlaced LLs enclosing the date-letters ij for 1786, with below the marks of Pierre-Joseph Rosset (blue) and Henri-Martin Prévost (gold). Incised mark: 25.
Cistern: H. $13\frac{5}{8}$ in. (34.7 cm.); W. $8\frac{5}{16}$ in. (21.1 cm.); D. (less spigot) $5\frac{11}{16}$ in. (14.4 cm.)
Basin: H. $3\frac{9}{16}$ in. (9 cm.); W. 13 in. (33 cm.); D. $9\frac{7}{16}$ in. (24 cm.)
Provenance: Bought from Jacques Seligmann, Paris, on 22 May 1903
1917.993 a–b, 994

The cistern and basin were used for washing hands. Plaster models and molds of two types of cistern were made in 1754, one described as "*à roseaux*" and the other as "*unie*."[1] The more elaborate one, which survives, is decorated in low relief with reeds and bulrushes; its spigot is in the form of a dolphin.[2] The other type, which has the same outline but lacks the relief decoration, came in two sizes.[3] These cisterns of rococo shape were almost certainly designed by Jean-Claude Duplessis. Two outline drawings of the basin and cistern are preserved in the Sèvres Archives. They are dated 6 March 1754, and on the evidence of the annotations, they relate to a version, probably the original one, which was destined for the Dauphine, Marie-Josèphe de Saxe.[4]

The Wadsworth cistern may well have been bought by the *marchand-mercier* Lazare Duvaux between 1 October and 31 December 1755.[5] Together with its basin, it cost 600 *livres* and is described in the Sales Ledger as painted in monochrome with cartouches containing scenes of children, their skin flesh-colored. Though we do not know the identity of the ultimate purchaser, it was probably a member of the royal family. In any event, when the replacement basin was made it was Louis XVI who bought it for 192 *livres* on 31 May 1786.[6] It may be that the replacement basin was supplied for the King's personal use at Versailles. In an inventory of 1792 a Sèvres cistern and basin are listed in the King's *cabinet de géographie* at Versailles, valued at 600 *livres*.[7]

Chavagnac has rightly noted that the decoration of the replacement basin is markedly inferior in quality to the painting on the cistern. One might have been tempted to conclude that the basin had been decorated outside the Sèvres factory, if it were not for an entry under Rosset's name in the Artists' Ledger which probably refers to it. On 21 April 1786 he received for decoration a basin for a cistern, which he painted in monochrome blue with a landscape, flowers, and figures and a jagged ("*déchiré*") band.[8]

The cisterns and basins made at Vincennes and Sèvres are typically Louis XV in style. With their serpentine outlines, bulbous shapes, and clasp-like handles, they are totally out of character with the later neoclassical style of the last quarter of the eighteenth century. It is, therefore, surprising to find a cistern and basin of the same pattern as the Wadsworth version being sold on 1 February 1788 to "Madame" (almost certainly Madame Elisabeth, Louis XVI's sister).[9]

Notes:
[1] MNS, I.7, Stock List dated 1 January 1755.
[2] The model was valued at 12 *livres* in the Stock List of 1 January 1755 (MNS, I.7).
[3] Their models were valued in the Stock List of 1 January 1755 at 6 *livres* and 4 *livres* 10 *sols* respectively (MNS, I.7).
[4] MNS, R.1, L.1, d.4, fo.2; R.1, d.1, L.17, fo. 13. A version of the *fontaine à roseaux* is in the C.-L. David Collection, Copenhagen (Eriksen, *David Collection*, nos. 43–4). It bears the date-letter for 1755 and incorporates in its decoration the French royal cipher formed by interlaced LLs. Three examples of the *fontaine unie* are known. The second example, which is without a basin, is in the Musée National de Céramique, Sèvres. It bears the date-letter for 1757 and is painted in blue with sprays of flowers (Préaud and Faÿ-Hallé, *Vincennes Cat.*, no. 92). The third example, which is in the Mansfield Collection at Scone Palace, Perthshire, is painted in gold with garlands and a fountain. The cistern bears the date-letters for 1788 and the mark of the gilder H.-M. Prévost; the basin, which is undated, bears the mark of the gilder, Vincent *jeune*. The Sèvres museum's version, which is 32 cm. in height, may be of the smaller size.
[5] Chavagnac, *Morgan Cat.*, no. 83, p. 7.
[6] Brunet and Préaud, *Sèvres*, fig. 68 *bis*. The comte de Chavagnac and Marcelle Brunet have suggested that the replacement basin, though paid for by the King, may have been intended for his aunt, Madame Louise, the Carmelite nun who died in 1787. The entry in the Sales Ledger which they cite is, however, ambiguous.
[7] Brunet and Préaud, *Sèvres*, fig. 68 *bis*.
[8] MNS, Vj'4 fo. 227.
[9] They cost 144 *livres*, the metal fittings amounting to a further 78 *livres* (MNS, Vy10 fo. 234v). The basin was evidently shattered shortly after delivery, for on 3 June 1789 a replacement was sold to Madame Elisabeth for 84 *livres* (MNS, Vy10 fo. 335v), which had been fired in the kiln for painted and gilded decoration on 25 May 1789 (MNS, V1.3 fo. 136). The gilder was Vincent. The 1788 cistern and the 1789 replacement basin are very probably those now in Scone Palace.

Literature: Chavagnac, *Morgan Cat.*, no. 83; *Wadsworth Atheneum Handbook* (Hartford, Conn., 1958), p. 98; C. C. Cunningham, *The Pierpont Morgan Treasures* (Hartford, Conn., 1960), p. 23, no. 58, plate X; Graham Hood, "French Porcelain from the J. P. Morgan Collection at the Wadsworth Atheneum," *Connoisseur* 158 (February, 1965), p. 133, fig. 5; Graham Hood, "French Porcelain from the J. P. Morgan Collection at the Wadsworth Atheneum," *Wadsworth Atheneum Bulletin* 1, no. 3 (Winter, 1965), pp. 5–7, fig. 4; Brunet and Préaud, *Sèvres*, fig. 68, 68 *bis*.

STANDISH (*écritoire*)
France, Sèvres, 1758
Composed of an oval, two-handled tray fitted with two pairs of matching containers. Of the two center ones, the one with a loose cover is an inkwell and penholder and the other may have been intended for a sponge used to wipe quill pens or as a receptacle for a bell.[1] The left-hand pot with a loose pierced cover is a pounce pot, and the other (cover missing) may have been intended for wax pastilles. Soft-paste porcelain painted green and with polychrome single sprays of flowers on a white ground.
Marks: in blue on the tray, interlaced LLs enclosing the date-letter F for 1758 and below, the mark of the flower painter, Jean-Baptiste Tandart. Incised marks: none
Tray: H. 2 3/16 in. (5.5 cm.); W. 11 13/16 in. (30.1 cm.); D. 7 9/16 in. (19.2 cm.)
Inkwell and penholder: H. 1 7/8 in. (4.8 cm.)
?Container for a sponge or a bell: 1 13/16 in. (4.6 cm.)
Pounce pot: H. 2 1/4 in. (5.8 cm.)
?Container for wax pastilles: 2 3/16 in. (5.6 cm.)
1917.1013

Very few standishes of this pattern seem to have been made. Entries dated 1755 in the kiln ledgers for biscuit and glost porcelain record the firing of three *écritoires*, each made up of five components. Tamara Préaud has plausibly suggested that these entries refer to standishes of this model.[2] Apart from the Wadsworth example, the only other version known to survive is in the Louvre. Dated 1755, it is painted with scattered flowers and lines of gold and blue.[3]

In the Sèvres Sales Ledgers there are references to *écritoires* of differing models ranging in price from 15 to 1,200 *livres*. Examples of the most expensive, which belonged to Madame de Pompadour and Madame Adélaïde, are in the Residenz-Museum, Munich[4] and in the Wallace Collection respectively.[5] Though the Wadsworth example would not have cost anything like 1,000 *livres*, it is not a conventional model and would probably have been priced at three figures. Bearing in mind that it is dated 1758 and that relatively few were made around that date, it may be possible to identify it in the Sèvres records. In the Stock Lists of 1 January 1759 two *écritoires* are listed, one valued at 168 *livres* and the other at 216 *livres*.[6] By 1 October of the same year only the *écritoire* priced at 216 *livres* remained unsold.[7] Then in December 1759 Madame de Pompadour bought at the Versailles sales an *écritoire* for 216 *livres* described as "*verd fleurs*."[8]

If the *écritoire* is indeed the one Madame de Pompadour bought on this occasion, it would be singularly appropriate as she, more so than any other figure in the public eye, exemplifies this eighteenth-century passion for writing notes and letters. In many a portrait she is represented engaged in this occupation. The marquis de Barbé Marbois, in a fictitious but plausible letter published in 1771, which he would have us believe had been penned by Madame de Pompadour in 1760, writes, "You ask me what I do when I have neither a migraine nor boring company. I write, Madam, I scribble, as do so many others."[9]

Notes:
[1] The precise function of each receptacle remains unclear. In the divisions for writing materials, which are incorporated into one of the drawers of desks and writing tables made in France in the eighteenth century, one is generally for the inkwell, another for the pounce pot, and the third for the sponge. In the case of freestanding standishes with three receptacles, the sponge is frequently replaced by a hand bell which is sometimes shown in contemporary engravings resting in a container (information kindly supplied by Pierre Ennès, who has drawn the writer's attention to an engraving illustrating "L'art d'écrire" in the *Encyclopédie méthodique* [begun in 1782]). Perhaps the last word should go to Diderot and d'Alembert. In their *Encyclopédie* under the word *Ecritoire* they write: "*Il y en a bien des sortes*" (vol. V publ. 1775).
[2] Préaud and Faÿ-Hallé, *Vincennes Cat.*, p. 48, no. 79.
[3] *Idem*. It is fitted with three covers for the containers, two of which are of pierced metal. The third, which is in porcelain, is crowned by simulated wax pastilles painted red, black, and turquoise blue. While accepting that the bronze covers are contemporary in date, Pierre Ennès has expressed reservations to the writer about the authenticity of the porcelain cover.
[4] Pierre Verlet, *Le Style Louis XV* (Paris, 1943), plate 32; Verlet, *Sèvres*, p. 211.
[5] Verlet, *Sèvres*, plate 56.
[6] MNS, I. 7.
[7] MNS, I. 7.
[8] MNS, Vy3 fo. 7v. No Sèvres *écritoire*, other than the one now in the Residenz-Museum, Vienna, can be identified in the inventory drawn up after her death in 1764.
[9] [Marquis F. de Barbé-Marbois], *Lettres de la Marquise de Pompadour . . .*, 2 vols. (London, 1771), I, p. 159.

Literature: Chavagnac, *Morgan Cat.*, no. 96.

OVAL CHESTNUT BASKET, COVER, AND ATTACHED STAND (*marronnière*),
ONE OF A PAIR

France, Sèvres, about 1760

Soft-paste porcelain with green ribbons looped through angular pink lattice-work forming diamonds. The ribbons and the lattice-work are edged with gold.

Marks: in blue, interlaced LLs. Incised mark: ℘.

H. 5¼ in. (13.4 cm.); W. 10½ in. (26.6 cm.); D. 8⁵⁄₁₆ in. (21.2 cm.)

1917.1010

Charles de La Varenne in *Le Confiturier François* (1687) provides three different recipes for chestnuts. In all cases they had to be roasted first. They were served either as a compote, "dry" with a covering of sugar, or glazed with a coating of icing. Gilliers in *Le Cannameliste François* (1768) also refers to grilled or boiled chestnuts which were served hot.

Marronnières were first made at Sèvres in 1757. They came in a variety of shapes and sizes. The earliest reference, in the Stock List of 1 January 1758, is to models and molds of two types, one described as "*unie*" (that is, plain and in this context presumably unpierced) and the other as "*à compartiments*" (that is, with divisions).[1] As the models and molds for their stands are entered separately, they clearly did not correspond to the Wadsworth pieces. Another type, described as "*forme pompᵣ* [Pompadour]," was recorded in August/September 1758.[2] There is no way of knowing whether it was of the same shape or different from the basket described as "*contourné*" (that is, shaped), which is included in the list of the new models and molds for 1758.[3] The earliest mention of chestnut baskets with attached stands, as is the case with the Wadsworth examples, occurs in 1759.[4] Yet another variant, of cabbage leaf design ("*à feuilles de choux*") is recorded in 1777.[5]

Marronnières could either be pierced or unpierced. All the covered bowls which have been identified to date as chestnut baskets are of the pierced variety.[6]

Marronnières were generally sold singly or in pairs. When they were included in a service they always came in pairs. Though by their very nature pierced chestnut baskets do not allow for elaborate decoration, they were comparatively expensive. The repairers must have spent many hours shaping and refining the details of the ribbons and lattice-work. Among the cheapest were those priced at 120 *livres* each, which were decorated with "*ornemens bleus*" or "*filets bleus*" — expressions which probably refer to the blue lines and minor blue ribboning sparingly used on other examples, such as on the version dated 1759 in the Wadsworth Atheneum (1917.1016). Among the more expensive chestnut baskets were those painted with green ribbons (360 *livres* in 1758),[7] with a pink ground (360 *livres* in 1758),[8] or with a mosaic pattern and birds (240 *livres* in 1760).[9]

On 1 January 1774 there were four pink and green *marronnières* in the Sales Shop at Sèvres. They were each valued at 168 *livres*.[10] If this entry is correctly interpreted as meaning that the four were painted with a combination of two colors, it is possible that the pair at the Wadsworth Atheneum are two of the survivors. A possible explanation for their relatively low valuation is that by 1774 the two-color combination, which had been popular in the late 1750s and early 1760s, was no longer in fashion and that they represented old stock which had been reduced in price.

Notes:

[1] MNS, I.7.

[2] IF, MS 5673 fo. 113v/115v, recorded as removed from a biscuit kiln after firing between 8 August and 16 September 1758.

[3] MNS, I.7, Stock List dated 1 January 1759.

[4] IF, MS 5674 fo. 97/105, recorded in a glost kiln examined on 2 April 1759.

[5] MNS, Vy6 fo. 204v, factory sale record dated 26 July 1777.

[6] The distinction is made in a Stock List dated 1 October 1759 which contains the first specific reference to pierced examples ("*à jour*"); MNS, I.7.

[7] MNS, Vy2 fo. 85.

[8] MNS, Vy2 fo. 81.

[9] MNS, Vy3 fo. 29.

[10] MNS, I.8.

Literature: Chavagnac, *Morgan Cat.*, no. 93; Brunet and Préaud, *Sèvres*, fig. 101; Gillian Wilson, Adrian Sassoon, and Charissa Bremer-David, "Acquisitions Made by the Department of Decorative Arts in 1982," *The J. Paul Getty Museum Journal* 11 (1983), p. 50, fig. 68.

MOUNTED VASE AND COVER (*vase cloche*[?] or *gobelet cloche*)
France, Sèvres, about 1763
Soft-paste porcelain, green ground, fitted with mounts of chased and gilt bronze. These include satyr handles, laurel garlands, and a stem chased with foliage. When the cover is removed a spring is released and the silver and gold model of Edmé Bouchardon's equestrian figure of Louis XV emerges from the body of the vase.
Marks: inscribed on the rim of the cover, *DULAC. M^D RUE S^T HONNORE JNVENISTE.* Engraved on a tablet at one end of the pedestal, *Posé Le 20 Juin 1763*, and at the other, *Louis Le Bien Aimé.*
Silver mark: unidentified

Overall H. (closed) 10⅞ in. (27.6 cm.);
Overall H. (open) 11⅞ in. (30.2 cm.); W. 7¼ in. (18.4 cm.);
H. of figure and pedestal, 3½ in. (8.9 cm.).
Provenance: Bought from J. S. Goldschmidt, Frankfurt am Main, 29 June 1905
1917.1065

On 20 June 1763 Edmé Bouchardon's equestrian bronze figure of Louis XV was unveiled to universal acclaim in the Place Louis XV (now Place de la Concorde), Paris. It stood on a marble base with, at the four corners, a bronze allegorical figure modeled by Bouchardon. It was completed by Jean-Baptiste Pigalle, who had taken over the project following Bouchardon's death in 1762.[1]

The Wadsworth porcelain vase with its hidden "surprise" — which anticipated by some 120 years Carl Fabergé's first Easter eggs with their comparable "surprises" — was clearly intended to entertain. It very probably belonged to Madame de Pompadour, a fitting acknowledgment of her dual role of mistress to the King and unofficial minister of the arts with a special interest in the Vincennes/Sèvres factory.[2] Following her death on 15 April 1764 it passed to her brother, the marquis de Marigny who, at her instance, had been appointed in 1751 *directeur général des bâtiments du roi*. Following his death it is listed in the inventory of his estate[3] and in the catalogue of his effects sold in Paris between 18 March and 6 April 1782.[4]

The fitting of mounts to Sèvres vases was an innovation of the 1760s, promoted no doubt by the *marchands-merciers* (dealers) in imitation of the oriental-mounted porcelain which proved so popular in France in the eighteenth century. Though the earliest reference to "vases à monter" in the surviving Sèvres archives is dated 31 December 1765,[5] the Wadsworth example establishes that the first prototype, if such it was, had already been made by the first quarter of 1764, if not earlier.

That the *marchand-mercier* Dulac should have inscribed his name on the mounts of the Wadsworth vase suggests that he may have been responsible for its design.[6] Judging from the number of mounted vases of this pattern which survive, the model must have proved popular in the middle years of the eighteenth century. They were designed for the most part as potpourri vases.[7]

It has not been possible to identify the Wadsworth vase in the Sèvres records. By the 1770s the model may have acquired the names *gobelet en cloche* and *vase en cloche* — a reference to the distinctive reversed bell shape of the porcelain. Made in two sizes, possibly three, they were sold (presumably without mounts) for 84, 60, and 54 *livres* each.[8]

Notes:
[1] Solange Granet, "Images de Paris: La Place de la Concorde," *La Revue géographique et industrielle de France* (Paris, 1963), pp. 43–57. In addition to two bronze reductions modeled by Pigalle for the Hôtel de Ville de Paris, seven others were ordered from Louis-Claude Vassé, Bouchardon's pupil. Cast in 1764, they were presented by the City of Paris to the King, Madame de Pompadour, and five other public figures.
[2] Jean-Cordey, "Inventaire des Biens de Madame de Pompadour . . .," *Société des bibliophiles François* (Paris, 1939), p. 207, item 2518, "*Un vaze de porcelaine verte, garny en bronze doré, contenant la statue équestre de la place de Louis quinze.*" I am indebted to Rosalind Savill for bringing this to my attention.
[3] No. 961. Item. "*Un vase de porcelaine verte garni de bronze doré renfermant la statue equestre de Louis XV en or et argent prisé soixante-douze livres.*" Inventaire après décés de Marquis de Marigny et de Menars, 1781. Minutier Centrale, XCIX 657.
[4] Lot 251, "*Une très-petite Statue équestre de Louis XV en or et argent, renfermée dans un vase de 10 pouces de haut, en porcelaine verte, garnie d'ornemens de bronze doré.*" Bought by Paillet for 196 *livres*. The identification of the Wadsworth vase in the Marigny inventory and sale was made by Alden Gordon who has generously agreed to my publishing this discovery.
[5] IF, Ms. 5675 fo. 29/32, list of pieces removed after firing from a glost kiln on 31 December 1765.
[6] Similar inscriptions occur on a closely related pair in Poland (cited in a catalogue entry of a sale held by Sotheby's, New York, on 16 May 1981 [Lot 34]).
[7] They are broadly of two types: those such as the Wadsworth vases which are fitted with satyr head handles joined by laurel garlands (examples in the British Royal Collection, The Vyne, Hampshire and Waddesdon Manor, Buckinghamshire); and those which are fitted with lion head handles joined by lion pelts disposed in the manner of garlands. Some examples of the second model were designed as candelabra holders. When their lids are removed three-branch candelabra emerge, as in the manner of the Louis XV equestrian model, and unfold (pair in the Stroganoff Collection, Leningrad [sold Rudolph Lepke, Berlin, 12, 13 May 1931, Lots 164-5, illus.; the porcelain described as Chinese]; another pair in the H.M.W. Oppenheim Collection [sold Christie's, London, 10 June 1913, Lot 76, illus.]).
[8] MNS, Vy5 fo. 53v; Vy7 fo. 105v; Vy7 fo. 214v.

Literature: Chavagnac, *Morgan Cat.*, no. 139; Eriksen and Bellaigue, *Sèvres Porcelain*, no. 136.

TEA SET (*déjeuner octogone*) COMPRISING A TRAY (*plateau octogone*), TEAPOT (*théière Calabre* or *Verdun*), SUGAR BOWL AND COVER (*pot à sucre Calabre*), MILK JUG (*pot à lait à trois pieds*), CUP AND SAUCER (*gobelet Hebert*)

France, Sèvres, 1764

Soft-paste porcelain, white ground, painted with a narrow border of a bright tone of dark blue overlaid with *caillouté* decoration in gold and a broad band hung with polychrome garlands. The band is composed of cartouches, which contain mosaic panels in red, blue, and gold, and are enclosed in interlacing laurel branches painted red and purple.

Marks: in blue on all pieces, interlaced LLs enclosing the date-letter L for 1764, with below the mark of Jacques-François Micaud. Incised marks: on the tray, fj; on the teapot and saucer, 2.

Tray: H. $1\frac{1}{8}$ in. (2.9 cm.); D. $9\frac{3}{16}$ in. (23.4 cm.)
Teapot: H. $3\frac{5}{8}$ in. (9.2 cm.); W. $4\frac{13}{16}$ in. (12.2 cm.)
Sugar bowl: H. $2\frac{1}{16}$ in. (5.3 cm.); D. $2\frac{3}{8}$ in. (6 cm.)
Milk jug: H. $3\frac{1}{8}$ in. (8 cm.); W. $3\frac{3}{8}$ in. (8.6 cm.); D. $2\frac{7}{16}$ in. (6.8 cm.)
Cup: H. $2\frac{1}{8}$ in. (5.5 cm.); W. $3\frac{5}{16}$ in. (8.4 cm.); D. $2\frac{11}{16}$ in. (6.8 cm.)
Saucer: H. $1\frac{1}{16}$ in. (2.7 cm.); D. $4\frac{5}{8}$ in. (11.7 cm.)
1917.1032–1036

The *déjeuner*, consisting of a tray and various components for drinking coffee, chocolate, or tea, was an eighteenth-century development which followed the introduction of these beverages into Europe from the East in the previous century. Porcelain *déjeuners* were first made at Meissen. At Vincennes and later at Sèvres a multiplicity of such tea, coffee, and chocolate sets were produced. Those without porcelain trays, named *cabarets*, were often sold with trays of lacquered metal. The *déjeuner* invariably included porcelain trays which came in a variety of shapes:

circular, triangular, octagonal, lozenge, square, rectangular, punt-shaped, trapezoidal, and basket-shaped (of oval, square, circular, and diamond patterns). Whatever the composition of the sets — the components varied from one type of tray to another and also, but less frequently, among sets with matching trays — they took their name from that of the tray.

The tray of this particular design was called a *plateau octogone*. The first reference to trays of this shape occurs in a Stock List dated 1 January 1758.[1] The first *déjeuner* specifically named *déjeuner octogone* was sold on 18 December 1760.[2] The trays evidently came in two sizes and were produced concurrently in two different designs. Whereas on the tray which is exhibited there are no handles and the eight rounded projections are double-lobed, on a comparable tray of a *déjeuner octogone* at the Wadsworth Atheneum, which is dated 1783, the projections form an unbroken curve and the tray is fitted with two handles.[3] The majority of such *déjeuners* consisted of a teapot, sugar bowl, milk jug, and cup and saucer. The individual components did, however, vary in size and shape.

The elaborate painted and gilded decoration, characterized by strong colors of red, purple, and blue predominating, mosaic panels, speckled grounds, and boldly painted garlands, are typical of the 1760 decade. Two broth basins and stands dated 1763 and 1764, which are painted in very much the same spirit, also form part of the Wadsworth Atheneum collection.[4]

Notes:
[1] MNS, I.7.
[2] MNS, Vy3 fo. 28v.
[3] 1917.1108–1111.
[4] 1917.1163 and 1917.1164.

Literature: Chavagnac, *Morgan Cat.*, no. 117.

PAIR OF ORANGE TUBS (*caisse*)
France, Sèvres, about 1765–1770
Soft-paste porcelain, dark blue (*bleu nouveau*) ground partly speckled in gold. Each tub is painted in polychrome colors with landscape scenes in four upright rectangular reserves.
Marks: on both in blue, interlaced LLs. Incised marks on both: sp.
H. 5⅞ in. (15 cm.); W. and D. 4¹⁄₁₆ in. (10.4 cm.)
Provenance: Bought from A. B. Daniell & Sons, London, on 19 April 1904
1917.963–964

The traditional orange tub with square corners was produced in three sizes, the models and molds for the first and third sizes dating from 1754.[1] Versions of the second size were, however, made in 1753, if not earlier.

Caisses were intended for potted plants; to allow for draining, the bottom panels are invariably pierced with five holes. Clearly this piercing poses problems and in order to collect the drips square trays were designed. The models and molds of such trays of the first and second sizes date from 1755. Paradoxically, few tubs were sold with drip-trays.[2] Another solution was to replace the living plants with artificial, porcelain flowers on metal stems lacquered green.

Two variants of the traditional square tub were made, one with rounded corners and the other with incurved corners. The Stock List of 1 January 1765 lists among the new models of the preceding year a *caisse* of the second size "*à angles arrondis*" (with rounded corners).[3] This probably refers to tubs with slightly recessed rounded corners of which versions dated 1766 (two pairs), 1768, and 1769 are known.[4] There is no mention in the Stock Lists of the rarer variant with incurved corners. Apart from the Wadsworth pair, the only other examples which have been traced are a pair in the Ephrussi de Rothschild Collection, Cap Ferrat, which are dated 1766. They are painted with trophies by Charles Buteux.[5]

It is not known whether the tubs with incurved sides were also produced in three sizes. The Rothschild pair, though shorter than the Wadsworth versions (12.5 cm. compared to 15 cm.), are nevertheless marginally broader (11 cm. compared to 10.4 cm.).

Chavagnac dates the tubs to the Vincennes period. While accepting that they may have been molded in the 1750s, Marcelle Brunet rightly dates the decoration to the 1760s. The *bleu nouveau* ground, the square frames of the reserves, and the sober interlacing of the gilded myrtle leaf trails on the corners all point to a mid-1760s date. That they may also have been potted at the same time seems plausible as the incised mark, sp, occurs with the greatest frequency on wares dating from 1764 to 1769. Among these pieces is one of the four *caisses* with rounded corners, dated 1766, which are at Goodwood House.

Notes:
[1] MNS, I.7.
[2] Eriksen, *Waddesdon Cat.*, p. 42.
[3] MNS, I.7.
[4] A pair dated 1766 at the Fondation Ephrussi de Rothschild, Villa-Musée "Ile-de-France," Cap Ferrat; four dated 1766 at Goodwood House, Sussex; a pair dated 1768 at Upton House, Warwickshire (Upt/C/148); a pair dated 1769 in The Frick Collection, New York (Brunet, *Frick Cat.*, pp. 276–283).
[5] Fondation Ephrussi de Rothschild, Villa-Musée "Ile-de-France," Cap Ferrat.

Literature: Chavagnac, *Morgan Cat.*, no. 59; Brunet and Préaud, *Sèvres*, fig. 48.

67 (previous pages)

PAIR OF VASES WITH COVERS (vase ferré)
France, Sèvres, 1766
Soft-paste porcelain, green ground, richly gilded. The bosses and oves around the rim are painted turquoise blue. On each vase a pastoral scene is painted on the front reserve and double interlocking wreaths of foliage and flowers on the three others. These include laurel, bay, and oak, roses, cornflowers, and pansies.
Marks: in blue on 1046, interlaced LLs enclosing the date-letter n for 1766. Incised within the foot of the same vase, a square.
H. 17 in. (43.1 cm.); W. 7⅜ in. (18.8 cm.)
1917.1045–1046

This model proved to be one of the most popular; numerous versions in two sizes were made in the 1760s and 1770s. The Wadsworth pair are of the larger size. The earliest examples date from 1763. The plaster model, which differs, however, from these examples in the disposition of the cords, corresponds to an undated pair in the Louvre.[1] The Louvre vases which could date from 1762 may be, therefore, the first versions based on the original model before it was subsequently modified.[2] In later years some of the vases were made to a simplified design. This is in line with a trend in the 1770s towards a less aggressive form of neoclassicism, as has also been noted in the context of the vase chinois (see no. 69).

Though vases of this design bore the name of vase ferré, the first mention of a vase so named only occurs in a Stock List of 1 January 1772.[3] Earlier references to vases à cordes or à cordons may refer to this model. However, many must also have been given the generic title vases d'ornements, which explains our inability to identify many of them in the Sèvres records, as is the case with the Wadsworth pair.

A distinctive feature in the decoration of the Wadsworth vases are the turquoise blue oves and bosses which contrast with the green ground color. This sharp juxtaposition of colors, which may not appeal to our taste, evidently found favor in the 1760s in France. Similarly decorated vases are in the Louvre[4] and the British Royal Collection.[5] Other combinations of colors were also tried: turquoise blue oves and bosses with ground colors of green, dark blue (bleu nouveau), or pink streaked blue and gold; dark blue (bleu lapis) oves and bosses with a pale turquoise blue ground; green oves and white bosses with a pale turquoise blue ground.

The decoration of cartels with interlocking wreaths of differing flowers was another innovation of the 1760s (see also no. 68). Grouped in twos or threes, they are sometimes held by brightly colored ribbons seemingly tied in a bow around a gold stud. Jean-Baptiste Tandart evidently specialized in this type of decoration. At the piece rate of 3 livres per cartouche, which is approximately what he was paid in overtime, it would have taken him one day to complete each cartouche.

The pastoral scenes on the front reserves reproduce engravings. On 1917.1046 elements from two prints after François Boucher have been copied: the seated shepherdess from Les Enfans du Fumier engraved by Louis Michel Habou; and the cow and sheep from Pastorale engraved by Gabriel Huquier.[6] On 1917.1045 the scene reproduces an untitled English engraving after a Dutch or Flemish seventeenth-century master. The particular engraving which served as the model almost certainly survives in the Sèvres Archives. It was printed for J. Dubois of the Strand.[7]

Linda Roth, the Louvre center vase and the Wadsworth pair, which match each other in every particular, could well have made up the original garniture.
[5]Queen's Gallery, Sèvres, no. 46, illus.
[6]Jean-Richard, nos. 1072 and 1089. Information kindly supplied by Pierre Ennès.
[7]The inscription reads: "Printed for and Sold by J. Dubois at yᵉ Golden Head near Cecil Street in yᵉ Strand." Information kindly supplied by Pierre Ennès.

Literature: Chavagnac, Morgan Cat., no. 127.

68

PAIR OF EWERS (vase en burette)
France, Sèvres, about 1767
Soft-paste porcelain, dark blue (bleu nouveau) ground, in part gilded. The central register of each vase is painted on a white ground with six wreaths of alternating roses and cornflowers which are knotted with lavender-colored bows.
Marks: On both in blue interlaced LLs enclosing a dot.
Incised marks: none.
H. 8¹¹⁄₁₆ in. (22.1 cm.); D. 3⁹⁄₁₆ in. (9.1 cm.)
1917.1043–1044

The model and molds of burettes of the larger and second sizes are first recorded in Stock Lists of 1 January 1766 and 1 January 1767 respectively.[1] They may correspond in shape to the Wadsworth ewers, which are examples of the smaller size. In the same year that produced the model of the larger version, namely 1765, a model of a vase described as a "queue de poisson" was also made. It is perhaps significant that the forked terminals of the handles springing from the shoulders of the Wadsworth vases also bear a family resemblance to fish tails.

Chavagnac provides a detailed account of the history of the pair of vases. He identifies them in the Sales Ledgers as the pair of ewers bought for 600 livres on 31 December 1767 by Jean-Baptiste de Machault d'Arnouville who had been contrôleur général des finances between 1745 and 1754. They are described in the Sales Ledger — where they are recorded as a gift and not a purchase — as of dark blue (bleu nouveau) ground and painted with wreaths.[2] Following Machault's death in 1794 (not 1793 as stated by Chavagnac), they passed to his son and then his granddaughter, the marquise de Valanglart. Her son, the marquis de Valanglart, inherited them. Finally, following the death of his widow (née Marie-Louise-Séraphine Le Paige d'Orsenne) in 1901, they were sold, and were presumably acquired then or shortly afterwards by J. Pierpont Morgan.

Though it has not been possible to identify with any certainty the vases in the inventory drawn up on 25 February 1795 following Machault d'Arnouville's death, the family tradition linking this particular pair of vases to the financier is plausible.[3] As Monsieur Paul Rouet has kindly pointed out to the writer, Xavier de Chavagnac was the nephew by marriage of the last owner, M.-L.-S. Le Paige d'Orsenne. He could well have had access to family papers which confirmed their provenance.[4]

Notes:
[1]Musée du Louvre, OA.10593; Brunet and Préaud, Sèvres, plate 43.
[2]Eriksen, Waddesdon Cat., p. 104.
[3]MNS, I.8.
[4]Set of three vases formerly in the Harewood Collection (sold by Christie's, 1 July 1965, Lot 19, illus.). It is possible that the three vases did not originally form a set. On the center vase the front reserve is painted with a pastoral scene and the other three with double wreaths. On the flanking vases the center reserves are painted with mythological scenes, the side reserves with double wreaths, and the one on the back with a bouquet of flowers. As pointed out by

Notes:
[1]MNS, I.7.
[2]MNS, Vy4 fo. 139v.
[3]AN, Minutier Central, Etude LXXXIX liasse 925.
[4]In overtime payments in 1766 J.-B. Tandart received 72 livres for four sets of six wreaths painted on four burettes (MNS, F.8). It is conceivable that two of the four ewers to which this payment refers are the pair in the Wadsworth Atheneum.

Literature: Chavagnac, Morgan Cat., no. 126.

69

PAIR OF VASES AND COVERS (*vase chinois* or *vase à pied de globe*)
France, Sèvres, 1769
Soft-paste porcelain, dark blue (*bleu nouveau*) ground enriched with gilding. The two oval reserves on each vase are painted, on the front with a pastoral scene, and on the back with a landscape.
Marks: on both in blue, interlaced LLs enclosing the date-letter q for 1769 and below the mark of Charles-Nicolas Dodin. Incised marks: on one vase, R, and on the other, N, in script.
H. (including the base) 14¼ in. (36.3 cm.);
H. (excluding the base) 12¹³⁄₁₆ in. (32.5 cm.);
W. 5¹⁄₁₆ in. (12.9 cm.); D. 4⁵⁄₁₆ in. (11 cm.)
Provenance: Bought from Charles Wertheimer, London, on 7 April 1906
1917.1060–1061

Vases of this design illustrate the difficulty we have when trying to identify pieces in eighteenth-century Sèvres records. The model evidently has more than one name and at the same time shared one of these names with another model of totally different design.

The plaster model of the Wadsworth type of vase is still preserved in the Sèvres factory. It differs, however, from known examples as two heads of Chinamen are fitted to the shoulders. It is devoid of strapwork. This plaster model can be related to entries in the Stock Lists of 1 January 1769 and 1 January 1770 recording new models and molds of a *vase chinois* of the second and third sizes made in 1768 and of the largest size made in 1769.[1] At the same time a pair of vases of this design has been traced by Svend Eriksen in the Sèvres records for overtime payments where they are named *vases à pied de globe*.[2] As no versions with Chinamen as handles seem ever to have been produced, it might be assumed that the name *vase à pied de globe* prevailed over *vase chinois*. This does not seem to have been the case. No other mention of a *vase à pied de globe* has been found, whereas there are references to *vases chinois* from 1770 up to the end of the century. These references also relate to vases of two different types — the center one incorporating Chinamen for handles — which were modeled at a later date, possibly as early as 1773, and which were known collectively as *vases chinois*.[3] Hence the confusion.

The Wadsworth vases were among the earliest of this model to have been made. They are of the smaller size.[4] The two pastoral scenes are copied from engravings: *Le berger récompensé* and *Le panier misterieux*, both engraved by René Gaillard after François Boucher.[5] The gold frame of the front reserve is elaborately tooled with a repeating wavelike motif, which appears principally on pieces bearing date-letters for 1770 to 1774. The earliest example may date from 1769.

Notes:
[1] Brunet and Préaud, *Sèvres*, fig. 164.
[2] Eriksen, *Early Neo-Classicism*, p. 373, plate 282.
[3] Queen's Gallery, *Sèvres*, no. 40, plate III.
[4] Also dating from 1769 are a pair of the second size in the Wallace Collection (I 18,9;). Other dated versions are known. One bearing the date-letter for 1773 is in the Wallace Collection (IV A 23) and another pair made one year later in the Walters Art Gallery, Baltimore (inv. nos. 639, 640). This later pair is of a simplified design. The fluted cover and flattened, bun-shaped molding separating the bottom of the vase from the stem have been replaced by plain ones. The triglyphs and fluted straps around the bottom of the vase have been eliminated. This process of simplification occurs in a number of other models of vases in the early neoclassical style which originally date from the 1760s (see entry on *vases ferrés* for example).
[5] Jean-Richard, nos. 1032 and 1030-1.

Literature: Chavagnac, *Morgan Cat.*, no. 134; Graham Hood, "French Porcelain from the J. P. Morgan Collection at the Wadsworth Atheneum," *Connoisseur* 158 (February, 1965), p. 135, fig. 9; Graham Hood, "French Porcelain from the J. P. Morgan Collection at the Wadsworth Atheneum," *Wadsworth Atheneum Bulletin* 1, no. 3 (Winter, 1965), pp. 8–9, fig. 6.

WATER JUG AND BASIN (*pot à eau ordinaire*)

France, Sèvres, 1769

Soft-paste porcelain decorated in different tones of cobalt blue with garlands and trails of flowers which are combined with stylized laurel trails in gold. The thumb-piece is silver gilt.

Marks: in blue on both, interlaced LLs with above a stippled crown (jug only) and below the date-letter Q for 1769. Incised marks: on the jug, a Saint Andrew's cross within a square; on the basin, 6 or 9.

On the thumb-piece the discharge mark of the *sous-fermier* Julien Alaterre (1768–75).

Jug: H. (with thumb-piece) 6⅝ in. (16.1 cm.); (without thumb-piece) 6 in. (15.3 cm.); W. 5³⁄₁₆ in. (13.3 cm.); D. 4¹⁄₁₆ in. (10.3 cm.)
Basin: H. 2³⁄₁₆ in. (5.5 cm.); W. 10⁷⁄₁₆ in. (26.5 cm.); D. 7³⁄₁₆ in. (18.2 cm.)
1917.1178-1179

Water jugs of this shape, which are of traditional design, derive from those made at Meissen, Saint-Cloud, and Chantilly.[1] The Wadsworth example marks the final development, evolved at Vincennes, from a squatter and more globular shape. Made in four sizes, ranging in height from about 22.5 cm. to 12 cm., they remained in production at Sèvres throughout the eighteenth century. This jug is probably a version of the third size.

An unusual feature of the markings on the jug is the stippled crown, which in this instance does not denote hard paste. It features on a number of other pieces of soft-paste porcelain dating principally from the late 1760s, many of which are also painted in monochrome with garlands and trails of flowers. The stippled crown was not, however, used solely in the 1760 decade. It appears as early as 1753 on a teapot painted in monochrome with scattered flowers,[2] and as late as 1787 on a *gobelet litron* painted in polychrome with garlands and a floral initial.[3]

Loose, meandering trails of flowers and garlands in monochrome blue, which are sometimes threaded with stiff laurel trails in gold, often occur in the late 1760s. A close parallel to the Wadsworth pieces is provided by a water jug of the shape known as *broc Roussel*, accompanied by a basin of the same design as the Wadsworth example. Not only are they painted in the same style, but their markings also comprise a stippled crown above interlaced LLs with the date letter Q below.[4]

It is unlikely that this type of decoration was the work of a single artist at Sèvres, though one painter who certainly did decorate pieces in this style was Pierre-Antoine Méreau.[5] On the evidence of the overtime records dated 1766, 1767, and 1769 two other names can be suggested, Nicolas Catrice and Antoine Toussaint Cornaille. They were paid for painting on a variety of pieces "*guirlandes camayeux*" and "*guirlandes bleues*."[6]

Notes:
[1] Eriksen and Bellaigue, *Sèvres Porcelain*, plate 41.
[2] Private Collection in the United States.
[3] Fondation Ephrussi de Rothschild, Villa-Musée "Ile-de-France," Cap Ferrat, no. 2711A.
[4] Christie's London, 2 February 1981, lot 29, illus.
[5] Queen's Gallery, *Sèvres*, no. 63.
[6] MNS, F.8, F.9, F.11.

TEA OR COFFEE SET (*déjeuner à tiroir*) COMPRISING A TRAY (*plateau à tiroir*), SUGAR BOWL AND COVER (*pot à sucre Bouret*), MILK JUG (*pot à lait à trois pieds*) AND CUP AND SAUCER (*gobelet Bouillard*)
France, Sèvres, 1770
Soft-paste porcelain, turquoise blue *oeil-de-perdrix* ground, painted in grisaille in reserves with putti in clouds and trophies. They are linked by white bands decorated with laurel trails and berries painted naturalistically. The inclined rim of the tray is in the form of a pierced, foliate wave band.
Marks: On the tray, cup and saucer in blue, interlaced LLs enclosing the date-letter R for 1770 (lower case on the cup and saucer), with below the mark of Jacques Fontaine; on the milk jug, in blue, interlaced LLs. Incised marks: on the saucer, a Saint Andrew's cross within a rectangle.
Tray: H. 1⅛ in. (2.8 cm.); W. 9¾ in. (24.7 cm.); D. 6¹³⁄₁₆ in. (17.3 cm.)
Sugar bowl: H. 3⅞ in. (9.8 cm.); D. 3⅛ in. (8 cm.)
Milk jug: H. 4 in. (10.1 cm.); W. 4³⁄₁₆ in. (10.6 cm); D. 2¹⁵⁄₁₆ in. (7.4 cm.)
Cup: H. 2⅞ in. (6.1 cm.); W. 3⅝ in. (9.2 cm.); D. 2¾ in. (7 cm.)
Saucer: H. 1⅜ in. (3.4 cm.); D. 5¼ in. (13.4 cm.)
1917.1066–1069

The first recorded sale of a *déjeuner à tiroir* is dated 21 December 1756. Trays of this shape were, however, produced at an earlier date. One bearing the date-letter for 1755 is at Waddesdon Manor.[1] They were made in two sizes, the Waddesdon tray being an example of the second size and the Wadsworth one of the larger size. Some versions are fitted with feet — either bun-shaped or of square tapering design. The rim of the tray can be plain or pierced. Models and molds for the latter, produced in two sizes, are first recorded in the Stock List of 1 January 1759.[2]

When used as a tray for a *déjeuner*, the components which made up the set could number two, three, or four. The Wadsworth set would have constituted a three-piece set, the cup and saucer being treated as a single entity. The tray seems to have been invariably excluded when calculating the number of components making up a *déjeuner*. Judging from the records for overtime work in the 1760s, a teapot was more often than not included in the three-piece sets of the *déjeuner tiroir* to the exclusion of the milk jug.[3] There was, however, no inflexible rule. The composition of a *déjeuner* could be varied to suit the wishes of the purchaser. For example, on 3 October 1758 Lazare Duvaux sold to the King for 252 *livres* a *déjeuner* for which he specifically states that he had to provide a teapot in the place of a cup.[4]

By 1770 the *déjeuner à tiroir* is rarely mentioned by name in the Sales Ledgers. No doubt a number were sold but under the generic title *déjeuner*. One rare entry of a *déjeuner à tiroir* could refer if not to the Wadsworth set then to one similarly decorated. In December 1772 the King bought for 240 *livres* a *déjeuner à tiroir* of the larger size which was decorated with a "*fond tailandier*" ground.[5]

The turquoise blue *oeil-de-perdrix* ground, when combined with putti and trophies in grisaille or in polychrome colors and laurel trails and berries in natural colors, was a fashionable even if relatively expensive form of decoration in the early 1770s. It was favored by Lord Melbourne in 1771 and by the comtesse du Barry in 1770.

Notes:
[1] Eriksen, *Waddesdon Cat.*, no. 16.
[2] MNS, I.7.
[3] MNS, F.8 – F.10.
[4] Lazare Duvaux, no. 3230.
[5] MNS, Vy5 fo. 42.

Literature: Chavagnac, *Morgan Cat.*, no. 140; Graham Hood, "French Porcelain from the J. P. Morgan Collection at the Wadsworth Atheneum," *Wadsworth Atheneum Bulletin* 1, no. 3 (Winter, 1965), pp. 7–8, not illustrated.

BROTH BASIN, COVER AND STAND (*écuelle et plateau*)
France, Sèvres, 1772
Soft-paste porcelain, turquoise blue (*bleu céleste*) ground. Painted with marine scenes in six reserves and decorated in gold with interlaced laurel garlands.
Marks: on the bowl, traces of indecipherable painted marks; on the tray in brown, interlaced LLs enclosing the date-letter t for 1772 and above the letter n (probably a partly erased m, the mark of Jean-Louis Morin). Incised marks: on the bowl, du; on the stand, H. Scratched in the glaze, the cipher WJG (William James Goode).
Basin and cover: H. 4$\frac{13}{16}$ in. (12.2 cm.); W. 6$\frac{3}{4}$ in. (17.2 cm.); D. 5$\frac{5}{16}$ in. (13.5 cm.)
Stand: H. 1$\frac{3}{8}$ in. (3.5 cm.); W. 8$\frac{15}{16}$ in. (22.7 cm.); D. 7$\frac{3}{16}$ in. (18.3 cm.)
Provenance: W.J. Goode (see Marks). Probably Lot 80 of the Goode sale (Christie's 17 July 1895; bought by A. Wertheimer for £90); Bought from Cartier et Fils, Paris, on 20 May 1899
1917.1073

Broth basins of this design proved the most popular of all those made in the Vincennes/Sèvres factory. Models and molds in four sizes are listed in the inventory of October 1752 and versions continued in production up to the Revolution.[1] The stands varied in shape, being either round or oval. A design for the basin and cover inscribed, "*Ecuelle tourne No 3 Rectifie . . .*" (revised drawing of a turned basin, No 3 [? of the third size]) is dated 19 February 1753.[2] The Wadsworth version is probably an example of the third size.

There seems little doubt that the painting of the reserves is by Morin, the painter at Sèvres who made quayside scenes his speciality. The same scenes regularly recur on wares which either bear his mark or can be attributed to him. For example, the two scenes on the stand are repeated—sometimes exactly, even to the repetition of the same

markings on bales—on other pieces dated 1772,[3] 1775,[4] 1777,[5] and 1780.[6] If undated examples of Sèvres porcelain were included, the list could be further extended. Clearly, originality within a given genre was not considered of importance when selecting designs to be reproduced on individual pieces.

Broth was sometimes taken on awakening in the morning, though in the eighteenth century, coffee or chocolate was generally preferred. Madame Campan tells us that Marie-Antoinette ate sparingly, her supper consisting of broth, a chicken wing, and biscuits dipped in water.[7] In December 1772, Marie-Antoinette bought two broth basins and stands. One, priced at 324 *livres*, was painted a dark blue (*beau bleu*) ground and was decorated with marine scenes. The other, costing 300 *livres*, was of turquoise blue (*bleu céleste*) ground. It too may have been painted with marine scenes.[8] Though it would be straining credulity to suggest on this evidence that the Wadsworth example had once belonged to Marie-Antoinette, the figure of 300 *livres* could well approximate its sale price.

Notes:
[1] Préaud and Faÿ-Hallé, pp. 49–50.
[2] MNS, R.1, L.3, d.2.
[3] Two *gobelets litrons* and their saucers, one in the Royal Collection (Queen's Gallery, *Sèvres*, no. 118), the other formerly in the Earl of Harewood's collection (sold by Christie's, London, 1 July 1965, Lot 31, illus.).
[4] A saucer which is part of a *déjeuner à baguettes* in the Kress Collection, Metropolitan Museum of Art (C. C. Dauterman, J. Parker, and E. A. Standen, *Decorative Art from the Samuel H. Kress Collection at the Metropolitan Museum of Art* [London, 1964], no. 57a–h, fig. 203).
[5] A *gobelet enfoncé* in the Wallace Collection (IV A-32).
[6] A *vase cassolette* in the Bearsted Collection, Upton House (C/106).
[7] Madame Campan, *Mémoires sur la vie privée de Marie-Antoinette* (London, 1823), I, p. 296.
[8] MNS, Vy3 fo. 42v.

Literature: Chavagnac, *Morgan Cat.*, no. 144.

CUP AND SAUCER (*gobelet litron et soucoupe*)
France, Sèvres, 1776
Soft-paste porcelain, yellow ground, elaborately gilded. The cup is painted with the portrait of a fashionably dressed woman in polychrome colors, and the saucer with a cipher formed by the letters M (gold scrolls), L (roses), and C (cornflowers) in three reserves.
Marks: on both in blue, interlaced LLs enclosing the date-letter Y for 1776 and below the marks of Charles-Nicolas Dodin (blue) and Etienne-Henry Le Guay (gold).
Cup: H. 3 in. (7.6 cm.); W. 3 15/16 in. (10 cm.); D. 2 15/16 in. (7.5 cm.)
Saucer: H. 1 15/16 in. (3.7 cm.); D. 5 15/16 in. (15.1 cm.)
Provenance: Bought from A. B. Daniell & Sons, London, on 19 April 1904
1917.1089

Portraits painted on Sèvres porcelain were at their most popular during the period 1773 to the Revolution. The earliest example that is known, however, dates from 1761. It is a portrait of Louis XV painted in grisaille on a plaque within a polychrome wreath.[1] Though some portraits were also painted on vases and very occasionally on plates, cups of the *gobelet litron* pattern were most frequently used.

The range of "sitters" was considerable. Perhaps the most often repeated portraits were those of the King and Queen and members of the Royal Family, a number of which were commissioned by the sovereign himself and were intended as gifts. Another practice was to present a visiting foreigner of note with a cup bearing his or her likeness, as occurred in 1782 on the occasion of the visit of Grand Duke Paul Petrovitch and his wife Maria Feodorovna traveling under the assumed names of Comte and Comtesse du Nord.[2] Figures in the public eye were similarly honored: Benjamin Franklin between 1778 and 1780 who, since his arrival in France in 1776, had become something of a cult figure; the

Marquis de Lafayette in 1790 who had been elected head of the National Guard the previous year; Jean-Sylvain Bailly, also in 1790, who had been proclaimed the first mayor of Paris in 1789. Scientists, men of letters, and heroes (real and legendary) were also included in the pantheon: Diderot, Rabelais, Homer, Hercules, Archimedes, and Cromwell, for example. Even the Duke of Marlborough's portrait was painted on one cup in 1783. This posthumous tribute to the bogeyman *par excellence* of the French may owe something to the revival in popularity at the Court of Versailles of the ditty "*Malbrough s'en va-t-en guerre*," which Madame Poitrine, the aptly named wet nurse of the Dauphin, sang as a lullaby.[3] Finally, portraits of the less exalted were painted at the special request of friends or relations, such as those of the children of the Marchioness of Carmarthen in 1777, and of an anonymous burgomaster in 1788.

Although the Wadsworth cup is signed by Dodin and is dated 1776, and even though we know the initials of the "sitter," MLC, it has not been possible to identify the cup and saucer in the Sèvres records.[4]

Notes:
[1] The plaque is in the Hermitage Museum, Leningrad.
[2] MNS, Vy8 fo. 215v, entry dated 13 June 1782.
[3] Jacques Urbain, *La Chanson populaire en Suisse Romande* (Yverdon, 1978), II, p. 119. The compiler is indebted to Giles Barber for this reference.
[4] On 12 November 1776 Madame de Bourbonne bought for 288 *livres* a *gobelet litron* of the second size, richly gilded and painted with an unnamed portrait (MNS, Vy6 fo. 136v). Though it is tempting to relate this entry in the Sales Ledger to the Wadsworth cup, it would be wrong to do so as the cup is undoubtedly of the largest and not of the second size. Another entry dated 1776 which appears in the records for overtime work refers to the payment of 120 *livres* for the painting of a portrait on a cup (MNS, F.18). Once again this entry cannot refer to the Wadsworth cup as the payment was made to Pierre-Nicolas Pithou and not to Dodin. Be that as it may, these two entries give an idea of the large sums involved in the production of portrait cups and saucers similar in quality to the Wadsworth examples.

Literature: Chavagnac, *Morgan Cat.*, no. 160.

75

BROTH BASIN, COVER AND STAND (*écuelle et plateau nouvelle forme*)
France, Sèvres, 1784
Soft-paste porcelain, dark blue (*beau bleu*) ground. Painted with
allegorical and mythological scenes in six reserves and decorated in
gold with bulrushes and garlands of flowers.
Marks: on both in blue, interlaced LLs enclosing the date-letters GG
for 1784 and above the mark of the painter Antoine Caton; on the
basin below the LLs, the mark in gold of the gilder Etienne-Henry Le
Guay. Incised marks: 13 and 45 on the basin, and 13 on the stand.
Basin and cover: H. 5 in (12.7 cm.); W. 7$\frac{3}{8}$ in. (18.7 cm.);
D. 6 in. (15.2 cm.)
Stand: H. 1$\frac{7}{8}$ in. (4.7 cm.); W. 9$\frac{13}{16}$ in. (25 cm.); D. 9$\frac{1}{8}$ in. (23.2 cm.)
1917.1112

Broth basins were produced at Vincennes and Sèvres in a wide variety of forms, varying in shape and size, as well as in the design of the knobs and handles. The type most often repeated, and which remained in favor from the early years of production at Vincennes right up to the Revolution, incorporates a berried branch for the knob and pairs of twisted branches for the handles. Its stand, which is very rarely fitted with handles, is either circular (often with a lobed rim) or oval with a raised undulating rim (see no. 73).[1]

On 6 April 1773 Madame du Barry bought for 192 *livres* a broth basin of a new shape ("*forme nouvelle*") which the Director of the factory, Melchior-François Parent, delivered personally to Louis XV's mistress.[2] It may well have been one of the first of this new line to have been successfully produced at Sèvres.

The Wadsworth basin and stand probably represent a later example of this new shape which was made in two sizes.[3] It can probably be identified with an entry in the Artists' Ledger under Caton's name which is dated 6 July 1784. On that date he received for decoration a broth basin of the new shape in the larger size, which was painted a *beau bleu* ground and which he decorated with miniature scenes. In the course of firing, the original cover was damaged and had to be replaced.[4] It was probably the same basin and stand which were placed in the kiln for painted decoration on 27 December 1784. The entry reads, "*1 Ecuelle forme nouvelle beaux bleu figure* [painter] *Caton*, [gilder] *Cornaille*."[5]

Figure painting was the most costly form of decoration on Sèvres porcelain. Only the finest and most highly paid artists were employed to do this work. For the most part they copied engravings. Four out of six of the compositions on this basin and stand have been traced to prints.[6] Two of these prints were copied in 1789 by Nicolas-Pierre Pithou and Pierre-André Le Guay on a shell-shaped fruit which forms part of the famous service, now largely at Windsor Castle, commissioned in 1783 by Louis XVI for his own personal use at Versailles.[7] It was half completed on the King's execution ten years later. Among the pieces which were never made were four *écuelles*, each costing 720 *livres*. The gilding apart, the Wadsworth version gives us some idea of their likely appearance.

Notes:
[1]Préaud and Faÿ-Hallé, *Vincennes Cat.*, nos. 83 and 85.
[2]MNS, Vy5 fo. 135v.
[3]It differs from the earlier traditional type in the pomegranate knob of the cover, in the loop-like handles of the basin, each formed of a single branch bifurcating at the top, and in the even, circular outline of the shallow stand which is fitted with projecting handles. Although some of these features vary on other versions of broth basins judged to be of the new shape, there is documentary evidence to suggest that the Wadsworth example was indeed classed as "*forme nouvelle*."
[4]MNS, Vj'3 fo. 66.
[5]MNS, Vl'2 fo. 125. As the basin bears the mark of the gilder Le Guay, and not that of the painter and gilder Antoine-Toussaint Cornaille, this identification may seem unconvincing. However, as there are no other *écuelles* listed in the kiln records which were painted at the time by Caton, and as some entries in this class of document have been proved inaccurate in the past, too much should not be made of this apparent conflict of evidence.
[6]The engraved source on the reserves of the basin are "Jupiter and Antiope" by Etienne Fessard (1758) after Carle Vanloo, and "The Joys of Summer" by Pierre-Etienne Moitte (about 1770) after François Boucher. The two scenes on the stand are taken from illustrations to Fénelon's "The Adventures of Telemachus," both engraved by Charles-Emmanuel Patas after designs by Charles Monnet and published between 1776 and 1782. They represent Venus bringing Cupid to the help of Calypso, and Telemachus recounting his adventures to Calypso.
[7]G. de Bellaigue, *Sèvres Porcelain in the collection of Her Majesty The Queen*, vol. 1: "The Louis XVI Service" (Cambridge, England, 1986), no. 125, pp. 200–201.

Literature: Chavagnac, *Morgan Cat.*, no. 175.

PLATE (*assiette unie*)
France, Sèvres, 1785
Soft-paste porcelain, turquoise ground. Painted with classical scenes in
grisaille on a brown ground in three reserves on the border, with
garlands and in the center with the crowned cipher of Catherine the
Great, all in polychrome colors and gold.
Marks : in blue, interlaced LLs enclosing the date-letters hh for 1785
with above, the mark of Nicolas Bulidon and below, the mark of
Etienne-Henry Le Guay in gold. Incised mark : 24.
D. 9⅜ in. (23.8 cm.)
Provenance : Bought from A. B. Daniell & Sons, London,
on 17 April 1902
1917.1095

Though the plate differs in size and outline from those which formed part of the famous Sèvres service commissioned by Catherine the Great in 1776 and delivered in 1779, the decoration is identical, even to the reproduction of the Empress's cipher.[1]

This service, which, at the Empress's wish, was to be "in the best and newest style," posed a challenge to the Sèvres factory. New shapes, new colors, and new designs had to be devised and tested within a very short span of time. Despite the many difficulties encountered, they were overcome and the service was hailed a *tour de force* of the potter's craft. To satisfy the curiosity of courtiers, the Russian ambassador, Prince Ivan Sergeyevich Bariatinsky, was asked by Henri Bertin, the minister in charge of the French royal household, whether the pieces from the service could not be exhibited at the end-of-the-year sale held in the King's private apartments in Versailles.[2] On 20 May 1779 Louis XVI paid a visit to Sèvres where he would have seen the complete service shortly before its dispatch to Russia.[3]

After completion of the service, a few additional pieces were sold to private individuals and dealers. It is thus that Madame du Barry bought a teapot for 216 *livres* on 14 July 1779 and another for 144 *livres* on 29 April 1788.[4] The Wadsworth plate could have been produced as a collector's item.[5]

Evoking Catherine II's passion for the collecting of gems, the major theme of the decoration of the service was a series of medallions containing cameos. Mythology and Greek and Roman history were the sources for the bas-relief scenes. On the Wadsworth plate they are all taken from Roman history and represent Numa Pompilius establishing the laws of the city; Hannibal vowing that he would destroy Rome; and the Roman army passing under the Candine yoke.

Notes:

[1] Rosalind Savill, "'Cameo Fever': Six Pieces from the Sèvres Porcelain Dinner Service Made for Catherine II of Russia," *Apollo* (November 1982), pp. 304–311.

[2] MNS, Ebl.

[3] Savill, "Cameo Fever," p. 309.

[4] MNS, Vy7 fo. 152; Vy10 fo. 243. As the teapots forming part of the service were priced at 633 *livres*, it follows that the two bought by Madame du Barry must have been either undecorated or decorated much more simply.

[5] Though the plate cannot be identified in the Sèvres Sales Ledgers, one priced at the low figure of 150 *livres* — Catherine II paid 242 *livres* for each of her plates — formed part of the factory's stock on 30 March 1786. It is listed as "*1 Assiette du Service de Russie*" (MNS, I.8). In any event a plate, which may well be the Wadsworth version, was placed in the kiln for painted decoration on 1 August 1785. It is described as "*1 assiette unie bleu celeste Pareille au Service Russe*" (MNS, Vl'2 fo. 145). The gilder was E.-H. Le Guay. No artist's name is given. A possible candidate for the painter of the cameo scenes was François-Pascal Philippine. On 30 April 1785 he received for decoration "*1 Assiette bleu celeste Service de Russie*" (MNS, Vj'3 fo. 220v). Another entry in the Artists' Ledger, dated 14 May 1785, could refer to Nicolas Bulidon's contribution. On that date he took delivery of a turquoise-blue ground plate which he painted with garlands of flowers (MNS, Vj'3 fo. 58v).

Literature: Chavagnac, *Morgan Cat.*, no. 166.

CUP AND SAUCER (*gobelet litron et soucoupe*)
France, Sèvres, 1788
Soft-paste porcelain, yellow ground painted in manganese with
continuous landscape scenes interrupted by oval reserves containing
diminutive polychrome landscapes.
Marks: on both in blue, interlaced LLs above the mark of André-
Vincent Vielliard and the date-letters KK for 1788.
Incised marks: on the cup 21 and 46; on the saucer 40.
Cup: H. 2⅜ in. (6 cm.); W. 2¹⁵⁄₁₆ in. (7.5 cm.); D. 2³⁄₁₆ in. (5.6 cm.)
Saucer: H. 1³⁄₁₆ in. (3 cm.); D. 4¹³⁄₁₆ in. (12.2 cm.)
1917.1127

This *gobelet litron* is of the third size and is possibly one of six yellow
ground cups of this size which Vielliard received for decoration in 1788
(four on 31 January and two on 3 March).[1] On the evidence of the entries
in the Artists' Ledger, he painted landscape scenes on each of these cups
and saucers. A cup and saucer identically decorated and marked, and of
the same size, is in the Fitzwilliam Museum, Cambridge.[2]

Vielliard was a prolific artist whose work closely reflects the changing
fashions of the times. In the 1750s he favored putti in clouds and children
in pastoral scenes, many of whom were based on François Boucher's
designs (cf. the Wadsworth *déjeuner Hebert*, 1917.967–971); in the late
1750s and 1760s Teniers-like scenes and still lifes of gardening implements; in the 1770s and 1780s panoramic landscape and lakeside
scenes, such as are painted on the Wadsworth cup and saucer, and on a
broth basin and stand dated 1780 also at the Wadsworth Atheneum
(1917.1126). In 1784 we find him painting balloon ascents commemorat-
ing the first ascent by man in the previous year. During the late 1770s
and 1780s he combined such miniature scenes with geometrically
designed borders forming broken lines, zigzags, and angular patterns
reminiscent of the ground plans of military redoubts. It is perhaps to
these that the terms "*bordure de Vielliard*" and "*frize de Vielliard*" refer
which occur in the Artists' Ledgers under different painters' names and
which also feature in Kiln Ledgers during the period 1778 to 1785.

Notes:
[1]MNS, Vj'4 fos. 256v, 257.
[2]Inv. no. C61-1961.

Literature: Chavagnac, *Morgan Cat.*, no. 192.

CUP AND SAUCER (*gobelet litron et soucoupe*)
France, Sèvres, 1789
White ground, painted with a rebus and floral trails.
Marks: in blue on the cup, interlaced LLs with above an unidentified artist's mark (a loosely formed Y) and below a Y, probably the mark of Edmé-François Bouillat. Incised mark: on the saucer, 46.
Cup: H. 2⅜ in. (6.1 cm.); W. 2¹⁵⁄₁₆ in. (7.5 cm.); D. 2³⁄₁₆ in. (5.6 cm.)
Saucer: H. 1⅛ in. (2.9 cm.); D. 4¹³⁄₁₆ in. (12.2 cm.)
Provenance: Probably one of a pair of cups and saucers bought from Cartier et Fils, Paris, on 24 May 1901
1917.1134

For a brief period of three years, from 1787 to 1789, artists at Sèvres were employed to paint *gobelets litrons* and their saucers with an eccentric type of decoration, the rebus.[1] There are three such examples in the Wadsworth Atheneum, two bearing date-letters for 1789 and one for 1788.[2] If we are to judge from their thinly veiled messages, generally couched in terms appropriate to a *billet doux*, they were aimed at a restricted market, that formed by love-sick gallants pining for their mistresses.

In translation the rebus on the cup and saucer which are exhibited read:

> *Show yourself as nature has made you without artifice and you will be adored by every mortal.*
> *To captivate forever more the swain who loves you, you need no finer apparel than yourself unadorned.*[3]

Edmé-François Bouillat was one of about twelve artists who are known to have been employed at Sèvres to paint rebuses on cups and saucers. On 22 December 1788 he took delivery of six cups and saucers of the third size, which he painted in this manner, no doubt completing the decoration in 1789.[4] The Wadsworth *gobelet litron* which is of the third size could well have been one of these.

Notes:
[1] According to Antoine Furetière (*Dictionnaire universel*) these punning verbal or pictorial images, which were at their most popular in the seventeenth century, had by 1727 fallen out of favor and were only used on coats of arms and by sign writers. Their appearance at Sèvres in the 1780s suggests that they enjoyed a revival of popularity. The evidence is provided by entries in the Artists' Ledger (Vj'4) and Kiln Ledger (Vl'3) and in the records for overtime payments in 1788 (F.30).
[2] 1917.1133; 1917.1174.
[3] Saucer: "*De vos seuls agréments | montrez vous décorée et de tous les mortels | vous serez adorée.*" Cup: "*Pour fixer sans retour le pâtre qui vous aime vous êtes à vous même votre plus bel atour.*"
[4] MNS, Vj'4 fo. 43.

Literature: Chavagnac, *Morgan Cat.*, no. 198 (part).

PLATE (*assiette unie*)
France, Sèvres, 1794
Soft-paste porcelain, yellow ground. Painted in the center in polychrome colors with a single bird in a landscape setting and on the border in black with stylized ornaments.
Marks: in blue, interlaced LLs enclosing the date-letters qq for 1794 with below the marks of Etienne Evans (in blue) and Sophie Binet (in black). Incised mark: JB.
D. 9$\frac{11}{16}$ in. (24.6 cm.)
Provenance: Bought from Jacques Seligmann, Paris, on 29 May 1903, together with three other plates from the same service (1917.1147, 1149–1150)
1917.1148

From the very earliest times in the history of the Vincennes and Sèvres factories, birds were reproduced as decoration. Their popularity was second only to that of flowers. At first they were largely imaginary and stylized. Later, from the 1760s onwards, in line with the trend towards realism which affected all branches of the decorative arts, identifiable species were reproduced and the names of the birds were inscribed on the reverse of the pieces.

In order to achieve the accuracy demanded, illustrated editions of ornithological books were consulted. This was already the practice in other European factories. At Chelsea, for example, many of the factory's models of birds were based on George Edward's illustrations. It was perhaps with some of these in mind that George Edwards in the sixth edition of *Gleanings of Natural History* (1760) complained, "I have observed that several of our manufacturers that imitate China ware, . . . have filled the shops in London with images . . . copied . . . and coloured after the figures in my History of Birds, most of which are sadly represented both as to shape and colouring."[1]

At Sèvres during the last quarter of the eighteenth century, the engravings which were most frequently copied were the colored illustrations by François-Nicolas Martinet which accompanied the ten-volume edition of the Comte de Buffon's *Histoire naturelle des oiseaux* (1770–1786). The set when completed numbered 1,008 plates. From 1781 onwards, services were made at Sèvres which reproduced these illustrations. The bird on the piece exhibited, which is inscribed on the reverse *Oiseau-Mouche à larges tuyaux de Cayenne*, is based on Martinet's Plate 672 published in Volume VII (1783).[2]

This porcelain plate, together with three others bearing the same date-letters and a pair of monteiths dated 1795, all five now at the Wadsworth Atheneum, may have formed part of a service sold to the *citoyen* Speelman on 6 *brumaire an* IV (28 October 1795).[3]

Notes:
[1]Mireille Jottrand, "La Porcelaine de Tournai et le décor d'oiseaux copiés de livres d'ornithologie," *Cahiers de Mariemont* 5 (1974) and 6 (1975), p. 43.
[2]The year 1783 may not provide an approximate dating for the engraving, as the engravings are not in numbered order in the ten volumes.
[3]1917.1147, 1149–1150; 1917.1151–1152. This service is described in the Sales Ledger as a yellow ground service painted with Buffon's birds. Each plate was priced in the debased currency of the times at 1,080 francs and the monteiths at 7,200 francs each (MNS, Vy12, fo. 67v). Entries in the Artists' Ledger may refer to the production of this service. Probably in April 1794 Evans received for decoration twelve yellow ground plates which he painted with Buffon's birds at a cost of 6 francs per plate (MNS, Vj'6, fo. 41). On 9 July or shortly afterwards Sophie Binet took delivery of fourteen yellow ground plates which she decorated with a "*petite frize noir*" — no doubt the term used at Sèvres to describe the black stylized border decoration (MNS, Vj'6, fo. 20).

Literature: Chavagnac, *Morgan Cat.*, no. 203.

1: *Silver Dish: David and Goliath*, Byzantine (Cypress), about 610-630. The Metropolitan Museum of Art, Gift of J. Pierpont Morgan, 1917.

ANTIQUITY
Glass, bronze, pottery, and marble objects from the Julian Gréau collection, ranging in date from about 3000 B.C. to fifth century A.D. (approximately 800 pieces, not including fragments, which brings the total to over 2000).

Assyrian Art
Six alabaster reliefs from Ashurnasir-pal.

Egyptian Art
Approximately 700 works, including the Ward Collection of Egyptian scarabs and small material, some works from the Gréau Collection, and other items Morgan bought during trips to the Metropolitan's excavation in Egypt.

Greek, Etruscan, and Roman Art
At least fifty-four pieces from classical antiquity, including Greek and Etruscan terracottas and bronzes, and Roman bronzes, ivories, bone, and glass.

Merovingian, Gallo-Roman, and Germanic Art
Over 600 Merovingian and Gallo-Roman antiquities, and about 400 Germanic antiquities from the Quackenberg Collection. These objects range in date from the end of the Roman Empire to the beginning of the Carolingian period (fourth–eighth centuries). Most of them were discovered in tombs in France and Germany. They are primarily of gold, bronze, and glass, and all are articles of personal use or adornment, such as jewelry, belt buckles, and daggers.

2: *Shrine or Sacrement house: scenes from the Life of Christ*, French, Limoges, champlevé enamel, thirteenth century. The Metropolitan Museum of Art, Gift of J. Pierpont Morgan, 1917.

BYZANTINE AND MEDIEVAL

Primarily ecclesiastical objects made of precious materials, especially gold, enamel, and ivory.

Byzantine Art

Objects from the fourth through eleventh centuries, the majority being cloisonné enamels, ivory diptychs, book covers, boxes, and devotional tablets, and gold and silver pieces. These last include a group of objects found on Cyprus, most notably six silver plates decorated with figural reliefs (Figure 1) and a very rare group of gold jewelry.

Medieval Art

A comprehensive collection of ivories, enamels, stone and wood sculptures, and metalwork, including about 130 pieces of French enamels, Limoges and champlevé, in the form of plaques, panels, reliquaries, and crucifixes (Figure 2), and French and German ivory plaques, diptychs, triptychs, figural groups, and caskets. Many of the objects were made for liturgical purposes, among them censers, chalices, and ciboriums; crucifixes, croziers, and miters. From the Gothic period, thirteenth–fifteenth centuries, are many French and Flemish sculptures, and a large collection of furniture, ivories, woodwork, and architectural fragments from the Georges Hoentschel Collection. Noteworthy also are the *Pieta* and *Entombment* from the Chateau de Biron, France, and five Sacrament tapestries.

RENAISSANCE

Sculpture, including Della Robbian terracottas, decorative items such as mirror frames, some small bronzes, and a collection of small boxwood and honestone carvings; about 80 Italian, fourteenth–sixteenth-century enamels, among them plaques and ewers; metalwork, primarily silver and silver-gilt, from Northern and Southern Europe, made for both ecclesiastical and domestic purposes, including reliquaries, chalices, incense burners, cups, beakers, tankards, and salvers; over fifty pieces of jewelry, such as gold necklaces, brooches, rings, pendants, medals, and medallions; ceramics, including some important examples of sixteenth-century French Pallisy and St. Porchaire ware, and the much larger Gaston LeBreton collection, comprised of over 200 examples of French faience, mostly from Rouen (these date from the sixteenth through the eighteenth centuries); the *Negroli Casque*, a masterpiece of European armor, dated 1543; paintings from the Flemish and Italian Schools, including works by Jan van Eyck, Roger van der Weyden, and Mabuse, Sebastiano del Piombo, and Raphael's magnificent *Colonna Madonna* (Figure 3).

BAROQUE

Seventeenth- and eighteenth-century French decorative arts from the Hoentschel collection (given to the Metropolitan in 1907), numbering over 1000 pieces, made up primarily of furniture, decorative paintings, and decorative woodwork; several hundred snuff boxes, scent bottles, patch boxes, and dance programs (*carnets de bal*), made of gold and other precious materials, and decorated with jewels, enamels, and miniature paintings; a large collection of watches, many from the Marfels Collection, dating from the sixteenth-eighteenth centuries, from England, France, Germany, Italy, Austria, Switzerland, and the Netherlands. They are cased in gold, silver, copper-gilt, and crystal, and decorated with enamels and jewels; paintings from the French, Dutch, and Flemish Schools, including works by Terborch, Metsu, Maes, and Peter Paul Rubens, and eight paintings by Hubert Robert.

3: Raphael, *Madonna Enthroned* (*The Colonna Madonna*). The Metropolitan Museum of Art, Gift of J. Pierpont Morgan, 1916.

The Wadsworth Atheneum

Ancient Bronzes

The Wadsworth Atheneum received over eighty ancient bronzes from Morgan's collection (1917.815–897) (Figure 1). A small number of important pieces remained at the Morgan Library. The Atheneum's collection contains a handful of Egyptian bronze statuettes, most of good quality, the best and most impressive of which is the *Seated Bronze Cat* (1917.520). Close to life-size, this cat is technically of high quality, with incised details, and in excellent condition. Of the Greek bronzes in the collection, the small statuette of a helmeted and *Cloaked Warrior* (1917.815) has long been recognized as a masterpiece. Dating to the archaic period, from which few bronzes have survived, its nearly perfect condition, as well as its subject and form, make it unique. The Hellenistic period is represented by the statuette of a *Running Fawn* (1917.843), which may have originally been intended to decorate a piece of furniture or to have been part of a group of figures.

Perhaps the technically best bronze in the Morgan collection is a dog-headed *Patera Handle* (1917.850). While broken from its patera, its condition otherwise is perfect, preserving a smooth glossy surface and all the original silver inlay. On the base of the handle is the remains of a scrolled floral motif typical of Augustan art, making it one of the best examples of decorative bronzes that survive from the early empire.

Another good example of Roman decorative bronzes is the *Seated Actor on an Altar* (1917.886). The bronze was originally a container: the actor is hinged to serve as a lid, sliding to one side to reveal a container in the altar. A weight in the form of a *Bearded Man* (1917.891) was actually created as a portrait bust, and only later was converted to use as a weight by the addition of a ring on the top, a practice of the late empire. Stylistically it can be dated to the late first century or early second century A.D. While its subject is unknown, the beard on the lower jaw may indicate that it is of provincial or even barbarian origin.

1 : Ancient Roman Bronzes. The Wadsworth Atheneum, Hartford, Gift of J. Pierpont Morgan, 1917.

Ancient Glass and Pottery

In addition to ancient bronzes, the Morgan collection contains 228 pieces of ancient glass, mostly from the Roman Empire (1917.586–814). They all were part of the Gréau collection which Morgan bought *en bloc*. Other portions of this collection are at the Metropolitan Museum of Art. Some noteworthy examples are an East Mediterranean, "Sidonian" type *Jug*, first century A.D., the body of greenish glass blown in a mold and a blue glass handle; an East Mediterranean *Bowl* of the late Hellenistic period which is cast and lathe-polished, with lathe-cut grooves below its rim, and an East Mediterranean blown glass *Beaker* from the fourth century A.D., with bobbed decoration.

The pottery, also from the Gréau collection, is mostly of Gallo-Roman origin. In general this group consists of small vessels and some fragments. Much of it is from the area of Auvergne.

The Atheneum also received two large-scale ancient works, a pair of marble *Lions*, four and one-half feet long, and a very large Roman porphyry *Bathtub*.

Majolica

The Wadsworth Atheneum received forty-nine pieces (1917.406–454) of the over one hundred pieces originally in Morgan's collection. There are examples from the fifteenth and sixteenth centuries representing the many centers of majolica production in Italy, including Urbino, Florence, Deruta, Caffaggiolo, Castel Durante, and Siena. There is also a small group of wares in the style of Orvieto but which date mostly from the nineteenth century.

Silver

There are forty-eight pieces of Continental silver and silver-gilt, primarily from Germany, dating from the seventeenth and eighteenth centuries (1917.248–295). Many of the great German metalwork centers are represented, including Augsburg, Breslau, Dresden, Nuremberg, Danzig, and Hamburg.

Ivories

A very small portion of the Morgan collection consists of ivories, twenty-two in all (1917.296–317). They are mostly Flemish or German seventeenth-century examples, including tankards, covered goblets, and statuettes.

European Glass

The European glass from the Morgan collection comprises a rather small group, thirty-six pieces (1917.319–354). They are mostly from Venice or in the Venetian style (*façon de Venise*), but there are some examples from France. They date primarily from the seventeenth century, with a few pieces from the sixteenth century (Figure 2).

The most important sixteenth-century piece is a *Pilgrim Flask* (1917.336), probably from Venice, dating about 1500–1525. It is elaborately enameled with birds, animals, and landscapes. From the seventeenth century there are several goblets and wine glasses. Among them there is one probably from Venice, with a stem decoration of a large yellow and white flower with blue and green leaves (1917.341), and another, colorless *Wine Glass* with a flared, saucer-like top (1917.347). Perhaps the most important Italian seventeenth-century work is the green blown and molded *Vase* with copper-gilt mounts, which probably came from Venice (1917.354).

French glass is represented by a colorful *Bottle* of translucent light blue, yellow, red, and white non-lead, blown glass (1917.323), from about the late seventeenth century. The colors are applied as random splotches on the blue body.

2: Venetian Glass, The Wadsworth Atheneum, Hartford, Gift of J. Pierpont Morgan, 1917.

3 : *Pair of Chinese Figures*, French, St. Cloud, eighteenth century.
The Wadsworth Atheneum, Hartford, Gift of J. Pierpont Morgan, 1917.897-898.

5 : *The Magic Lantern*, French, Mennecy-Villeroy, mid-eighteenth century.
Wadsworth Atheneum, Hartford, Gift of J. Pierpont Morgan, 1917.924.

German Porcelain

There are 362 pieces of German porcelain (1917.1186–1547), the vast majority from the Meissen factory. All but about twenty-five are figures or groups of figures. There are very few tablewares, those mostly late rococo examples. The collection contains no Böttger stoneware or early figures, and no Kaendler figures from before about 1740. The successive years of production, however, are represented by numerous examples. There are many different types of figures in the collection: Italian comedy figures, including several from the Duke of Weissenfels series; courtly genre groups; and pastoral groups from the 1740–1755 period. There are also several charming chinoiserie groups. Surprisingly, there are no works by the later Meissen artists Acier or Punct, and no truly neoclassical pieces.

Other German factories are sparingly represented. There is a pair of *Sweetmeat Dishes* made at the Du Paquier factory, Vienna (1917.1229–1230), and a wonderful Frankenthal *Shepherd and Shepherdess* (1917.1540) from about 1770. Finally there are several individual figures from other porcelain centers, such as a lovely *Female Figure* from Kloster-Veilsdorf (1917.928).

French Porcelain

The Atheneum has 290 pieces of French porcelain from Morgan's collection (1917.897–1185), over 200 of them Vincennes and Sèvres. All of it dates from the eighteenth century. There are several early figural groups in white glazed porcelain. Other works made while the factory was at Vincennes illustrate some of the early colors and shapes developed. Most of the colors and many of the forms used subsequently at Sèvres can also be found in the collection. The collection ranges in date from the 1750s through the Revolutionary period. Of special interest are biscuit figures from the 1760s and 1770s. Notable also are pieces from the aristocratic services of Madame du Barry and Charlotte Louise, Queen of Naples.

There are about fifty works from important French factories other than Sèvres. From St. Cloud, the earliest French center for porcelain production, there is an important pair of white glazed *Chinese Figures* (1917.897–898) (Figure 3). Probably dating from the second quarter of the eighteenth century, they illustrate the potter's ability to create animated, small-scale sculpture in porcelain.

The Chantilly porcelain factory, founded about 1725 under the patronage of the Prince de Condé, is represented by several pieces. There are two covered jars with almost identical kakiemon-style decoration with coats of arms in the center (1917.901–902). In addition, there is a notable pair of candelabra with Chinese figures mounted in gilt-bronze, from about 1745 (1917.950–951) (Figure 4) Figures in this style were typical of the production of the Chantilly factory.

Many other pieces in the collection can be attributed to the Mennecy-Villeroy factory, which was founded in 1734 in Paris and transferred to Mennecy in 1748. These include several small figural groups, often representing children with animals, decorated in pastel enamels for a charming effect. There is also a larger, more important figural group, *The Magic Lantern* (1917.924), which illustrates Mennecy's ability to create well-modeled, three-dimensional compositions, decorated with muted colors (Figure 5). A more unusual example from Mennecy is the *Ewer and Basin* (1917.921–922), with an extraordinary pea-green ground and red, yellow, and black decoration of flowers and parrots. Finally, there is the monumental, white glazed *Bust of Louis XV* (1917.1509), dating from about 1750–55, after a model for a marble sculpture by Jacques-François-Joseph Saly of 1752. It is extraordinary in its size (it had to be fired in two pieces in order to fit into the kiln) and in the grandeur of the conception. It is also very rare, for it is one of only two known examples of this model, the other recently acquired by the J. Paul Getty Museum, Malibu.

English Ceramics

Morgan's collection does not contain very many examples of the English ceramicists' art. In fact, it includes only a small, specialized group of salt-glaze ware from Staffordshire, numbering forty-eight pieces (1917.358–405). The group is comprised of teapots, cups and saucers, pitchers, and some small animal figures, all dating from the middle of the eighteenth century. Typical of the objects in Morgan's collection of salt-glaze are three teapots, two decorated with a form of underglaze blue called "Littler blue" and afterward enameled with pink and green roses (1917.372 and 1917.374), and a third teapot decorated with a portrait of Frederick III, King of Prussia (1917.377).

4: *Pair of Candelabra*, French, Chantilly, eighteenth century. The Wadsworth Atheneum, Hartford, Gift of J. Pierpont Morgan, 1917.950–951.

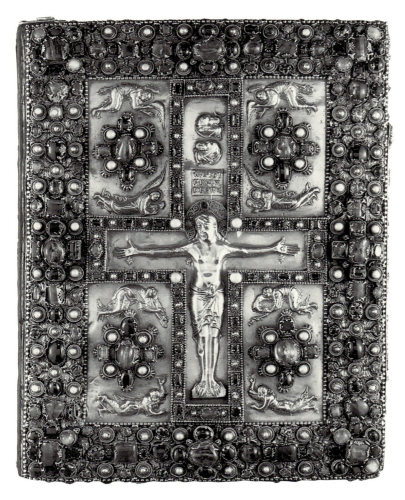

1: *Jeweled Cover of the Lindau Gospels*, Carolingian, ninth century. M1, front cover. Courtesy of The Pierpont Morgan Library, New York.

The Pierpont Morgan Library

Morgan's books, autographs, historical documents, manuscripts, binders, prints, and drawings are all housed at The Pierpont Morgan Library in New York. Although the Library has been adding to its collection since Morgan's death in 1913, making it difficult to separate what Morgan bought from what was purchased later, it is possible to summarize the Library's holdings in very general terms.

Ancient and Oriental Manuscripts
Egyptian, Coptic, and Greek papyri, many of them from the collection of Lord Amherst of Hackney; the Hamouli collection of Coptic liturgical papyri (almost sixty volumes from the ninth century), and Coptic bookbindings dating from the sixth–tenth centuries; Oriental manuscripts in Arabic, Armenian, Ethiopic, Syriac, Persian, and the Indian languages.

Medieval and Renaissance Manuscripts
Preeminent collection of illuminated manuscripts, from the James Toovey Collection, the Theodore Irwin Collection, and the Richard Bennett and William Morris Collection. Noteworthy among these are the *Golden Gospels of Henry VIII* (MS 23), the *Lindau Gospels* (MS 1), and superb examples of medieval works collected by William Morris, including psalters, bestiaries, and Books of Hours. There are also many manuscripts whose importance lies more with their texts than with their illuminations, such as a seventh-century Merovingian *St. Augustine*, early texts of Chaucer, and many volumes of French medieval romances.

Autograph Manuscripts and Documents
Literary autographs include the manuscripts, letters, and documents of important authors, dating from the early fifteenth century to the twentieth century. There are more than 400 bound volumes of English material, about 200 volumes of American material, and about eighty French volumes. This does not include thousands of unbound documents also in the collections. Authors include Pope, Swift, Poe, and Milton. The historical autographs are primarily letters and documents, dating from the twelfth–twentieth centuries. Interesting among them are papers relating to the Rulers of England (Henry VI–George VI), documents of the popes, and a set of autographs of the signers of the Declaration of Independence. Also noteworthy is the group of letters and documents of the bishops of the Episcopal Church, comprising about 2,000 manuscripts, and three volumes of documents related to the siege of Yorktown by American forces in 1781.

Printed Books
Early printed books, many from the Toovey and Morris-Bennett Collections (over 700 incunabula in the latter), including the first printing of Augustine's *De civitate Dei* (1467) and a 1470 edition of Cicero's *Rhetorica ad Herennium* from Venice. There are early blockbooks, three Gutenberg Bibles, one on vellum, one on paper, and one Old Testament only. There is the very rare *Indulgence* of Pope Nicholas V (1455), a 1459 *Psalter* printed on vellum, and a strong holding of early Mainz printings. Outstanding groups include bibles, ranging from the "Gutenberg" to eighteenth-century American examples, early printed books on the liturgy of the Roman Catholic church, early printings of ancient classics, an important collection of works printed by the Aldine Press, another group of books by England's first printer William Caxton, and first editions of English and American authors of the eighteenth and nineteenth centuries, first editions of French writers of the seventeenth and eighteenth centuries, medieval romances, Reformation literature, the history of Mary Queen of Scots, early illustrated books, and English caricatures.

Bookbindings

Of monumental importance is the cover for the *Lindau Gospels*, an extraordinary example of goldsmith's work during the Carolingian period (Figure 1). Other medieval bindings include the ivory cover for the *Cologne Gospels*, and the oak cover for the *Anhalt Gospels* (tenth century). From the Renaissance period there are examples of *cuir-ciselé*, blind-stamped, and panel-stamped bindings. Later centuries are represented by works of the best publishers of France and England. There is an unusual collection of armorial bindings, the earliest dating from the sixteenth century.

Drawings and Prints

Old Master drawings which rank among the best of any American collection, from the fourteenth–nineteenth centuries. The major part of these come from the Fairfax Murray Collection, which Morgan purchased in 1910. Several artists are represented by many drawings, for example Albrecht Dürer, Parmigianino, Claude Lorraine, Nicolas Poussin, Rubens, van Dyck, and Rembrandt. There are over thirty illustrations by William Blake, acquired by Morgan from the Earl of Crewe in 1903. There is also an impressive collection of prints, including an important group of Rembrandt etchings.

The Frick Collection

Many objects from Morgan's collection were sold by his son after 1913 and later by his son's estate in 1943. Some of these were bought by Henry Clay Frick. The following is a summary listing.

Paintings

John Constable's *The White Horse*, Rembrandt's *Portrait of Nicolaes Rut*, Sir Joshua Reynolds' *General John Burgoyne*, and the impressive group of panels painted by Fragonard entitled *The Progress of Love*, originally painted for Madame du Barry.

Sculpture

Approximately forty fifteenth- and sixteenth-century Italian bronzes, mostly statuettes by artists such as Pollajuolo, Ricci, Bertoldo, Sangallo, and Soldani; bronze lamps, candlesticks, and a casket; bronzes from the Netherlands, Germany, and France; five pieces of French eighteenth-century sculpture, including works by Clodion and Falconet; and thirty-seven Limoges enamels.

Oriental Porcelain

Almost fifty examples of Oriental porcelain, including blue and white wares, *famille verte* wares, and *famille noire* pieces, primarily from the Garland Collection.

Furniture

There are pieces of French eighteenth-century style furniture, which were at one time part of the furnishings of Morgan's Princes Gate house in London.

Other Collections

To trace the present location of every object from the Morgan collection is beyond the scope of this book. In some cases, however, we can provide this information.

Boston Massachusetts
> The Boston Museum of Fine Arts: six pieces of Sèvres porcelain, three pieces of English silver, and a majolica *Bust of a Lady*.

Cincinnati, Ohio
> The Taft Museum: fifteen examples of Chinese porcelain and stoneware, including several *famille verte* figures, two *famille rose* vases, a Ming stoneware vase, and a *famille noire* vase.

Cleveland, Ohio
> The Cleveland Museum of Art: four pieces of French soft-paste porcelain (Vincennes, Chantilly, and St. Cloud), a pair of mounted Meissen vases, and a French silver soup tureen by Meissonnier.

Corning, New York
> The Corning Museum of Glass: *The Morgan Cup*, Roman Empire, probably Italy, late first century B.C.–first century A.D.

New Haven, Connecticut
> Yale University Art Gallery: Frans Hals, *Portrait of a Man (Herr Bodolphe)* and *Portrait of a Woman (Mevrouw Bodolphe)*.

Indianapolis, Indiana
> The Indianapolis Museum of Art: Mendert Hobbema, *The Water Mill (The Trevor Landscape)*, 1667, and Corneille de Lyon, *A Man with a Glove*, about 1540–50.

Los Angeles, California
> The Los Angeles County Museum of Art: sixteen Limoges plates, including a complete series of zodiacal plates, given to the museum by William Randolph Hearst who purchased them from the Morgan family (date unknown).

Lugano, Switzerland
> The Thyssen-Bornemisza Collection: Fra Angelico, *Madonna Enthroned*, Jacques Daret, *Nativity with the Annunciation to the Shepherds*, and Domenico Ghirlandaio, *Giovanni Tornabuoni*.

Malibu, California
> The J. Paul Getty Museum: Sèvres, *Vaisseau à Mat*, about 1761, and pair of *Vases à flambeaux*, 1759 (these were sold by the Morgan family in 1944), pair of drug jars, Faenza, about 1510, one with man leaning on a crutch, and a *Berettino Bocale*, Faenza.

New York, New York
> The Robert Lehman Collection, The Metropolitan Museum of Art: Hans Holbein, *Erasmus of Rotterdam*, about 1523.

Pittsburg, Pennsylvania
> The Frick Art Museum: Chinese porcelains from the Garland Collection and Renaissance bronzes.

Toledo, Ohio
> The Toledo Museum of Art: Peter de Hooch, *Courtyard, Delft*, about 1657.

Washington, D.C.
> National Gallery of Art: Andrea del Castagno, *Portrait of a Man*, Gerard David, *Rest on the Flight into Egypt*, M. Hobbema, *A Wooded Landscape*, Sir Joshua Reynolds, *Lady Elizabeth Delmé and her Children*, George Romney, *Lady Broughton*, and Agostino di Duccio, *Madonna and Child* (sculpture); all acquired 1937.

Williamstown, Massachusetts
> The Sterling and Francine Clark Art Institute: Nicolas Lancret, *Les Deux Amis* and *Nicaise*.

Later Sales from the Morgan Collection

Catalogue of the Famous Collection of Miniatures of the British and Foreign Schools, the Property of J. Pierpont Morgan, Esq. Christie, Manson and Woods, Ltd., London, 24–27 June 1935.

Exhibition of Paintings: Collection of J. P. Morgan, for the Benefit of the Citizens Committee for the Army and Navy, Inc. M. Knoedler and Co., New York, 23 November–11 December 1943, (included Constable's *The White Horse*, Gainsborough, Goya, Greuze, Hobbema, Hogarth, Holbein, Lawrence, Raeburn, Rembrandt's *Nicolas Ruts*, Reynolds, Romney, Rubens, J. Ruisdael, Turner, and West. Many had already been sold — see appendix).

Furniture and Objects of Art, Property of the Estate of the Late J. P. Morgan. Part 1. Parke-Bernet Galleries, Inc., New York, 6–8 January 1944. (Battersea enamels, gold and enamel objects of vertu, Chelsea scent bottles, Sèvres, Mennecy, and other French porcelain).

Furniture and Objects of Art, Property of the Estate of the late J. P. Morgan. Part 2. Parke-Bernet Galleries, Inc., New York, 22–25 March 1944. (Roman, Byzantine, and other antiquities, Gothic, Renaissance, and Near Eastern art, Battersea enamels, Chelsea scent bottles, Meissen snuff boxes, objects of vertu, French porcelain, French decorations).

Catalogue of Old English and French Furniture, Porcelain, Objects of Art and Eastern Rugs and Carpets, The Property of J. Pierpont Morgan, Esq. Christie, Manson and Woods, Ltd., London, 22, 23, 29, 30 March 1944. (English pottery and porcelain, especially Worcester and Chelsea; English furniture, including Sheraton and Hepplewhite; Chinese porcelain, including *famille verte*, *famille rose*, and blue and white; Dresden porcelain; Sèvres porcelain; continental porcelain and pottery; miscellaneous objects of art; French decorative objects and furniture; Dutch furniture; Oriental rugs; provenance not indicated which would distinguish which objects belonged to J. Pierpont Morgan, Sr.).

Catalogue of Ancient and Modern Pictures and Drawings and Engravings, the Property of the Late J. Pierpont Morgan. Christie, Manson and Woods, Ltd., London, 31 March 1944. (Mezzotints, old master and modern drawings, old master paintings, including Paolo da Siena, Greuze, Hobbema, Largillière, Nattier, and van Dyck; unclear whether objects were in Morgan, Sr.'s collection).

Catalogue of the Library of Books from Wall Hall, Aldenham, Herts., the Property of the Late J. Pierpont Morgan. Christie, Manson and Woods, Ltd., London, 4 April 1944, (art books, Morgan catalogues, broadsides, historical engravings, many probably from Morgan, Jr.'s collection).

Catalogue of Decorative Furniture and Porcelain removed from Wall Hall, Aldenham, Herts., . . . the Property of the Late J. Pierpont Morgan. Christie, Manson and Woods, London, 1–2 June 1944. (English porcelain, table glass, decorative furniture [inherited from Morgan, Sr.?], various pieces of continental porcelain, Chinese *famille rose* and *famille verte* porcelain).

Superb Old English Silver from the Reign of Elizabeth to George IV, Notable Continental and Modern Silver, Property of the Estate of the Late J. P. Morgan. Parke-Bernet Galleries, Inc., New York, 30 October–1 November 1947. (Old English and German silver, much published in E. Alfred Jones, *Illustrated Catalogue of the Collection of Old Plate of J. Pierpont Morgan, Esq.*, 1908).

Highly Important English and Continental Silver and "objects of vertu," the *Property of Members of the Morgan Family,* Christie, Manson and Woods, New York, 26 October 1982. (Snuff boxes [no provenance listed], Morgan, Jr.'s English eighteenth-century silver, English silver from Morgan Sr., including George II Condiment Urns with ladles, Paul de Lamerie Candlesticks, a 1525 Henry VIII Beaker, and the Aldobrandini Vespasian Tazza).

Selections from the J. Pierpont Morgan Collection: Greek and Roman Coins. Stacks, New York, 14 September 1983. (Coins which had been on long-term loan to the American Numismatic Society until 1949 — the Morgan Library trustees sold the collection in 1953 — comprised of 101 silver and gold coins from Magna Graecia and Sicily, the Roman Imperial aurei of the first and second centuries; many of the gold coins from the Strozzi collection).

J. Pierpont Morgan Selected Bibliography

Adams, Frederick B., Jr. *An Introduction to the Pierpont Morgan Library.* New York, 1974.

Allen, Frederick Lewis. *The Great Pierpont Morgan.* New York, 1949.

Boyce, George K. "The Pierpont Morgan Library." *The Library Quarterly* 22, no. 1 (January, 1952): 21–35.

Breck, Joseph and Meyric R. Rogers. *The Pierpont Morgan Wing.* New York: The Metropolitan Museum of Art, 1929.

Brimo, René. *L'Évolution du gout aux États-Unis.* Paris, 1938.

Brown, David Alan. *Raphael and America.* Washington, D.C., 1983.

Canfield, Cass. *The Incredible Pierpont Morgan: Financier and Art Collector.* New York, 1974.

Constable, William George. *Art Collecting in the United States.* London, 1964.

Corey, Lewis. *The House of Morgan.* New York, 1930.

"Editorial." *Burlington Magazine* 23, no. 122 (May, 1913): 65.

Harris, Frank. *Latest Contemporary Portraits.* New York, 1927.

Hellman, George Sidney. *Lanes of Memory.* New York, 1927.

Hovey, Carl. *The Life Story of J. Pierpont Morgan.* New York, 1911.

Hoyt, Edwin P. *The House of Morgan.* New York, 1967.

Josephson, Matthew. *The Robber Barons.* New York, 1962.

Lawrence, Bishop William. *Memoir of John Pierpont Morgan (1837–1913);* written in the form of a letter to Herbert L. Satterlee, 6 January 1914. Boston 1914. Unpublished typescript in The Pierpont Morgan Library, New York.

Metropolitan Museum of Art. *Guide to the Loan Exhibition of the J. Pierpont Morgan Collection.* New York, 1914.

————. *The Pierpont Morgan Wing: A Brief Guide.* New York, 1918; second edition, 1925.

Morgan, J. P. and Co. *Morgan Papers.* New York, 1939.

"The Pierpont Morgan Gift." *Bulletin of the Metropolitan Museum of Art* 13, no. 1 (January, 1918): 2–20.

"The Pierpont Morgan Wing." *Bulletin of the Metropolitan Museum of Art* 13, no. 6 (June, 1918): 128–129.

Pitkin, Albert H. *The Morgan Collection.* Hartford, Conn., 1918.

Reitlinger, Gerald. *The Rise and Fall of Picture Prices, 1760–1960.* London, 1961.

————. *The Rise and Fall of Objets d'Art Prices since 1750.* London, 1963.

Rigby, Douglas and Elizabeth. *Lock, Stock, and Barrel: The Story of Collecting.* Philadelphia and New York, 1944.

Saarinen, Aline. "When J. P. Morgan Played the Art Market." *New York Times Magazine* (16 December 1956): 20–22, 25, 27, 30.

————. *The Proud Possessors: The Lives, Times and Tastes of Some Adventurous American Art Collectors.* New York, 1958.

Satterlee, Herbert L. *J. Pierpont Morgan: An Intimate Portrait.* New York, 1939.

————. *The Life of J. Pierpont Morgan.* Privately printed, 1937.

Seligman, Germain. *Merchants of Art: 1880–1960: Eighty Years of Professional Collecting.* New York, 1961.

Shenker, Israel. "J. Pierpont Morgan and The Princely Library He Founded." *Smithsonian* 10, no. 6 (September, 1979): 76–83.

Taylor, Francis. *Pierpont Morgan as Collector and Patron: 1837–1913.* New York, 1970.

Teall, Gardner. "An American Medici: J. Pierpont Morgan and His Various Collections." *Putnam's Magazine* 7, no. 2 (November, 1909): 131–143.

Tomkins, Calvin. *Merchants and Masterpieces: The Story of the Metropolitan Museum of Art.* New York, 1970.

Towner, Wesley. *The Elegant Auctioneers.* New York, 1970.

Valentiner, W. R. and G. C. Pier. *The Wing of Decorative Arts.* New York: Metropolitan Museum of Art, 1910.

Vitry, Paul. "Les Collections Pierpont Morgan." *Gazette des Beaux-Arts,* series 4, vol. 11 (1914): 425–440.

Wadsworth Atheneum. *The Pierpont Morgan Treasures.* Hartford, Conn., 1960.

Wheeler, George. *Pierpont Morgan and Friends: The Anatomy of a Myth.* Englewood Cliffs, New Jersey, 1973.

Woolf, Virginia. *Roger Fry.* New York, 1940.